BARCLAY

Miniature Toy Vehicles, Transports, Cars, Trucks, and Trains 1932-1971

Howard W. Melton

Schiffer Publishing Ltd

4880 Lower Valley Road • Atglen, PA 19310

Other Schiffer Books by the Author:
Barclay Toys: Transports & Cars, 1932–1971.
ISBN: 978-0-7643-2127-6. $24.95

Designed by Molly Shields
Type set in Calibri/Zurich BT

ISBN: 978-0-7643-4913-3
Printed in China

Published by Schiffer Publishing, Ltd.
4880 Lower Valley Road
Atglen, PA 19310
Phone: (610) 593-1777; Fax: (610) 593-2002
E-mail: Info@schifferbooks.com

For our complete selection of fine books on this and related subjects, please visit our website at www.schifferbooks.com. You may also write for a free catalog.

This book may be purchased from the publisher. Please try your bookstore first.

We are always looking for people to write books on new and related subjects. If you have an idea for a book, please contact us at proposals@schifferbooks.com.

Schiffer Publishing's titles are available at special discounts for bulk purchases for sales promotions or premiums. Special editions, including personalized covers, corporate imprints, and excerpts can be created in large quantities for special needs. For more information, contact the publisher.

Dedication

This book is dedicated to my wife, Jo Anne Melton, and my children, Heather C. Melton and Patrick W. Melton, both of whom are published authors in their own right. Jo Anne deserves special credit for both continuously encouraging this project and spending many hours editing this manuscript.

Contents

Introduction

The Barclay Manufacturing Company, Inc., ("Barclay," "Barclay Manufacturing Company," or "Barclay Company") introduced its first miniature toy vehicles in the early 1930s and produced various ranges of these toys for forty years until the company closed in 1971. There are four ranges of these inexpensive toys, Transport Toys, Miniature Trucks, Miniature Cars, and Miniature Trains.

The first Transport Toys were introduced in 1932 or 1933 and consisted of a slush cast cab, pressed steel trailer, slush cast sedan, and slush cast coupe. At about the same time, the first Miniature Trains were introduced, consisting of a slush combination engine-tender and four slush cars in two configurations, a freight train, and a passenger train. In various designs, both the Transports Toys and the Trains were produced continuously until the day Barclay closed its doors.

In the mid- to late 1950s, Barclay introduced Miniature Trucks and Miniature Cars in numerous designs, which were distinctly different from the trucks and cars found in the transport sets. These toys were produced in varying designs and finishes until the company ceased production in 1971.

These toys were meant for play. The toys were not expensive, had great styling, would endure hard play and abuse, and were colorfully painted. The toy transports and the small semi-trailers had pivoting trailers. All of the transports, trucks, cars, and trains had wheels that rolled and a considerable degree of detail in their design, particularly the vehicles designed in the 1930s and 1940s. The colors varied, but they were generally primary and bright. Colors such as red, orange, blue, and green remained throughout the production period. Other colors were added or dropped as the various series evolved and as tastes changed. As production moved into the late 1960s, the colors became more varied, brighter, and included neon colors in the final years leading up to the closure of the company.

The Compilation of This Book

This book has two major components. First, the book updates the author's earlier work, *Barclay Toys: Transports & Cars, 1932–1971* (referred to as "*Barclay Toys*"), written with co-author Robert E. Wagner and published by Schiffer Publishing, Ltd., in 2004. Since *Barclay Toys* was published, any number of new varieties and new color variations have surfaced and been added, corrections to the original detailed listings have been made, and additional research has added substantial detail explaining how these toys were designed and produced, as well as how some of the unusual variations evolved. Unless noted otherwise, all references to the toys discussed in this volume refer to the Barclay miniature toys produced between the early 1930s and 1971, in contrast to the larger vehicles that the company produced prior to World War II.

The second major component of this book is the inclusion of three additional ranges of miniature Barclay toy vehicles: the Miniature Trucks that were produced from the mid- to late 1950s or early 1960s until the company closed in 1971; the Miniature Cars that were produced from the mid- to late 1950s or early 1960s until 1971; and the Miniature Trains that were first introduced in the early 1930s and continued to be produced in various styles until 1971. These three ranges of toys include a multiplicity of designs and variations. When combined with the Transport Toys, these four vehicle ranges represent virtually the entire post-World War II production of vehicles by Barclay. While Barclay manufactured cars, trucks, and other vehicles in a number of sizes prior to World War II, the only larger vehicles produced after 1945 were a limited number of toy military vehicles produced in the late 1940s and the 1950s, a larger pickup truck produced continuously until the company closed in 1971, and a mid-sized fire truck produced in the early 1950s. Examples of the latter two vehicles are pictured in the Appendix.

This book includes knowledge accumulated over several decades of collecting by any number of collectors, discussions with former employees of Barclay, store sale catalogs, and other sources. The project actually began as an attempt to put together a collection inventory for the transport trucks and cars. As is the case with many types of toys made by defunct toy companies, very little has been documented concerning the toys produced by Barclay. Few records exist from the company itself including an almost complete absence of Barclay catalogs and other contemporary materials.

The scarcity of information is one of the challenging aspects facing collectors in many collecting categories. This is particularly true of items from a company such as Barclay, which produced a wide variety of inexpensive toys and then simply closed its doors.

This book is written from a collector's perspective. In contrast to the typical collectible reference book, this book provides detailed descriptions, drawings, and pictures including variations, paint colors, and identifiers. In addition to the author's collection, the author had access to several major collections of Barclay miniature vehicles, as well as the assistance of any number of collectors and former Barclay employees.

With respect to Barclay's Transport Toys, this book builds upon, supplements, and expands our knowledge regarding these toys. With regard to the Miniature Trucks, Cars, and Trains, this volume represents the first significant attempt to comprehensively identify and catalog the many varieties that exist for these toys. Since many of these toys, including very rare varieties, are still available at toy shows, flea markets, and other venues, it is hoped that this book will be an invaluable aid to those interested in these very fascinating toys.

Since *Barclay Toys* was published, many collectors and readers have supplemented our knowledge concerning the Barclay Company and its miniature toys. The author acknowledges that there is more to learn about each of the ranges covered. It is hoped that the collectors and other users of this book will continue to contribute their recollections and knowledge to clarify and augment the information that has been uncovered to date.

The book has four major parts. The initial section of the book includes historical information concerning the company and detailed discussions concerning the manufacturing process, distribution, packaging, and related issues. The second and longest part of the book consists of detailed catalogs of each of the four ranges of toys. The third part (the Appendix) includes historical and supplemental material, including reproductions of original marketing photographs from the very few remaining documents from the Barclay archives, examples of related Barclay toys, and other material. The fourth and final part of the book reproduces the identification grids containing the detailed listings that are found throughout the book for use by the reader as a quick reference to the various listings. The identification grids are followed by a bibliography.

Updates and Authentication Services

The website www.barclaytoys.com includes updates to the tables of known varieties found in the book, updates to the text of the book, additional information that has been discovered, pictures of new varieties, and other information of interest to collectors of these toys. The website also gives information concerning authentication services for these toys as well as e-mail contact information for the author. Although this book is based on the examination of well over 100,000 examples, many of the varieties and colors listed in the book are quite scarce. Since color pictures can often be misleading, only those pieces that have actually been seen by the author or a contributor to the book are listed as "existing."

Editorial Conventions

When the name of a specific range of the Barclay miniature toy vehicles appears in the text, the reference is capitalized, but only when the reference applies to that entire range. The four ranges are Transport Toys, Miniature Trucks, Miniature Cars, and Miniature Trains. This convention is also utilized with respect to specific references to one or more of the four Transport Toy series, which are First or Vintage Series, Second or Streamlined Series, Third or Classic Series, and Fourth or Modern Series. Proper names, such as those of individuals and businesses, are capitalized throughout the text.

Acknowledgments

The author wishes to thank any number of people that contributed their knowledge concerning the Barclay miniature toys and, in several cases, loaned examples to be photographed for the book. In particular, the author wishes to acknowledge Douglas Ehrenhaft (deceased), Joe Evangelist, William "Bill" Lango, David C. Miller, William ("Bill") Rucci, Sr. (deceased), Bill Rucci, Jr., William "Bill" Adorjan, Jim K. Levey, Dave Rappaport, and Dr. Carl A. Restivo, Sr., for their contributions toward this project.

Special recognition must be given to Robert "Bob" E. Wagner for his continued contribution and insights with respect to what we know regarding these toys. As co-author of *Barclay Toys: Transports & Cars, 1932–1971*, many of the key observations concerning these toys are his. This is particularly true with respect to the Transport Toys, which are one of his collecting passions.

The author particularly wishes to thank Jo Anne Melton for editing of the final draft of the book before it was printed.

Photographic Credits

Pictures are the work of Jeff Brown of All Events Photography, Chicago, Illinois. The examples shown in the photographs are primarily from the collection of the author. Several examples, including a number of pieces of the Miniature Trains section, are from other collectors.

About the Barclay Manufacturing Company

The Barclay Manufacturing Company closed its doors very abruptly in 1971. There is relatively little detailed information written concerning the company and even less about the miniature toys. Even with limited published information and without detailed catalogs, the miniature Barclay toys are extremely popular with collectors. This book attempts to document everything that is known about these toys as well as provide a detailed catalog of the various ranges, series, and variations.

Our information concerning the Barclay Manufacturing Company comes from various existing toy catalogs, particularly those originally authored by Richard O'Brien, and from conversations with a variety of toy industry veterans, former employees, and collectors familiar with the company. The Barclay Manufacturing Company was organized in either late 1923 or early 1924.[1] It was named after "Barclay" Street (now 10th Street) in West Hoboken, New Jersey, and as it grew, the company moved to various locations in Northern New Jersey.

A great deal of what we know about the company and its operations is the result of interviews with the late William "Bill" Rucci, Sr., which occurred in 2005, subsequent to the publication of *Barclay Toys*. Rucci first worked for Barclay from 1939 to 1942 and again from 1948 to 1966. Since the plant did not make toys from 1942 to 1945 and closed permanently in 1971, Rucci was employed by Barclay during the greater part of the period of its operation between 1939 and 1971. Rucci's title was "Tool and Die Maker." Other than a supervisor, Rucci was the only tool-and-die man for most of his tenure and was responsible for many of the post-1939 designs[2].

Originally owned by Leon Donze, Michael Levy bought an interest in the company in the 1920s and eventually took control of the company. Until the late 1930s, most of Barclay's products were manufactured by the traditional slush casting method. In this process, a combination of metals, the main ingredient being lead, was poured into bronze molds. The mold was then rocked back and forth and the metal that was still liquid was poured out to create a hollow casting. In the late 1930s, the company began to switch to the injection, die-cast casting method, whereby metal was forced under pressure into a hollow opening in a mold. Once the metal cooled and hardened, the mold was opened to remove the finished casting. Although Barclay created a wide variety of toys, most of their success was with military and, later, civilian toy figures, as well as all types of vehicles, both military and civilian. The company prospered throughout the 1920s and 1930s and was said to be the country's largest producer of lead alloy vehicles during the 1930s and early 1940s.

Barclay ran its manufacturing operation at several different locations. Originally located on Barclay Street in West Hoboken, New Jersey, the factory moved to Paterson Plank Road in North Bergen, New Jersey, about 1930 and then to Hoboken Street in North Bergen, New Jersey, around 1931. From 1935 to 1946, Barclay operated a three-storey factory in West New York, New Jersey, where it employed one hundred twenty-five employees. Barclay's final location was 316 Palisade Avenue in Union City, New Jersey, where it relocated in 1947 and remained until it closed in 1971.[3]

William Lango, a noted toy collector and author, recounts a discussion with an elderly gentleman who lived near the factory when it was located on 52nd Street in West New York, New Jersey, in the late 1930s:

> The Barclay factory had cantilevered windows and some of the local kids would stand on the sidewalk outside the fence and shout at employees whom could see through the open windows. One time, the kids even tossed a few stones at the windows. Infuriated Barclay workers would get so angry that once a worker tossed both soldiers and vehicles at the neighborhood kids. The kids ran back, picked up the soldiers and vehicles off the sidewalk, and ran like hell.
>
> At the West New York Factory, Barclay stored damaged, unsalable soldiers outside, alongside the building in open-topped, 55-gallon drums. When the drums were filled up, they were wheeled back into the plant and their contents were re-melted. Neighborhood kids would sometimes climb the fence and help themselves to figures and vehicles.[4]

Barclay suspended toy production on April 1, 1942, and began manufacturing metal components, including weights for time bombs and grenade pins, for the United States military effort for the duration of World War II. At the time Barclay ceased toy production in 1942, the company had one hundred twenty-five employees. By the end of the war, the workforce had dwindled to five employees. During this period, much of the manufacturing facility was rented to other companies.

Toy production resumed in 1945, after the war ended. While Barclay achieved some success in the 1950s, it continued to produce the same types of toys that had been popular thirty years before and began a progressive decline. In its attempt to broaden the vehicle lines, the Miniature Cars and Trucks were introduced in the late 1950s and continued to be a major part of the Barclay product line until the company closed in 1971.

Throughout the post-war period, Michael Levy continued to lead the company. Levy normally came to work around noon, smoked cigars, and enjoyed life. Levy's daughter married Stanley Goldsmith. Goldsmith joined the company in 1961 and assumed control of Barclay in 1964 upon Levy's death, due to a heart attack. When he died, Levy was either 64 or 65 years old. At the time of Levy's death, his brother, Harry Bogaty, was the general manager. According to Rucci, Bogaty and Goldsmith did not get along and Harry retired.[5]

Whereas Levy had a love and empathy for toys, Goldsmith had little feeling for toys, but he did want to modernize the company. Among the changes that Goldsmith wished to make was to produce the toys from plastic rather than lead. Unfortunately, the molds for Barclay's toys would not accommodate plastic. While Goldsmith has been given credit for such innovations as the introduction of blister packs, Rucci stated that the idea for the blister packs was actually suggested by Levy's brother, Mike, who was head of sales. Regardless of the innovations introduced, Barclay continued to struggle and closed in 1971.[6]

It is not known what instigated Barclay's sudden closure. Residents of the area say that when Barclay closed, its owners simply walked away from the unsecured plant leaving molds, stacks of boxes, and much more. Rucci indicates that approximately eighty percent of the molds had been cut up into scrap by Goldsmith's brother-in-law, Charlie, the head of maintenance, and his crew prior to the closure.[7] Local scrap and antique dealers later picked up many of the remaining abandoned molds that remained. At least some of these molds eventually were sold to private collectors and dealers.

In 1976, Lango located one of the steel molds used to produce cars for the postwar transports. This mold was being used as a boat anchor in the Hudson River. Lango also has said that at the time the plant closed, a dumpster was parked in the street and was filled with all sorts of figures and castings. This dumpster and other dumpsters on the property were pilfered by neighborhood residents.[8] Even several years after the company closed, collectors visiting the shuttered plant found abandoned boxes, axles, and other components.

Barclay's failure undoubtedly can be traced to several causes. Among others, the market for toy soldiers and other figures declined rapidly after World War II, and to the extent that this market continued to exist, it switched to plastic figures rather than metal figures. While the market for metal vehicles remained strong in the 1950s and 1960s, the competition in this market became increasingly intense. The miniature Matchbox vehicles were introduced in England in 1953 and began to be sold in the United States by at least 1958 or, perhaps, earlier. Not only were these toys made of alloys containing no lead, they also featured recognizable vehicles with more detail in respect to both the design and the finishing. While some collectors have suggested that the introduction of the Hot Wheel vehicles by Mattel may have been a factor leading to the closure of Barclay, the Hot Wheel range was not introduced until 1968. Hot Wheels used a standard 1:64 scale and were very attractive, but Barclay's business was already in rapid decline before this new competitor entered the market.

Another factor leading to its closure was the fact that Barclay used an alloy that was primarily lead as well as lead-based paints. Lead in toys was first identified as a serious health risk to children in the late 1960s. At this time, the Toy Manufacturers of America (TMA) and the American Academy of Pediatrics called for drastic limitations on the use of lead and lead paint in toys. While Barclay did switch to non-lead-based paints in the late 1960s, changing Barclay's production to a non-lead alloy would have been extremely costly because, for the most part, their existing molds could not be used for the alternative metal alloys. Barclay also faced substantial potential product and environmental liability arising from past production methods.

We will most likely never know the exact reason or chain of events that lead to Barclay's closure. In all likelihood, it involved a combination of changing taste in toys, particularly with regard to the military toys, the switch to plastic toys with respect to the military and civilian figures, new competition with respect to the metal vehicles, and the significant problem faced by Barclay with regard to its use of an alloy that was primarily lead.[9]

The Major Categories
of Barclay Miniature Vehicles

The most extensive part of this book is a very detailed description of the four major ranges of Barclay miniature vehicles. At this point, each category will be only briefly described.

Transport Toys

Transport Toys: First or Vintage Series

Not a great deal is known about the Vintage Series of the Transport Toys. Other than color variations in the cabs, trailers, and cars, and die variations in the cabs, there are no other variations in the transport cabs and trailers and only minor variations in the cars. It is believed that the First Series was manufactured between 1932 and the latter part of the 1930s. The cabs and the cars were made from a lead alloy and were manufactured by the traditional slush casting technique. This method resulted in castings that are somewhat thicker than the castings in the later series, which were produced by the injection die-cast casting method. Wheels on both the cabs and trailers were made of white natural rubber with red wooden hubs or simply with white natural rubber. The trailers were

stamped from steel and painted. The cars exist in two varieties, sedans and coupes, and have metal wheels, a characteristic of all Barclay transport cars until the 1960s. There were no four-car transports in this series.

Vintage Series trailer sets

Transport Toys: Second or Streamlined Series

Streamlined Series trailer sets

As with the First Series of the Transport Toys, not a great deal is known about the Streamlined Series. It is believed that the series was manufactured from later 1930s through 1939 or slightly later. The cab clearly reflects the Streamline Moderne or Art Moderne design movement, which appeared in the later 1930s and is generally viewed as an outgrowth of the Art Deco design movement of the later 1920s and earlier 1930s. The cab has a modern, "streamlined" look and is cast out of a lead alloy by the traditional slush casting method. A notable feature of the cab is the word "Trailer" cast into the door area on each side of the cab. The wheels on the cab are the same as those described for the First Series; however, the wheels do not have the wooden hubs. The trailers were the same as the trailers in the First Series except they lack the wooden hubs. The cars were the same as and indistinguishable from the cars in the First Series. As was the case in the First Series, there were no four-car transports in the Streamlined Series.

Transport Toys: Third or Classic Series

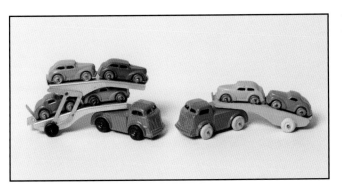

Classic Series trailer sets

The Third Series of the Transport Toys is what most people think of when the Barclay auto transports are mentioned. This series is notable given its length of production, 1939 through 1965, and its variety of colors and other variations. It was also the first series

to include both two- and four-car transports. As with the First and Second Series, the cabs and the cars were cast out of a lead alloy and painted; however, in this case they were manufactured by the injection die-cast casting process. Before World War II, the two-car trailers were also cast out of a lead alloy and painted. After World War II, all trailers, both two-car and four-car, were made from metal, primarily unpainted aluminum with side supports for the four-car trailers made from steel. The cars in this series include both sedans and coupes with metal wheels, which exist in a number of variations.

Transport Toys: Fourth or Modern Series

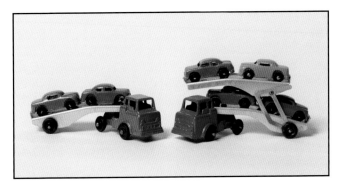

Modern Series trailer sets

The Fourth Series of the Transport Toys represented Barclay's attempt to modernize its line. The modern cars were first produced in the mid- to late 1950s. The modern cabs were introduced in early 1960s. The cabs were relatively detailed. While more modern in appearance, the cars lacked most of the detail found in the earlier series. As with the Third Series, the cabs and cars were cast using the injection die-cast casting method, while the trailers were aluminum. The earliest cars retained the metal wheels, but the later cars had rubber and then plastic wheels. The last type of car in the series had a single-piece plastic axle and wheel assembly. This final variety reflected the gradual deterioration of quality in the later years of Barclay's operation.

Miniature Trucks

Miniature Trucks: Initial Introduction

The Miniature Trucks were first introduced in the late 1950s or early 1960s. Initially introduced in only a few body types, primarily without labels and with metal wheels, this range eventually grew to eleven separate styles with many different variations. Contrary to what some collectors have speculated, the design of the initial version of the cab was not based upon any particular brand of truck that existed at the time. Rather, the design was generic, according to Rucci.[10] The scale of the vehicles is not clear, but it is very close to the scale of the classic and modern transport cars produced in the 1950s and 1960s.

Miniature Trucks: Subsequent Designs and Variations

While only eleven distinct body types of the Miniature Trucks were produced, multiple design variations evolved for most of the body types, as did variations in colors, labels, castings, and decorative elements. The Miniature Trucks were produced up until the days that Barclay closed. While the earlier trucks were relatively consistent with respect to colors and labels, many variations of colors, labels, and other elements appeared as the 1960s progressed. In general, the scarcest varieties are the multiplicity of neon-painted trucks produced in the last two or three years before Barclay closed.

Miniature Cars

Miniature Cars: Initial Introduction

The Miniature Cars were first introduced in either the late 1950s or early 1960s. While many variations exist in terms of castings, colors, wheel types, and labels, there are five distinct styles: antique cars; racers; generic sedans (assumed to be modeled after the Citroën of the era); sport cars in two variations; and Volkswagen Beetles. While about two inches in length, the scale is somewhat larger than the scale of the Transport Toys cars and the small trucks. The scale varies between the different styles of vehicles. As an example, the scale of the VWs is distinctly larger than the scale of the other vehicles in this range.

Miniature Cars: Subsequent Designs and Variations

While no additional body types were added, the Miniature Cars underwent numerous changes in terms of castings, color variations, wheel types, and labels. As with the Miniature Trucks, some of the scarcest variations of the Miniature Cars appeared in the last two or three years before Barclay closed.

This era saw significant experimentation in terms of colors (particularly the neon and metallic colors), casting modifications, and labeling. This last statement is particular true of the racers and the VWs. As will be noted, many of the variations of this later era are quite rare.

Miniature Trains

Various large- and medium-size trains

Miniature Trains: Prior to World War II

The Miniature Trains were introduced in the early 1930s. Barclay produced a number of trains during the 1930s and early 1940s in three distinct sizes varying from three to five pieces when counting the engine, tenders, and the various cars. Barclay also produced a single-piece three-car streamliner. The earlier trains were produced with the slush casting method and had metal wheels. The trains produced in the mid- to late 1930s, including the streamliner, had natural rubber wheels. As was the case with the Transport Toys, Barclay switched to the injection die-cast casting method of production beginning in the later 1930s.

Miniature Trains: After World War II

After toy production resumed in 1945, Barclay produced a five-car freight train with rubber wheels for a period of time; however, the primary product in the Train range from 1945 to 1971 was a three-car train produced by the injection die-cast method. Initially, these toys

had metal wheels; however, they were switched to rubber or plastic wheels in the late 1950s or early 1960s. The same castings for the three-car train were used throughout the post-World War II period; however, a variety of colors were used. In the late 1960s and early 1970s, the three-car trains came in bright neon colors and some trains were produced with white sidewall tires. In contrast to the Miniature Trucks and Cars, labels were never applied to the Miniature Trains.

How Barclay Miniature Vehicles Were Sold

As far as is known, the first two series of the Transport Toys were only sold as sets, although today you often see the pieces being sold individually or in partial sets. The trailers and cabs were sold as parts of sets that included the required number of cars throughout the production of the four series. At least by the early 1950s, the cars from the Third or Classic Series were being sold individually in five-and-dime stores for five cents apiece. From the late 1950s or early 1960s through the final days of production, the individual cars were sold primarily in blister packs. Initially the blister packs included seven cars to a pack, but later packs contained either five or ten cars. Toward the end of production of the Transport Toys, sets that included a cab, a four-car trailer, and five individual cars were sold in a blister pack. Detailed discussions of the packaging and distribution of the various series can be found later in the book under those titles.

The Miniature Trucks and Cars were most commonly sold individually or in sets of two or more related pieces. Beginning in the early 1960s and continuing until Barclay ceased doing business, trucks and cars were also sold in mixed sets of five pieces in a blister pack. So far as we know, the trains were always sold in sets in a variety of packaging, including sets attached to strips of cardboard, boxes, and eventually blister packs.

Classic cars priced at five cents

Modern car priced at five cents

Numbering, Varieties, and Nomenclature

Numbering, Varieties, and Nomenclature for the Transport Toys

As is the case with many collectible toys, numbering has been problematic and spotty. The numbering found in O'Brien's books is helpful, but it only focuses on the basic sets or types and does not address the multiplicity of variations or rarer varieties. The only official Barclay numbering system that is known is the numbers on packaged sets or individual vehicles and the numbering found in the few pages from Barclay wholesale catalogs that exist. While cross-references to both the O'Brien numbers as well as to the Barclay numbers are provided selectively, the toys require a much more specific and comprehensive numbering system. References to the O'Brien numbers appear with the letters "BV" followed by a number with two or three numerals, i.e. "BV153," whereas references to the Barclay numbers are simply a number with three numerals, i.e. "577."

For the Transport Toys, the numbering system that is adopted first identifies the piece as being a cab (C), a two-car trailer (2T), a four-car trailer (4T), a sedan (S), or a coupe (CO). The second component of the number identifies the series. There are four major series distinguished by the distinctive designs of the major components. The Third Series ran for approximately twenty-six years. The Fourth Series, in part, overlapped the Third Series and ran for twelve to fifteen years. The series also have names: the First Series is also referred to as the Vintage Series; the Second Series as the Streamlined Series; the Third Series as the Classic Series; and the Fourth Series as the Modern Series. These descriptions are used interchangeably throughout the book.

Although it was stated in *Barclay Toys* that the First Series cab had no variations, it has now been determined that a number of casting variations exist for this first cab. The basic cab is still identified as "C1," but a special table has been added outlining

various casting variations. The Classic and Modern Series, in contrast, include numerous variations for each of the components. The second number in the Third and Fourth Series represents a major variation. The third number in these series represents a less significant variation within a major variation; and in a few cases, a fourth number represents still another level of variation. As an example, a four-car trailer from the 1945–1964 era is numbered as 4T3.1.1, which identifies this piece as being a four-car trailer that is part of the Third Series. The second number after the piece identifier says the toy is the first major variation within this series of trailers and the third number identifies the toy as the first secondary variation of the first major variation of this trailer.

With very few exceptions, every known variation that was part of the regular production, even when produced for a very short time, is included in the numbered variations. A few unusual variations are simply noted at the bottom of the identification grids or in the text and illustrations. These latter variations were often created by mixing older parts with newer parts and may or may not have been part of regular production runs.

The decision to treat a particular variation as a major or a minor variation was based upon its apparent significance. As an example, the major variations in the sedans from the Classic Series represent the three distinctive variants in which this car appeared. Within the first variation of the sedan, called the "plain sedan," there are five sub-variations. The sub-variations are viewed as less significant as compared to the three distinctive variations in the external appearance of these cars; therefore, cars within the sub-variations are identified as S3.1.1 through S3.1.5. While reproductions and alterations made outside the factory are discussed in a later section, they are not considered collectible and, therefore, are not identified in the numbering system.

Variations were created in several ways. First, the four series represent the four major designs. Second, from time to time changes were made in one or more pieces within a series, such as the change from cast to aluminum trailers in the Third Series. Third, while maintaining the essential appearance of a piece, Barclay sometimes changed the molds, an example being when they went from open to closed wheel-wells in the Classic Series cars and cabs. Fourth, minor variations were created by changing components such as the various changes of wheels in the cars within the Modern Series. Fifth, as molds began to wear, there was evidently a tendency to rework the older molds. This fact appears to explain some of the variations in the cars of the Classic Series. Sixth, some varieties may have been created by various manufacturing practices. As an example, it is not clear whether the open- and closed-rear window varieties of the cars in the early part of the Fourth Series were the result of different molds or the result of some aspect of the manufacturing process that sometimes failed to punch out the back window.

We must remember that these were inexpensive toys. Consequently, there was an effort to never waste materials. Older or newer parts, if they happened to be available, were used on a transitional basis such as the use of copper-clad steel instead of aluminum for some of the early trailers. A number of transitional variations were created because parts for older varieties were used as parts on newer varieties. This same factor applies to color variations. On occasion, Barclay used the paints and parts that were available. While there appears to have been set color schemes for the various sets, from time to time other paint colors were used. With the exception of some of the neon and metallic colors in the later years of the Fourth Series, the new colors that appeared were typically colors that were being used on other Barclay products of the time, particularly the solders and other metal figures.

While all known variations are cataloged, there are minor differences that were not considered as legitimate variations. The most obvious example is minor paint shade and tint variations that arise in every series. In the case of every variation included, actual examples have been examined and authenticated as being produced in the Barclay factory.

Numbering, Varieties, and Nomenclature for the Miniature Trucks

The Miniature Trucks exist in eleven distinct body styles. While the castings of some body styles remained consistent, most were modified in one manner or another over the period of their production and many were modified any number of times. The numbers for the Miniature Trucks all begin with "MT." The first number following the letters identifies the specific body type. As an example "MT1" identifies a bottle delivery truck. The second number following the letters identifies a significant variety of a given body type, and the third number following the letters identifies a notable, but less significant variation of a given body type. As you will note on the identification grid, "MT1.3.2" identifies a bottle delivery truck with a traditional cab, a tank truck body, yellow cab, yellow body, plastic whitewall wheels, and a Coca-Cola label.

As was the case with the Transport Toys, the decision to treat a particular variation as a major or a minor variation was based upon its apparent significance. Beyond the identification of the specific body type, variations exist with respect to the cab castings, the body castings, the wheel material, the type of wheels, the colors of both the cab and the body or the trailers in the case of the semi-trailer sets. A further differentiation exists with respect to logos. Most of the earliest Miniature Trucks did not have logos, whereas most of the later trucks do have logos. With respect to the logos, multiple variations exist with respect to several logo types.

While no reproductions of the Miniature Trucks are known to exist, there are examples of alterations that have occurred outside the factory both with respect to paint colors and the attachment of cabs and body components in combinations that are not original. While alterations are reviewed in the detailed discussion of this range, reproductions and alterations made outside the factory are not considered collectible and, therefore, are not identified in the numbering system.

A particular problem is presented by the semi-trailer sets. The semi-trailer sets came in many variations. Since a given cab can theoretically be combined with any trailer, the listings include only the set variations actually found in unopened blister packs or set combinations that have been seen repeatedly online, at shows, and in collections.

Numbering, Varieties, and Nomenclature for the Miniature Cars

The identification grid for Miniature Cars is broken down into five major types of cars. As a group, the numbers for the cars begin with "MC." Within the various major types of cars, multiple castings and varieties exist. In addition to different castings, variations exist relating to colors, the type of wheels, trim details, and, in certain cases, logos. As with the numbering schemes that have previously been described, the number immediately following the letters represents a major variation and the subsequent numbers represent secondary variations and sub-variations. Thus, "MC1" identifies an antique car. "MC1.2" indicates a casting with cast headlamps and "MC1.2.3" identifies this specific casting as that of at Stutz vehicle with one bucket seat.

The decision to treat a particular variation as a major or minor variation was based upon its apparent significance. Particularly in the last three or four years prior to the time that Barclay ceased production, many variations appeared, particularly with respect to paint color and labels.

While it is certainly possible that cars have been repainted or otherwise altered, no reproductions of the Miniature Cars are known to exist. Unlike the Miniature Trucks, the Miniature Cars consist of one major casting so the problem of changing the combination of the two components of a particular vehicle does not exist. As with the other ranges and series, any reproduction or alteration outside the factory is not considered collectible.

Numbering, Varieties, and Nomenclature for the Miniature Trains

The Miniature Trains were produced in four distinct series. The numbering scheme for the Miniature Trains is largely based on size for the three major series, specifically, the large, medium, and small sizes. The fourth series is the streamlined train, which was only produced in a single variety. The trains are identified first by the letter "T." The series is then identified with the first number following the "T." Subsequent numbers identify significant and then less significant variations within a particular series. Thus, a train identified as "T4.3.1" would be a train in the fourth series and be the variety identified as "3.1."

The first trains were introduced in the early 1930s. Prior to World War II, the trains were produced in a number of varieties in all four series. It is believed that all major variations have been identified; however, it is certainly possible that one or more additional variations were manufactured by Barclay. Since any number of companies produced trains using the slush cast method during the 1930s, metal trains from this era are often misattributed as being made by Barclay when, in fact, they were not.

No reproductions of the Miniature Trains are known to exist; however, individual pieces are found that have been repainted. An even greater problem is finding cars and engines in combinations that are different than the way in which they were sold. This problem is acute in respect to the earlier trains, which are seldom offered as a set, and the trains that were produced in the late 1960s and early 1970s in a variety of neon and non-neon color combinations. This catalog only lists sets of the trains that are in older advertisements, in the few Barclay catalog pages that have been found, repeatedly seen in the same set combination, or, in the case of the trains from the 1960s and 1970s, found in original blister packs.

Production and Painting

Production

Although our knowledge of the production techniques utilized prior to 1940 is not substantial, a great deal is known regarding both the factory layout and the production techniques beginning in 1947 at the Palisade Avenue location in Union City, New Jersey. Our knowledge of this era has been greatly expanded as a result of the Rucci interview.[11]

The building on Palisade Avenue was two storeys with a basement. Production was organized into departments-casting, trimming, painting, finishing, inspection, and packing and shipping. The production functions were located on the main floor with the exception of painting, which was located in a paint shed outside the main building. The casting department was located near the windows, presumably for ventilation.

There was a separate storage shed adjacent to the main building. In addition to the production departments, the office was located in the front of the building on the main floor. As you walked in the front door, the lobby included cabinets displaying the products made by the company. The basement was used for the carpenter shop and storage. The packing and shipping department was located on the second floor. There was an extensive exhaust system throughout the factory, which Rucci states was very clean; however, in addition to the lead fumes and dust, there was a great deal of asbestos in the building.

By the time Barclay moved to the Union City location, all production took place using the die-cast or injection molding technique. Barclay employed a vertical manufacturing model where, with minor exceptions, the entire production process took place in the Barclay factory. Production started with antimonial lead slabs or pigs (crudely cast bars of lead containing a small percentage of antimony) and went through each manufacturing process ending with packaged toys ready to ship. With a few exceptions, such as the aluminum trailers for the Transport Toys and the printed cardboard bases for the blister packs, which were outsourced, every toy was manufactured from start to finish in the Barclay factory.

The toys were designed, the molds were created, and the plastic blister packs were manufactured in-house. At each step in the manufacturing process, specialized machinery and tools were utilized, most of which were created onsite in the machine shop.

It is not clear how the small metal wheels, which were used on many of the small vehicles beginning in the early 1930s, were initially produced; however, after die-cast molding was introduced, production was transferred to injection molds producing one hundred (100) wheels at a time. Given the number of wheels required, wheels were produced continuously.

The factory was organized by product line. During the post-World War II period, the Transport Toys were the most popular Barclay toys and were produced continuously. With regard to the vehicles, the first step was casting the body and the other components of the vehicles. The second step was trimming the castings. After the castings were trimmed, they were transported to the paint shed. In the paint shed, the castings were spray painted and then returned to the finishing department on large trays. Once the painted castings were returned and were dry, wheels were attached, various components were attached in the case of many of the small trucks and small cars, and the completed toys were sent to the packing department to be prepared for shipping.

Transport Toys: First and Second Series

Very little is known regarding the production methods utilized to produce the First and Second Series. Clearly, the cabs and cars were produced in bronze molds into which a hot lead alloy was poured. We do not know how many pieces were produced simultaneously by each mold. In the first two series, the cabs and cars were first painted and then had the wheels attached by putting the axle through axle holes and crimping one end of the axle. Consequently, there should never be paint on the axles or tires. The trailers were made from stamped steel and were painted after they had been shaped, but before the wheels were attached.

The trailers for these two series are the same except that the wheels in the First Series generally included red wooden hubs, which are found on many Barclay vehicles of this era. With one exception, which will be covered later in more detail, the cabs of the First Series had red wooden hubs, whereas the cabs in the second series did not have the red wooden hubs.

Transport Toys: Third Series

Beginning in 1939, most of the cabs and the cars were manufactured from molds using the injection die-cast casting method. The molds for the Third or Classic Series cabs produced two cabs at a time. The molds for the Classic Series cars produced four castings at a time. In both cases, the molds were made from steel, into which hot metal was injected under pressure to produce the castings. While we do not know how many sets of molds were used, we do know that there were two distinct varieties of the early sedans, the plain and parking light sedans, and one variety of the coupes, the plain coupes. Each of the three different types of early cars as well as the early cabs had open wheel-wells.

At various times the molds were reworked. A major change occurred in the late 1940s or early 1950s, when the wheel-wells were closed. Subsequent reworking of the molds or the creation of new molds produced the grill bars sedan. Reworking and gradual deterioration of the older molds appears to have eventually produced the crooked-line and the no-line coupes. With these three additional varieties, there are three major varieties for each of the Third Series sedans and the Third Series coupes. In the mid-1950s, new molds were again created to produce four cars at a time. In this case, all were plain sedans or plain coupes with closed wheel-wells. These molds were used until production of the Third Series stopped in the mid-1960s.

With the exception of some early examples produced just as the Third Series began, castings were painted after the castings were produced and before the wheels were attached. The final step in the production process was to attach the axles and wheels as had been done for the first two series.

Initially, trailers for the Classic Series were cast using the injection casting method and painted. In the final step in the production process, the axles and wheels were attached. When production resumed after World War II, Barclay began using stamped, unpainted metal trailers. These stamped trailers were manufactured for Barclay by Heyco Products, Inc., which was located in Kenilworth, New Jersey. According to Rucci, the first metal trailers were made out of steel, but production quickly converted to aluminum for the ramps, while the pieces connecting the ramps on the four-car trailers continued to be stamped from steel.[12]

A tab to hold the cars on the lower ramp on the four-car trailers was stamped from either aluminum or steel. After creating the various pieces, the components of the four-car trailers were connected by means of rivets and then the axles and wheels were added. As was the case with the cabs and cars, the axles on the trailers had a nub at one end and were crimped at the other. We do not know whether the wheels were attached by the trailer fabricator or were attached in the Barclay factory.

The aluminum trailers had three distinct advantages as compared to the cast trailers. The stamped trailers did not crack, which was a problem with the cast trailers; the aluminum trailers were lighter than either the cast or the steel trailers, which saved on shipping cost; and the switch to steel and then aluminum allowed the addition of a four-car trailer, which could be accomplished with steel or aluminum trailers, but which was not possible when using cast ramps.

Transport Toys: Fourth Series

Production of the cars in the Fourth Series began in the late 1950s and production of the cabs began in the early 1960s. The Fourth Series cabs and cars were produced by the injection die-cast casting method. The cars were produced from molds producing either eight sedans or eight coupes. Each car was numbered 1 to 8 on the inside roof, which was its position number inside the mold. After the hot metal was injected into the steel molds to produce the castings, the castings were painted and the axles and wheels were attached. There are a number of variations within the cars, which are also called "Shoebox"[13] cars due to their shape.

According to Rucci, the modern cars were not modeled after any particular vehicle; however, the modern cabs were based on a 1958 Ford Cab-over Truck in a scale of 1/124. With minor variations, the trailers used for the Modern transport sets were the same as the trailers in the Third Series.[14]

Miniature Trucks

The Miniature Trucks range was introduced in the late 1950s. Ultimately, there were eleven distinct types of trucks. Ten of the eleven styles consisted of a common cab and chasse ("cab") with different bodies attached to the cabs. The cabs and the body pieces were cast and painted separately and then attached to each other. The eleventh type was a two-piece semi-trailer truck. The cab of the semi was the same casting as the cabs for the other ten types of trucks; however, the body of the semi was not attached permanently as was the case for the other truck types. As will be explored in detail, the design of the cab component changed several times creating multiple varieties. Varieties were also created as color combinations changed, logos were added and changed, and wheel types changed. While the Miniature Trucks are often referred to as "two inch" trucks, their actual length varies. There is no consistent scale for these toys; however, the scale is roughly the same as the small cars from the Transport Toys range.

Production of the Miniature Trucks was relatively straightforward. The castings were produced and painted, and the cab and body castings were attached. Wheels were attached and, if applicable, logos were added. The trucks were then packaged in various sizes of blister packs that accommodated one, two, or three trucks. As will be discussed later, blister packs included up to five trucks or a combination of five Miniature Trucks and Cars.

Miniature Cars

Miniature Cars were introduced at the same time as the Miniature Trucks. There are five distinct series of the Miniature Cars; however, there are multiple types of vehicles in several of the series as well as variations relating to castings, colors, wheels, decorative labels, and other features. Most of these vehicles are approximately two inches long, but the scale of these cars is slightly larger than the Miniature Trucks and the cars in the various Transport Toys series. It should also be noted that the scale of the various cars varies as between the different types of cars.

As was the case of the Miniature Trucks, production of the Miniature Cars was relatively straightforward. Most of these vehicles had a single casting; however, vehicles such as the racers, the sports cars, and the antique cars often had decorative components added after the casting was completed and painted. The wheels were added either after the castings were completed or after any additional components or labels were added. The Miniature Cars were generally packaged in packs of either one or two vehicles; however, they were often included with the Miniature Trucks in packs of five vehicles.

Trains

Barclay introduced Miniature Trains at about the same time as the first Transport Toys were introduced in the early 1930s. In the 1930s, a number of train types were manufactured in three distinct sizes. With one exception, the trains manufactured after World War II were of the smallest size. The early trains were made using the slush casting method. Beginning in the late 1930s, the trains were manufactured using the die-cast injection casting process.

Production of the Miniature Trains was very straightforward. With the exception of the single-piece streamlined train, the train sets were made up of an engine and either two or four cars. In some, but not all, cases, one of the cars was a tender. Each piece was a single casting. The casting was created and painted. In contrast to the Miniature Trucks and Cars, there were no labels applied to any of the train components. With the exception of the lighted engines in the 1930s, there were no additional parts to be added. After the castings were painted, the wheels were attached, the engines and the cars were put into sets, and the sets were packed. As will be outlined in detail, Barclay manufactured a number of distinctly different train sets and numerous color variations of the various components exist.

Colors

Color is one of the most intriguing and appealing aspects of the Barclay Miniature toy vehicles. Colors, such as green, orange, blue, and red, are found throughout the various vehicle ranges. Other colors were added and existing colors were sometimes dropped. While most colors were used for a period of years or many years, colors such as gray, moss green, and clay appear to have been used for only a matter of weeks or months. These were inexpensive toys and care was not always taken to keep colors consistent from one batch to the next. Consequently, colors such as the greens, oranges, and blues come in a variety of shades and tints, particularly in the long-running Third Series of the Transport Toys range.

In the First and Second Series of the Transport Toys range, we see a limited pallet of bright, primary colors—green, orange, blue, red, and yellow. The initial years of the Third Series of the Transport Toys included relatively few colors. In addition to the five colors in the First and Second Series, multiple shades of green and blue appeared in the first ten to fifteen years of the Third Series. From the mid-1950s until the end of the Third Series in the 1960s, several other colors appeared including brown, camel, chocolate, clay, cream, flesh, gold, gray, khaki, lilac, pink, salmon, silver, tan, turquoise, and lemon yellow.

As the Third Series cars were being phased out, two metallic colors, steel blue and aqua green, appeared. In contrast to the earlier practice of continuing colors for a very long time, many of these colors appeared in the transitional period when cars from both the Third and Fourth Series were produced simultaneously. In some cases, colors appear to have been used for no more than a few weeks. While some colors were used on various combinations of cabs and cars, other colors only appear on one or both types of cars. In the detailed discussion of each series, the relative rarity of the various colors will be addressed as they relate to specific pieces within the various series. The colors in the Third Series that were introduced in the transitional period are among the scarcest in any series.

Colors in the beginning of the Fourth Series of the Transport Toys largely duplicated the colors used in the last part of the Third Series; however, the last version of this series includes a substantial expansion of colors including extensive use of "hot" or "neon" colors. The neon colors were achieved by using a white base paint and then spraying automobile paint over the base to give the piece a bright eye-catching color. Examples of these vehicles are often difficult to locate.

In large measure, the colors used for the Miniature Trucks and Cars were the same as those used for the Transport Toys. The earliest Miniature Trucks and Cars generally are found in primary colors. As the 1960s progressed, additional colors such as steel blue, silver, and lemon yellow appeared on a selective basis. In the final years of production, the neon colors were used extensively; however, examples with the neon colors are generally scarce and many are rare.

The colors of the Miniature Trains essentially followed the pattern of the other miniature ranges. In the 1930s, the colors are similar to those used for the First and Second Series of the Transport Toys: primary colors such as green, orange, blue, and red were used in addition to black, which was frequently used for the engines and tenders. One additional color, silver, was used on many of the engines and tenders in the late 1930s–1960s. In the late 1950s and early 1960s, additional colors appeared, such as steel blue, gray, and gold. Toward the end of the range, in the late 1960s and the early 1970s, trains appeared in various combinations of the neon colors. As one would expect, trains in the neon colors are difficult to locate, particularly in mint condition.

The criteria for including a specific color is that it be readily identifiable as a distinct color, there was consistency in its use, it is clearly a product of the factory, and it is not simply a shade or tint variation. Colors are discussed and illustrated extensively in the detailed catalogs. Shading and tint differences are particularly pronounced in the Third Series of the Transport Toys range. Differences occurred both at different periods of time, i.e. the forest green in the earlier years of the Classic Series differs from the forest green in the later years of the Classic Series; and within the same period of time when sequential batches of paint were mixed with slight differences. The only colors for which we know the names used by Barclay are Blue (we know this color as light blue), Gerard Green (known to us as light green), Sunset (known to us as orange) and Banner Red (known to us as red).

We also know that non-standard paint combinations were sometimes produced in the factory. According to William Lango, two older female ex-employees related how some of the young women in the finishing department would flirt with the men in the paint department to get them to paint figures in special colors. To prove the point many years later, they produced examples of metal sailors painted pink instead of the traditional white.[15]

Painting

Individual pieces of the Transport Toys and Miniature Trains as well as the Miniature Cars and Trucks were cast in groups of identical pieces. Once the castings were removed from the molds and trimmed, the raw castings were moved to the paint shed. A given group to be painted might only include one type of casting such as classic sedans or it might include two or more groups of castings, so long as they were all going to be painted the same color. The paint shed contained two stalls; however, normally only one stall was used at a time. Once the castings had been placed in the appropriate stall, they were spray painted by hand. When the painted castings were dry, they were placed on metal trays and moved back to the appropriate production line.[16]

With only one exception involving the early classic cars, the castings were always painted in mass before the axles, wheels, and additional parts were added. Since the pieces were spray painted, you can expect some paint on the inside of the pieces with open windows. Except in rare cases, pieces were never painted on the inside and never repainted with another color. Evidence of being painted by hand, paint of another color showing on the inside of the piece, a complete coat of paint on the inside, paint on a wheel, or paint on an axle is generally an indication that the piece has been painted outside the factory.

There are a very few examples of genuine cars and cabs in the Transport Toys range, which were painted one color and then were returned to the paint line and repainted a second color. When, on occasion, a casting turned over during the painting process and failed to receive a complete coat of paint, such pieces were put aside and later repainted. This could explain the very rare examples of a piece completely or partially painted on the inside in a given color and then painted on the outside with the same color or a different color. Rucci also stated that castings that were not properly painted were occasionally touched-up by hand.[17]

There is at least one example of a cab in the Transport Toys range that had already been repainted and then was again returned to the line and repainted with a third color. In these cases, there will be splashes of all the colors of paint in the inside of the pieces having open windows. There are also examples of early Classic Series cars, which were completely painted on the inside as well as early Classic and Modern cars that were painted after the wheels were attached. Various cars painted multiple times and/or with multiple colors are illustrated in the Appendix.

The castings for the Miniature Trucks, Cars, and Trains were painted in exactly the same process as described above for the Transport Toys. While they undoubtedly exist, examples of pieces within these three ranges that were painted more than once have not appeared. There is no evidence whatsoever, that any pieces from these three ranges were ever painted after their wheels were attached. There are, however, some examples of toys in these three ranges that have been repainted outside the factory.

While the castings for the vehicles and the base color for the military and civilian figures were spray painted, any additional painting details, such as the clothing colors on the figures, were painted by hand. Hand painting was done by young women seated at long tables. While examples of hand painted or hand sprayed details exist with regard to the larger vehicles of the 1930s, the only conclusive examples of an additional hand painted detail with respect to the miniature toy vehicles are found on a few Volkswagens and racers in the Miniature Cars range. According to Rucci, Barclay experimented with painting the Transport Toys in two colors, but found it too difficult to do and abandoned the idea.[18]

Although a single paint color was applied to each batch of castings in the paint shed, multiple types of toys might be painted at the same time. The paint was in five-gallon buckets. Barclay employees would experiment with paint colors, mixing colors themselves. If a color was created that the employees liked, the paint company was asked to provide that color. If the employees in charge of painting ran out of a color in the middle of a run of a particular group of toys, two things might occur. First, the painting staff might switch to another color even though it was not the standard color for a particular casting or group of castings. Second, the painting staff might mix two colors that they did have in stock to create a new color. In either case, it is very possible that a much rarer color or color combination was created for the toy or toys being painted.

Distribution and Packaging

Barclay toys were primarily sold in five and dime stores. They were commonly found at stores such as Woolworth's, S.S. Kresge, TG&Y, and many others as well as at value department stores such as The Fair in Chicago. For many years, Woolworth's was Barclay's largest customer. The use of this channel of distribution actually contributed to our limited knowledge concerning these toys. In contrast to more upscale retailers that produced extensive catalogs, most of the major outlets selling Barclay toys issued no more than an occasional sale flyer, compounding the difficulty of locating contemporary information concerning these toys. According to Rucci, Barclay shipped toys to every state in the United States and, also, to Canada, Europe, and Japan.[19]

In the 1930s through the mid-1950s, packaging was very simple. Toys were either packaged in lithographed boxes, lengths of cardboard with v-cuts to hold rubber bands wrapped around the toys, or simply wrapped in tissue paper or newspaper and placed in boxes holding multiple pieces to be shipped to retailers. In the later 1950s, the miniature vehicles were packaged either individually or in groups in blister packs, which consisted of a printed cardboard base and a plastic enclosure that was glued to the base. While the cardboard bases were contracted to a commercial printing company, the plastic enclosures were produced at the Barclay plant and the packages were assembled at the plant.

Early Packaging

The first of the Transport Toys and the Miniature Trains were introduced in the early 1930s. We do know that at least some of the early trains were sold in lithographed boxes; however, we do not know whether this was a universal practice or whether Barclay sold the trains with other packaging or simply wrapped sets in paper to be laid out on the sales counter by the retailer. The earliest packaging that we have for the Transport Toys is a set from the First Series placed on a heavy piece of cardboard with "v" cuts to hold the set to the cardboard by means of rubber bands.

After Barclay resumed production following the conclusion of World War II, the four-car Transport Toys sets were packaged in lithographed cardboard boxes. These boxes were used through the 1950s and until the introduction of the blister pack packaging. The only other packaging example that we have from the post-World War II period prior to the introduction of the blister packs is a train set issued shortly after the conclusion of World War II that was sold in a lithographed box. Although not considered a miniature toy, we do know that the small fire engine issued in the very early 1950s was sold in a lithographed box. (See an example in the Appendix.)

The cardboard boxes for the four-car Transport Toys sets are printed red, white, and blue on cardboard. On the back is a drawing of a transport unloading the cars. One piece that is often missing from the boxed sets is a flat piece of loose cardboard that fits in the bottom of the box. This piece served as an anchor for two rubber bands that were wrapped around the transport set to hold the set in place. When original rubber bands are present, they will be deteriorated. Given Barclay's tendency to produce product in parallel, it is quite possible that the cardboard boxes continued to be used at the same time that companion sets were being sold in the blister packs. Barclay did not mark these boxes with prices, although individual stores often did so. This packaging always contains a cab and a four-car trailer from the Third or Classic Series as well as two sedans and two coupes.

The cars in the boxed sets are normally the Third Series cars; however, there are also cardboard boxes that contain a mixture of cars from the Third and Fourth Series. While one could question whether the Shoebox cars were originally in these sets, the number of mint sets containing one or more Shoebox cars clearly suggests that this packaging continued until

Classic Series set, front view

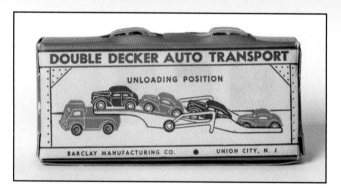

Classic Series set, back view

Classic Series set, cardboard inserts

Classic Series set, side view

Classic Series set, bottom view

As you look at its cardboard box, the typical early Classic Series' configuration within the box has the cab facing right with an orange sedan on the upper left, a green sedan on the upper right, a red coupe on the lower left, and a blue coupe on the lower right. As time evolved, other configurations can be found, frequently with straight substitutions, such as pink or salmon being substituted for red, camel or yellow being substituted for orange, forest green being substituted for light green, and light blue being substituted for blue. Third Series colors such as silver do not appear to have been included in the trailer sets. Colors that did not appear in trailer sets are thought to have been found only in circle packs, which began to be sold at least by the early 1960s.

sometime after the introduction of the Shoebox cars. Boxes of the four-car sets were wrapped in newspaper or tissue paper and shipped in cardboard boxes containing various quantities to retailers.

In contrast to the four-car transport sets, we do not know how the Miniature Trains or the two-car transport sets were packaged after World War II, but before the introduction of the blister packs. It is possible that they were mounted on a small piece of cardboard and held to the cardboard by means of rubber bands. We do know that individual cars were sold in the early 1950s without packaging; they were simply set on the retailers' counters and sold individually at five cents apiece. It is likely that the individual cars were wrapped in tissue paper and shipped in relatively large groups similar to the way Barclay shipped its military and civilian figures prior to the introduction of the blister pack packaging.

Blister Packs

In the late 1950s, Barclay began packaging its toys in blister packs, which have a printed cardboard base with a plastic cover that is glued to the cardboard. The blister packs offered several advantages. The toys could be more easily transported and displayed without damage, the bright colored cardboard backgrounds showed off the toys, and toys, such as the transport cars, could be sold in groups rather than singly. While Barclay outsourced the printed cardboard backs, the plastic enclosures were manufactured at the Barclay factory and all of the blister packs were assembled and filled at the factory.

It appears that Barclay began to use blister packs for all of its miniature toys at about the same time including all four ranges of toy vehicles. Although the Transport Toys two-car trailer sets and single cars as well as the Miniature Trains had been sold without packaging or with minimal packaging previously, there is no evidence that the Miniature Trucks and Miniature Cars were sold in any way other than in blister packs.

Over the twelve- to fifteen-year period when blister packs were used, a number of distinct styles were utilized. In some cases, a particular style of packaging was used for the product of all four ranges of miniature vehicles. In other cases, a particular style of packaging was used only on one or two of the four vehicle ranges. It is also apparent that multiple styles were used simultaneously, which could reflect the use of different styles of packaging for different customers or groups of customers.

While the following list is believed to be relatively comprehensive, it is almost certain that additional packaging styles do exist. This list is not necessarily in date sequence. Although the earlier styles are listed first, various packaging types were used simultaneously and certain styles were used for multiple ranges while other styles were specific to a given range or series.

While examples of the specific packaging used for the various ranges of miniature toys are found in the detailed catalogs, the basic styles of blister pack packaging are as follows:

Barclay Blister Pack Styles

Solid Yellow Card, Black Printing. One of the earliest packaging styles. While most commonly seen with respect to the Transport Toys, this packaging was used for all four ranges of miniature toy vehicles.

Blister pack style #1, transport set

Blister pack style #1, train set

Blister pack style #1, miniature trucks

Red Background, Vintage Cars. Very early packaging for the antique car series that identifies the specific cars included in this series. The flap identifying the four cars in the set is folded under the bottom half of the pack and then stapled to hold in the two cars. This design of the pack is very unsatisfactory, but it is a very scarce packaging example.

Blister pack style #2

Metal Miniatures Packaging, Version 1. An early packaging type used for single pieces of the Miniature Cars and Miniature Trucks ranges. Highway scene in background and no blue on the right side.

Blister pack style #3

Metal Miniatures Packaging, Version 2. An updated design of Version 1 above with a construction scene on the left and a highway scene with blue background on the right. Exists with both printed and unprinted prices.

Blister pack style #4 without printed price

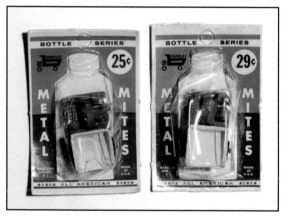

Blister pack style #4 with printed price

Metal Miniatures Packaging, Version 3. A slight variation of Version 2 above with the placement of the vehicle in a diagonal position rather than a straight vertical position. Scarce packaging example. *Blister pack style #5 not illustrated.*

Metal Mobile Miniatures (Trucks). A very early packaging type for three Miniature Trucks. There is a semi-trailer truck in the middle slot and two smaller trucks above and below the semi-trailer truck. All of the trucks have metal wheels and are from the earliest varieties within the various series. A very scarce packaging example.

Blister pack style #6

Miniature Autos Seven-Car Package, Lined Circle with Blue Triangles. Only used for seven-car packages. Center of package has a "stop" sign. Relatively scarce packaging example. Either all Classic Series or a mixture of Classic and Modern Series cars.

Blister pack style #7

White Base with Red and Blue Vertical Stripes. Used for all four ranges; however, this packaging is somewhat scarce.

Blister pack style #10, miniature trucks

Miniature Autos Seven-Car Package, Yellow Circle with White Triangles. Only used for seven-car packages. Center of package is plain. Somewhat more common than type 7 above. Either all Classic Series or a mixture of Classic and Modern Series cars.

Blister pack style #8

All American Packaging with Red on Top, Blue on Bottom. This packaging was used for all four ranges. While all Barclay blister packs are scarce, this version of the blister pack packaging is probably the most common.

Blister pack style #11, transport toys cars

Yellow Base with Red and White. Used for all four ranges. Examples include trailer sets of the Transport Toys and three-car trains. For the Miniature Trucks and Cars, this packaging variation was used for sets of two cars or two trucks. A somewhat more common type of packaging.

Blister pack style #9, miniature cars

Blister pack style #9, transport set

Blister pack style #11, miniature car, one car

Blister pack style #11, miniature car, two car

Paisley Background Packaging. This packaging was used toward the end of Barclay's existence. It is most frequently seen used for various Transport Toy and Miniature Train sets. The paisley background packaging was used for individual semi-trailer trucks and may have been used for other Miniature Trucks and Cars.

Blister pack style #12, transport sets, blue and black paisley

Blister pack style#12, transport set, yellow and green paisley

Wheel-a-Rific Packaging. This packaging was specifically designed for the Wheel-a-Rific car variations that were produced just prior to Barclay's closure. This type of packaging is scarce.

Blister pack style #15, Wheel-a-Rific miniature car

New Metal Mites—Ten Cars. This packaging was specifically for ten cars from the final version of Modern Series cars. The package includes the notation that non-toxic paints were used. This type of packaging is scarce.

Blister pack style #13, transport toys cars

New Metal Mites-Trailer Set with Five Cars. This packaging includes a four-car trailer and five cars from the final series of Modern Series cars. This type of packaging is very scarce.

Blister pack style #14, transport set and extra car

Metal Mites for Play— Three Toys. This packaging contained three individual Miniature Trucks and Cars. The toys in this packaging may be either the traditional colors or neon colors. The packaging was introduced in the final years before Barclay ceased operations and includes the notation that non-toxic paints were used. This type of packaging is scarce.

Blister pack style #16

Metal Mites for Play—Five Toys. This packaging contained five individual Miniature Trucks and Cars. The toys in this packaging may be either the traditional colors or neon colors. The packaging was introduced in the final years before Barclay ceased production and includes the notation that non-toxic paints were used. This type of packaging is scarce.

Blister pack style #17

All Metal Mighty Trucks—Three Semi-Trailer Toys. This packaging contained three semi-trailer trucks. The toys in this packaging may be either the traditional colors or neon colors. The packaging was introduced in the final years before Barclay closed and includes the notation that non-toxic paints were used. This type of packaging is scarce.

Blister pack style #18

As noted above, multiple types of blister pack packaging were used simultaneously. Since a given packaging design may have been used over a period of years, a number of different prices may be found for a specific type of toy. It is also clear that packaging was produced with both preprinted pricing and without any pricing. Examples of the packaging used for specific types of toys can be found in the detailed catalogs.

Prototypes for Products that Were Never Manufactured

According to Rucci and others, a number of products were designed, but never actually produced.[20] Three examples are a medium-size gasoline truck for which a mold was made, but was only used to produce prototypes (see Appendix for example); a troop transport truck in the Miniature Trucks scale for which a plaster prototype exists; and a Christmas manger set for which a portion of the prototype pieces exist. Since Barclay made hundreds of different toys over nearly a fifty-year period, it is reasonable to expect that any number of other products were designed, but never produced.

Reproductions and Out-of-the-Factory Alterations

The principal alteration encountered with respect to Barclay vehicles are toys painted outside of the factory. Examples include colors that do not match, colors that never existed, two-tone combinations, and colors painted by brush. Aside from the use of non-standard colors, it is almost impossible to paint the Barclay pieces with the wheels on and it is very difficult to take the wheels off and then duplicate the construction of the axle. Even when the color and painting technique is matched, pieces painted outside the factory generally contain traces of the original color on the underside as well as inside the wheel-wells. If there is any paint on the wheels, it is almost a certain indication that the toy has been repainted.

Since reproductions and out of the factory alterations are not considered collectible, this book does not dwell on these pieces. At a minimum, reproductions have been made of the First Series Transport cars, the Third Series trailers, both aluminum and cast, and the Third Series cabs. These reproductions can generally be spotted due to variations in the thickness of the metal, the cutting techniques used for the trailers, the type of axles and tires, the thickness and quality of the castings, the size of the castings, the paint colors, the method of painting, and other details.

Identification and Description

Dating

Dating the various components and variations found in the Barclay ranges of miniature toys is somewhat problematic. Dating is complicated by the almost total non-existence of contemporary information from the Barclay Manufacturing Company itself and the very limited number of contemporary catalogues with listings for these toys. So far as is known, no comprehensive, contemporary resource exists concerning these toys and the catalog pages that have been found are fragmentary at best.

The dates included in this book are based upon the best existing information and are subject to change. The production dates of the various ranges and series are generally correct. The dates of certain variations can be deduced from other facts, an example being the white rubber tires used on the first two series and the earlier varieties of the third series. We know that white rubber ceased to be used on toys in the early part of the World War II because rubber was needed for the war effort and was rationed.

Another technique to date the toys is to compare known mint sets. While the contents of most sets have been altered with various substitutions, there are examples of mint sets where the owner knows when a particular set was purchased or that it was purchased with all of its original wrappings. Additional information has been gained from store catalogs, former employees, and advertisements.

It should be noted that the dating of some pieces has changed since the publication of *Barclay Toys*. As an example, white tires are found on some later sets of the Classic Series in the Transport Toys range as well as some of the racers in the Miniature Cars range. We now know that this occurred when Barclay received a shipment of white tires rather than black tires. Rather than returning the incorrect shipment, Barclay went ahead and used the white wheels on these toys.[21]

Among the additional factors complicating dating for various Barclay toys was the company's tendency to continue to use old parts, the periodic reworking of the molds, the substitution of different materials, and the overlapping production of certain variations and/or series. These factors are particularly acute with regard to the various series in the Transport Toys range. Examples of the use of older parts and reworking the molds have already been mentioned. The fact that the cars of the Third and Fourth Series were produced simultaneously for several years is an example of the overlapping of some series. For the most part, discrete dates are used, meaning that one series is dated as ending a given year and the next set is assumed to have been manufactured in the next year. In reality, a new series or variation could have been produced at any time of the year. It is also likely that multiple series and/or variations were produced at the same time and, therefore, overlapped.

Condition

Throughout this catalog, the ten-point "C" scale frequently used in toy collecting catalogs and auctions has been adopted. On this scale, the collectible grades are roughly:

C6 Good: Played with condition with overall wear. While played with, all parts are present and all paint is original. Considered collectible by many collectors. Inside of castings may be discolored.

C7 Good Plus: Overall wear, but noticeably less wear than C6. All parts are present and all paint is original.

C8 Very Good: Minor overall wear, clean, very good color and overall condition. At least hints of luster on the inside of the casting and on the metal wheels of the various vehicles and train cars should be present.

C9 Excellent: Near mint, minor chips and abrasions. The inside of vehicles and train cars as well as the metal wheels should be bright and shiny. There should be little to no rust on the metal axles. The piece should be clean and the paint should be bright.

C10 Mint: Mint means exactly as the piece came from the factory. The piece may be self-standing, mint in a box (MIB), or mint on a card (MOC) in the case of the blister packs. Each piece must be clean and bright. There must be originally luster on the inside and any metal wheels of the vehicles or the train cars. There should be no rust on the metal axles.

Judging condition is complicated by several factors. Since the Barclay miniature vehicles were inexpensive toys, they were not necessarily delivered from the factory in pristine, flawless condition. It is not unusual to see one or more pieces with minor chips and abrasions even though they have never been out of their original packaging. This is even true of vehicles in blister packs with absolutely no possibility of having been used or otherwise damaged after leaving the factory. Pieces that are absolutely mint can also be found with manufacturing flaws such as cracks or holes in their casting.

Common manufacturing flaws include fragments of metal on the casting, extra metal in the windows, thin spots in the metal, and small cracks or holes in the casting. Painting is another issue. While the painting process was discussed earlier, the quality of the paint job can vary greatly depending upon when the piece was produced, the care or lack of care applied when the piece was painted, and the color of the paint. The most common painting flaw is incomplete coverage. Pieces can be found with little or no wear from play, but with rusted axles and discolored interiors and wheels. Rust is also frequently seen on the steel supports of the four-car transport trailers. The rust is typically the result of moisture. Discoloration of the lead is the result of oxidation. Oxidation occurs naturally; however, it can be hastened if the piece has been in a moist area for an extended period. Discoloration of the lead can also occur from the oils of the skin when it is handled with bare hands.

Rarity

Except in the case of the most knowledgeable collectors, rarity has not been widely acknowledged within the various ranges of Barclay miniature vehicles. In truth, there is a tremendous range of rarity with respect to these toys. This publication uses a rarity scale with rarity specified from R-1 (very common) to R-10 (unique):

- **R-1**: Very common
- **R-2**: Common, but less often seen than R-1
- **R-3**: Seen, but relatively infrequently
- **R-4**: Scarce, seen but difficult to locate
- **R-5**: Very scarce, difficult to locate
- **R-6**: Extremely scarce, seldom seen
- **R-7**: Rare, few examples known to exist
- **R-8**: Very rare, 5 to 10 examples exist
- **R-9**: Extremely rare, 2 to 4 examples exist
- **R-10**: Unique

We know that millions of pieces of the various Barclay miniature vehicles were produced. Based upon observations at toy shows and auctions, it appears that most of these toys were destroyed and/or discarded many years ago. While both sets and individual pieces are seen, most examples are used and are of the more common varieties. Certain pieces, varieties, and colors are scarce to rare and some pieces are in the R-8 to R-10 categories. Extremely rare pieces exist in all four ranges. The listings attempt to give some feeling for the relative rarity of various pieces. There is no attempt to differentiate the rarity of pieces in various conditions; therefore, only one rarity number is assigned to each piece. This is meant to give an indication of the relative rarity of that piece across all conditions. It is clear that true R-9 and R-10 pieces are scarce in virtually all varieties and very rare in the more scarce varieties.

Although it is believed that a number of pieces listed as R-7 should be in the R-8 to R-10 categories, most pieces are assigned rarity codes no higher than R-7. The rarity scales are based upon the actual observation of many thousands of examples on the part of a number of advanced collectors. As more information surfaces and more people become aware of the variations and their relative scarcity, these initial assignments will necessarily have to be updated.

Pricing

Pricing the Barclay miniature vehicles is difficult. While these items are actively sought after and rising in price, only the most knowledgeable buyers and sellers differentiate pricing between the relatively common and the much more scarce varieties. The prices listed in this catalog are the prices a knowledgeable collector is willing to pay for an example in an arms-length transaction. Given the fact that many transactions occur without rarity being fully recognized by one or both parties and that even mint specimens can vary in quality, prices are given in relatively large ranges.

Authentication

It is assumed that additional varieties may exist within the various ranges and series discussed. This is particularly true with respect to the existence of additional colors in each of the four ranges of vehicles. Information concerning authentication of Barclay miniature toys, whether new varieties or existing varieties, can be found at www.barclaytoys.com.

Detailed Catalog

Transport Range

First
or Vintage Series

Vintage Series sets

The First or Vintage Series of the Transport Toys range is quite scarce and many of the individual pieces are rare. Since none of the pieces have any indication of the manufacturer, many collectors of the Transport Toys from the Classic and Modern series have not realized that the transports and cars from the First and Second Series are related to the transports and cars of the later series. Since the publication of *Barclay Toys*, our knowledge regarding the Vintage Series has substantially expanded. While the only significant differences found with the trailers are color and wheel variations and the only significant differences with respect to the automobiles are color and window variations, significant casting variations are now recognized with regard to the cabs, in addition to their color and wheel variations.

The Series was first manufactured in 1932 or 1933 and production continued through most of the 1930s. The castings for the cabs and cars were created by the slush casting method where hot metal was poured into brass molds to produce the castings. Paint was applied to the castings by spraying. The trailers were stamped from steel and spray painted. Axles were inserted and the wheels were added after the paint was dry. Unlike the later Classic Series where the cars were sold separately, to the best of our knowledge, the Vintage Series components were only sold in sets consisting of a cab, trailer, sedan, and coupe.

Vintage Series Colors

The colors used in the Vintage Series are relatively straightforward. There are five distinct colors, blue, green, orange, red, and yellow. As is typically found with Barclay products, shading and tint differences exist with respect to the various colors. Blue was only used on the cars and is a darker shade. The darker green was used relatively consistently on the cabs and cars with a lighter shade used on the steel trailers. The shading and tint of red is relatively consistent, but there are slight variations. Orange was used on both the cars and trailers; however, there are significant shade and tint differences of the orange on the cars ranging from a very light shade to a dark shade similar to the burnt orange in the Modern Series. The orange used on the trailers was much lighter. Yellow was only used on the cars and this shade of yellow is the same bright shade seen on the early cars in the Classic Series.

Vintage Series cars (lacking the blue color)

Vintage Series Cabs, Trailers, and Cars

The detailed listing grid for the First Series is shown in two parts. The first section, shown immediately below, shows all of the major variations, which are known, with the exception of the casting variations of the cabs, which are shown in the second section. Each piece in the sets will be discussed below.

Scarcity and pricing is listed in italics after the detailed description for each piece. Due to variations seen in the market, prices are listed in ranges for examples in C-8 (Very Good) and C-10 (Mint) conditions.

As an aid to the users of *Barclay Toys*, listings that appear in *Barclay Toys* are shown in a darker color without an "x." New variations are shown in a lighter color with an "x." Each piece in the sets will be discussed below.

Type	Ref.	Years	Characteristics	Colors					
			First or Vintage Series (Cabs and Trailers)	Blue	Green	Green/Blue	Orange/Blue	Red	Red/Blue
C1	(BV152)	1932-37	Cast, white wheels, red hubs, Model A Ford. **See detail listing below.**		░		░	░	
C1.4	(BV152)	1937	Cast, white wheels, no hubs, Model A Ford. **See detail listing below.**		x				
2T1	(BV152)	1932-37	Steel, white wheels, red hubs, painted				x	░	
2T2	(BV152)	1937	Steel, white wheels, no hubs, painted		x				

Notes: (1) The 2T2 Trailer appears to be part of an original set with the C1.4 cab; however, it is the same trailer as is found in the Second Series.

Vintage Series Cabs

The cabs are two and one-quarter inches long and have an open window on each side. As was the case with all the cast pieces in the various series, the cabs were spray painted on the outside; the inside should be the original silver color just as it came out of the mold except where paint may have come through the windows. The cabs have a rectangular shape, look as if they belong to the 1920s or early 1930s, and appear to be modeled after the Model A Ford trucks of that era.

A distinguishing characteristic of most of the cabs and trailers is the addition of a red, wooden hub on each wheel, similar to the hubs on many Barclay vehicles of this era. On both the cabs and trailers, the wheels were made of natural, white rubber. A somewhat more scarce variation of both the cabs and trailers is the existence of some sets with plain white rubber wheels rather than the more common variety with hubs. It can be assumed that the variety without hubs was produced toward the end of the production cycle of the Vintage

Vintage cab, side view

Vintage cab, front view

Vintage cab, rear view

Vintage cab, bottom view

Series when Barclay was phasing out the use of hubs on all of its vehicles.

In *Barclay Toys*, there was no differentiation with respect to the castings for the cabs. Thanks to the observations of the late Douglas Ehrenhaft,[22] we now recognize that there are at least five distinct castings of the cabs, which are outlined below.

Scarcity and pricing are listed in italics after the detailed description for each piece. Due to variations seen in the market, prices are listed in ranges for examples in C-8 (Very Good) and C-10 (Mint) conditions.

As an aid to the users of *Barclay Toys*, listings that appear in *Barclay Toys* are shown in a darker color without an "x." New variations are shown in a lighter color with an "x." Each piece in the sets will be discussed below.

Type	Ref.	Years	Characteristics	Colors	
			Model A Cab—Detail of C1 cabs listed above: all cabs cast with wheels having red hubs unless noted as having solid wheels.	**Green**	**Red**
C1.1	(BV152)	1932–37	Plain hood, no hitch bars, plain tank, hubs	x	
C1.2	(BV152)	1932–37	Plain hood, no hitch bars, cross on tank, hubs	x	x
C1.3	(BV152)	1932–37	Plain hood, small hitch bars, cross on tank	x	
C1.4	(BV152)	1932–37	Plain hood, long hitch bars, plain tank, solid wheels	x	
C1.5	(BV152)	1932–37	Hood louvers, small hitch bars, cross on tank, wheels with hubs or solid wheels	x	

Notes: (1) C1.1–1.5 hitches vary in height, flashing on some pieces look like radiator caps.
(2) C1.1–1.5. Although these variations have been identified, it is very likely that additional variations exist.

Vintage Series Cabs (Casting Details)

You will note that the primary differences in the castings for the Vintage Series cabs relate to the hood, the hitch, and the gas tank. Undoubtedly these differences evolved as brass molds deteriorated and new molds were created. Whether these changes reflected an attempt to increase the detail of the toy or reflected the creative impulses of the designers and the tool-and-die men, we will probably never know.

With respect to the Vintage Series cabs, green is by far the most common color. The red cab is by far the scarcer variety. Particularly with this series, finding examples in mint or near-mint condition in this series is challenging. Of particular concern is the condition of the rubber tires, which, if original, more often than not are cracked. While original tires are clearly preferred, it is not unusual to find examples of these cabs with replacement tires. Since these toys are seventy to eighty or more years old, they are scarce in all conditions.

R4: Green ($25-35) ($40-65)
R5: Red ($35-45) ($55-80)
R4/R7: Specialized Cab Castings ($25-80) ($40-100)

Vintage Series Trailers

In contrast to the later transport trailers, the trailers in the First Series are made from stamped metal with paint on both sides of the trailer platform. The trailers are three and one-quarter inches long. The underside is painted a light blue, whereas, the upper part of the trailers are light green, orange, or red. As with the cabs, the green trailers are the most common and the red trailers are somewhat scarcer. The orange trailers are extremely scarce. The wheels are white rubber with a red hub on each wheel.

R4: Light Green, Red ($25-35) ($45-65)
R7: Orange ($80-100) ($150-200)

Vintage cab, C1.1

Vintage cab, C1.2

Vintage cab, C1.4

Vintage cab, C1.5

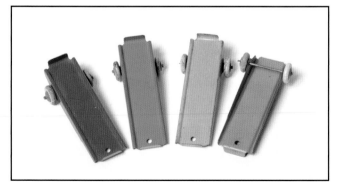
Vintage trailers

Vintage Series Cars

Scarcity and pricing is listed in italics after the detailed description for each piece. Due to variations seen in the market, prices are listed in ranges for examples in C-8 (Very Good) and C-10 (Mint) conditions.

As an aid to the users of *Barclay Toys*, listings that appear in *Barclay Toys* are shown in a darker color without an "x." New variations are shown in a lighter color with an "x." Each piece in the sets will be discussed below.

As is the case throughout the various Transport Toy series, the cars come in two varieties, sedans and coupes. All of the cars have metal wheels, a characteristic of all Barclay transport cars until 1965. The sedan is one and one-half inches long, whereas the coupe is one and five-eighths inches long. Unlike the later cars, most examples of these cars do not have open win-dows. The sedans are commonly seen in various shades of orange, ranging from a very light shade to a burnt orange shade. Less common sedan colors include blue, green, red, and yellow. The coupe is most commonly found in red, with minor shade and tint variations. Additional colors found on the coupes include blue, green, and orange. The orange sedans and the red coupes are by far the most common. Please note, however, that these cars should not be confused with similar Barclay vehicles that measure two inches long.

While there is agreement that a few examples exist of both the sedans and coupes that were manufactured with open windows, these are relatively rare and most likely were manufactured in the early 1930s. Most examples that are seen with open windows were altered outside the factory.

Type	Ref.	Years	Characteristics	Colors				
				Blue	Green	Orange*	Red	Yellow
First or Vintage Series (Sedans and Coupes)								
S1	(BV152 or 114)	1932-38	Cast, metal wheels, closed windows	x	x		x	
S2	(BV152 or 114)	1932-38	Cast, metal wheels, open windows					
CO1.1	(BV152 or 114)	1932-38	Cast, metal wheels, closed windows	x		x		
CO1.2	(BV152 or 114)	1932-38	Cast, metal wheels painted black, closed windows		x			
CO2	(BV152 or 114)	1932-38	Cast, metal wheels, open windows		x			

Notes: * Exists in two shades-orange and burnt orange.

Vintage sedan, side view

Vintage sedan, front view

Vintage sedan, rear view

Vintage sedan, bottom view

Sedans Closed Windows

R3: Orange ($10-15) ($25-30)
R5: Red ($20-25) ($35-45)
R6: Yellow, Blue, Green ($50-70) ($90-110)

Vintage sedan, dark orange

Vintage sedan, green

Vintage sedan, light orange

Vintage sedan, yellow

Sedans Open Windows

R6: All Colors ($25-85) ($40-135)

Vintage sedan and coupe, open windows

Coupes Closed Windows

R3: Red ($10-15) ($25-30)
R5: Orange ($15-20) ($30-50)
R6: Blue, Green ($50-70) ($90-110)

Vintage coupe, red

Vintage coupe, orange

Coupes Open Windows *(See Example Above)*

R6: All Colors ($25-85) ($40-135)

Vintage Series Original Sets

Original sets are made up of pieces of similar age and condition. A matched original set is more difficult to locate than a set that combines pieces from multiple sources, which vary in age and condition. A set consists of a cab, trailer, sedan, and coupe. Pricing is for a set with the most common pieces. It should be noted that near mint sets that include the rare orange trailer have sold for up to $500.00.

Vintage Series trailer sets

R5: Matched Set ($100-120) ($140-200)

Vintage Series: Other Characteristics, Packaging, and Availability

Axles on all of the pieces are made from a pin with a nub on one end that is crimped on the other end; however, there are some examples of axles on the earlier cars that were made from nails. Over time, the white natural rubber on tires of the cabs and trailers tend to accumulate dirt, turn a darker color, and become dry and brittle. Even when an older tire is washed, the tire will still appear to be off-white rather than the bright white of a new tire. All of the tires on an original set should show a similar degree of aging. If you find a white, new-looking tire on these pieces, it is most certainly a replacement. If faced with the choice of a set with original tires that are cracked or a set with replacement tires, many collectors prefer the set with original tires even if the older tires must be glued together.

Recognizing mint or near mint specimens is somewhat challenging. Aside from a lack of chips, abrasions, and rust, the cast pieces in this series should be bright and shiny in the inside except where paint might have entered through open windows.

Some pieces may appear to be mint, but have a darkened inside as the result of natural oxidation, which may have been compounded by the presence of moisture. Even on mint specimens, the tires will appear off-white and may have cracks. This is a natural part of the aging process for this material and does not necessarily indicate use. In contrast to the later series, there were no four-car transports in the First Series.

As far as is known, this series was sold in sets with a matching cab and trailer and two cars, one sedan and one coupe, in various colors. The most common color combination was a green cab and trailer with an orange sedan and a red coupe. As is illustrated above, these sets came attached to a flat piece of cardboard with slits cut for wheels and with the toy attached to the cardboard with rubber bands. Some stores may have removed the cardboard and laid out the trailer sets for sale individually.

All pieces in this series are scarce. Mint or near mint pieces are extremely scarce.

Example of early transport toys packaging (recreated from original example by Robert E. Wagner)

Second
or Streamlined Series

Not a great deal is known about the Second Series of the Transport Toys. The Second Series was most likely manufactured in 1938 and 1939. As with the First Series, there is no indication on any piece identifying the manufacturer; therefore, the various pieces are often incorrectly identified. Except for color, there are no variations in either the cabs or trailers. The cars are the same as in the First Series. As with the First Series, the cabs and cars were cast by pouring hot metal into brass molds using the traditional slush casting method. The trailers were stamped from steel. After each piece was painted, axles were inserted and the wheels were attached.

As has been discussed, the most interesting aspect of the Streamline Series is the design of the cab, which reflects the design concepts of the Streamline Moderne or Art Moderne design movement. This design movement is normally viewed as a direct outgrowth of the Art Deco design movement, which became an international sensation after the International Exposition of Modern Decorative and Industrial Arts show in Paris in 1925. The Streamlined Series cab,

as well as a number of other vehicles that Barclay manufactured in the latter part of the 1930s, with its sculptured lines and modern look, reflects the influence of Streamline Moderne design concepts found in many American-made consumer products of this era.

Streamlined Series Colors

The colors used in the Streamlined Series are straightforward. Only one color, green or light green was used for the cabs. In contrast, the trailers exist in at least six colors, dark blue, blue, green, orange, red, and white. To further complicate matters, the various trailers may or may not be painted on the underside. Those that are painted on the underside may be painted the same color as the top of the trailer or a different color. The green used on the trailers is lighter than that used in the First Series and the blue is a light blue. The colors are relatively consistent and tend not to have the extreme shading and tint differences found in the later series.

Streamlined Series Cabs, Trailers, and Cars

Streamlined Cabs and Trailers

Scarcity and pricing is listed in italics after the detailed description for each piece. Due to variations seen in the market, prices are listed in ranges for examples in C-8 (Very Good) and C-10 (Mint) conditions.

As an aid to the users of *Barclay Toys*, listings that appear in *Barclay Toys* are shown in a darker color without an "x." New variations are shown in a lighter color with an "x." Each piece in the sets will be discussed below.

Type	Ref.	Years	Characteristics	Colors							
				Blue-Dk.	Blue/Plain	Green	Green/Green	Orange/Red	Red/Plain	Red/Blue	White/White
Second or Streamlined Series (Cabs and Trailers)											
C2	(BV114)	1938	Cast, white wheels, no hubs, "Trailer" on side								
2T2	(BV114)	1938	Steel, white wheels, no hubs, painted	x	x		x	x	x	x	x

Notes: (1) Related cab variety-C2 in red with built-up hitch. Not considered a part of this series; see Appendix.
(2) A transitional variety cab and trailer with red hubs may or may not be original. Pictures of those seen appear to have been restorations that took place outside of the factory.

Streamlined Series Cabs

The cabs are two and one-half inches long with windows on each side. The cab is clearly a more modern, streamlined design. The cab is cast from a lead alloy by the traditional slush casting method. A notable feature of this cab was the word "Trailer" cast into the door area on each side. As with the First Series, the inside of a mint cab should be the original silver color just as it came out of the mold except where paint may have come through the windows. The wheels on the cab are the same white, natural rubber material described for the First Series. The wheels do not have the red wooden hubs that are found on most of the cabs in the First Series.

Cabs from the Second Series occasionally are seen with red wooden hubs; however, an example that was in fact made at the factory has never been authenticated. If authentic cabs with red wooden hubs exist, it can be assumed that they were manufactured during the transitional period as production moved from the First Series to the Second Series. The Second Series cab is only seen in green.

R4: Green ($15-20) ($30-60)

Streamlined Series cab, side view

Streamlined Series cab, front view

Streamlined Series cab, rear view

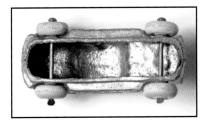
Streamlined Series cab, bottom view

Periodically examples of a red Streamlined Series cab with black wheels and a built-up hitch are seen. Since this cab does not fit the Streamlined Series trailers or the later Classic Series trailers, it is assumed that it was intended for another Barclay toy. This cab variety is pictured in the Appendix for reference only.

Streamlined Series Trailers

The trailers are stamped steel from the same die as the trailers in the First Series; however, they may or may not be painted on the underside. The trailers are three and one-quarter inches long. One notable difference between the trailers in the First Series and the Second Series is that the newer trailers do not have the wooden hubs on the wheels. If authentic Streamlined Series cabs exist with red wooden hubs, it is assumed that these cabs were sold with the older style trailer from the First Series that had wooden hubs.

The white, natural rubber wheels are attached directly to the axles. The trailers are normally found in either green or red. Both colors are seen attached to green cabs. The blue trailers are a light shade in contrast to the darker shade frequently seen on the cast trailers in the early days of the Third Series. Second Series trailers are also found in dark blue, orange, and white. Of these additional colors, blue is the most often seen, but is still quite scarce. Dark blue, orange, and white are all rare.

R4: Green, Red (Plain or Blue Reverse ($20-25) ($40-70)
R6: Blue ($60-80) ($120-180)
R7: Dark Blue, Orange, and White ($75-95) ($110-250)

Streamlined Series Cars

In all respects, the cars in the Streamlined Series are the same as the cars in the First Series. Please refer to the First Series for discussion and pricing.

Streamlined Series Original Sets

Original sets are made up of pieces of similar age and condition. A matched original set is more difficult to locate than a set that combines pieces from multiple sources, which may vary in condition. A set consists of a cab, trailer, sedan, and coupe. Pricing is for a set with the most common pieces. A set made up of the rarer pieces could be priced as much as $400.

R5: Matched Set ($80-100) ($140-200)

Streamlined original sets

Streamlined trailers, top view

Streamlined trailers, bottom view

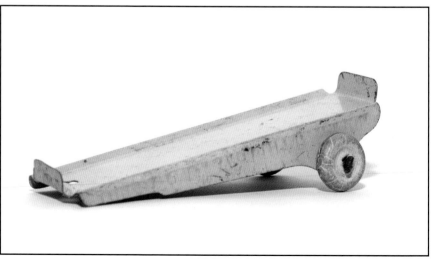

Streamlined trailer, white

Streamlined Series: Other Characteristics, Packaging, and Availability

Axles on the cabs, trailers, and cars are made from a pin with a nub at one end that is crimped on the other end. Over time, the white natural rubber on the cabs and trailers tends to change color and become dry and brittle. On an original set, all of the tires should show a similar degree of aging and/or wear.

The tires on the Streamlined Series cabs and trailers do not have hubs, are a larger piece of rubber, and tend to have survived in better condition than the tires on the Vintage Series sets. If a tire is white and looks new, it is almost certainly a replacement tire. If faced with the choice of a set with original tires that are cracked or a set with replacement tires, many collectors prefer the set with original tires even if the older tires must be glued together.

Aside from lacking chips, abrasions, and rust, mint specimens of the cast pieces should be bright and shiny on the inside except where paint has entered through open windows. Some pieces may have a darkened inside due to oxidation and excessive humidity. Even on mint specimens, the white rubber tires age naturally, will appear to be off-white, and may have cracks.

As far as is known, this series was only sold in sets of a cab, trailer, sedan, and coupe. Although no Streamlined Series set has been found with its original packaging, it is fair to surmise that these sets were shipped attached by rubber bands to a heavy piece of cardboard with cutout slits to hold the rubber bands.

The Second Series was sold with contrasting colors for the cab and trailer as well as with the cab and trailer in the same color. In the case of each color combination of cab and trailer, the set always came with two cars, most commonly a red coupe and an orange sedan. There were no four-car transports in the Second Series.

All pieces in this series are scarce. Mint or near mint pieces are very difficult to locate. Of the four components in the sets and for reasons that are unclear, the trailers seem to be the component that are the most difficult to locate. The cars of the First and Second Series are exactly the same. While we know that the orange and red cars were produced for both series, we do not know with certainty whether the secondary colors were produced for one series or the other or whether they were produced for both series.

Third
or Classic Series

When the Barclay Transport Toys are mentioned, most collectors think of the Third or Classic Series for several reasons. First, it is the most common of the four series. Second, this series includes both two-car and the four-car transport sets. Third, the Third Series was sold in sets of the cab, transport, and matching cars; in sets of cars only; and, for a period of time, the cars were sold individually. Fourth, there is a tremendous amount of variety in the series in terms of the castings, materials, and colors. The series was introduced in 1939 and continued until the mid-1960s. While the wheels were similar to the wheels in the Second Series, all of the pieces had a new design and used the die-

cast injection casting process, which produced a thinner, more refined casting.

The cab and the cars in the Third Series appear to be from the late 1930s and many collectors find this series the most aesthetically appealing of the four series of this toy. The early cabs and trailers in this series were marked with the "Barclay" name; however, the later cabs and trailers as well as all of the cars had neither the manufacturer nor the country of origin identified and are frequently misattributed to other manufacturers. A large number of varieties exist for each of the various pieces. In this section, we will systematically discuss and illustrate each of the known varieties and colors.[23]

Classic Series Colors

In the earlier years of the Classic Series, seven colors were used; light blue, blue, forest green, light green, orange, red, and yellow. With the introduction of the closed wheel-well versions of the cars, the colors camel, pink, and silver appeared. Moss green and gray are believed to have been produced in the 1957 to 1960 era, but they apparently were manufactured for relatively short periods and were sold as part of the trailer sets. In the final years of production, the colors brown, chocolate, clay, cream, flesh, salmon, tan, and lemon yellow appeared. Of these transitional colors, salmon, and lemon yellow were sold both in the seven-car circle packs as well as part of trailer sets. Cream and tan were definitely sold in the circle packs and may or may not have been sold as part of the trailer sets. It is not known when the colors brown, chocolate, clay, and flesh were manufactured; however, with the exception of chocolate, it is safe to assume that most of these colors appeared toward the end of the Classic Series production cycle, which ended in the mid-1960s.

Since the publication of *Barclay Toys*, seven additional colors have been authenticated for the Classic Series cars. Examples of steel blue, aqua green, and gold cars have been found for both the sedans and the coupes. In addition, examples of burnt orange, khaki, lilac, and turquoise have been found for the Classic Series coupes. In all likelihood all of these colors were sold in the seven-car circle packs and were manufactured toward the end of the Classic Series. All of these colors are very scarce. Examples of burnt orange, gold, khaki, lilac, and turquoise are rare.

In certain colors, there are considerable differences in shading and tint. Shades can differ both between the same color produced in the earlier and later years of the Classic Series as well as between colors produced in sequential batches.

Known shading and tint differences include:

Blue: A darker blue ranging from a very pure blue to almost a navy blue

Light Blue: Shades from light to somewhat darker

Steel Blue: Metallic blue, introduced toward the end of Classic Series production, consistent shading

Brown: Based on a small number of examples, the shade is a somewhat darker brown

Light Brown: A light milk chocolate brown, very rare

Camel: Many shades going from lighter to darker: the color always has a yellowish orange tint

Chocolate: Based on a small number of examples, a dark chocolate brown; however, the chocolate Classic Series cabs tend to be somewhat lighter

Clay: At least two shade variations with one slightly lighter than the other; clay has definite orange-brown tint in contrast to the various shades found in the orange color range

Cream: Relatively consistent light off-white shade

Flesh: Based on a small number of examples, a very light brown used to color the flesh on Barclay's military and civilian figurers

Gold: Introduced toward the end of Classic Series production, consistent shading

Gray: Varies from lighter to darker with one version of the lighter color appearing to have a pink tint

Aqua Green: Metallic green, introduced toward the end of Classic Series production, consistent shading

Forest Green: Earlier version has a blue tint; later version is close to an emerald green

Light Green: This common color varies from a relatively consistent lighter green to a somewhat darker version toward the end of the series

Moss Green: Relatively consistent with shading (light to dark) and tint variations, a grayish green

Khaki: Light yellow brown; rare color most likely introduced toward the end of Classic Series production

Lilac: A very light purple color based on very few examples, consistent shading

Burnt Orange: A dark orange with a blackish tint. Based on very few examples, consistent shading

Orange: Common color with relative consistency; however, in the later years of the series some examples tend to be darker, more of a tangerine

Pink: Color has considerable range with some examples appearing to be a washed out, light pink, while others are considerably brighter

Red: A common color used throughout the Classic Series that is fairly consistent, but can vary from a dark or burnt red to a very bright cherry red: differences are easiest seen on the cabs

Salmon: A relatively consistent color with minor shading differences; a reddish pink color with a bluish tint

Silver: Probably the most consistent color in the series

Tan: Introduced in the later years of the series with minor variations in shading

Turquoise: bluish green; rare color most likely introduced toward the end of Classic Series production

Yellow: Almost a chrome yellow with minor variations of color

Lemon Yellow: Introduced in the final years of the series with minor variations in shading; yellow with a white tint

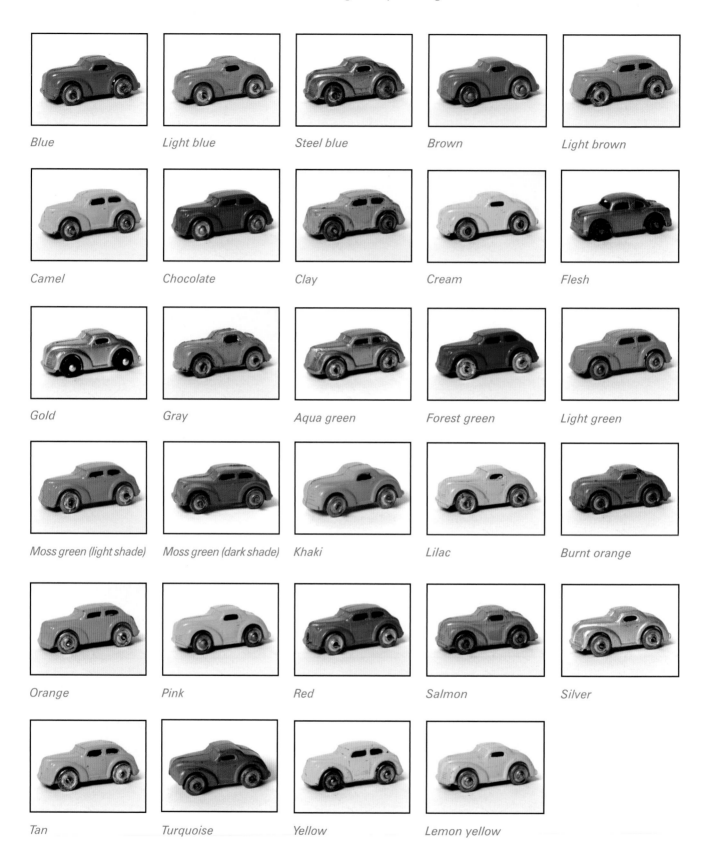

Blue	Light blue	Steel blue	Brown	Light brown
Camel	Chocolate	Clay	Cream	Flesh
Gold	Gray	Aqua green	Forest green	Light green
Moss green (light shade)	Moss green (dark shade)	Khaki	Lilac	Burnt orange
Orange	Pink	Red	Salmon	Silver
Tan	Turquoise	Yellow	Lemon yellow	

Classic Series Cabs

Scarcity and pricing is listed in italics after the detailed description for each piece. Due to variations seen in the market, prices are listed in ranges for examples in C-8 (Very Good) and C-10 (Mint) conditions.

As an aid to the users of *Barclay Toys*, listings that appear in *Barclay Toys* are shown in a darker color without an "x." New variations are shown in a lighter color with an "x." Each piece in the sets will be discussed below.

Type	Ref.	Years	Characteristics	Colors										
Third or Classic Series Cabs				Blue	Blue-Lt.	Chocolate	Green-Forest	Green-Lt.	Green-Moss	Gray	Orange	Pink	Red	Salmon
C3.1.1	(BV11)	1939-42	Cast, White Tires, Open Wheel-Wells, Low Hitch, '38 Ford Cab Over Engine		x			▓					▓	
C3.1.2	(BV11)	1939-40	Same as C3.1.1, Except Lights and Grill Mask, Painted Silver										▓	
C3.1.3	(BV11 or 157)	1945-46	Same as C3.1.1, Except Black Tires								x		▓	
C3.2.1	(BV11 or 157)	1945-49	Cast, Black Wheels, Open Wheel-Wells, High Hitch, '38 Ford Cab Over Engine			x								x
C3.2.2	(BV11 or 157)	1945-46	Same as C3.2.1, Except White Tires										▓	
C3.3.1	(BV11 or 157)	1950	Cast, Black Wheels, Half Open Wheel-Wells, High					▓						
C3.3.2	(BV11 or 157)	1950	Same as C3.3.1, Except Reinforced										x	
C3.4.1	(BV11 or 157) (330 or 440)	1950-65	Cast, Black Wheels, Closed Wheel-Wells, High Hitch, '38 Ford Cab Over Engine, Smooth Wheels	▓				▓			x	▓	▓	▓
C3.4.2	(BV11 or 157) (330 or 440)	1965	Same as C3.4.1, Except Ridged Wheels	x	x	x			▓		x		▓	▓
C3.4.3	(BV11 or 157) (330 or 440)	1960s	Same as C3.4.1, Except White Rubber Wheels										▓	

Note: (1) Classic cabs in yellow may exist, but an example has not yet been authenticated.

The Third or Classic Series cab is approximately two and one-half inches long with four open windows, one on each of the two sides and two in front. The cab is thought to have been modeled after the 1938 Ford "cab over engine" truck cab. The earlier versions of this cab are the only cabs in the Transport Series to have the manufacturer identified. In contrast to the cabs in the earlier two series, the Third Series cab was manufactured using the die-cast injection casting method. If the specimen is in mint condition, the inside of the cab should be shiny and silver in color with a small amount of paint having come through the windows.

With the possible exception of certain of the Third Series cars, the Third Series cab is probably the easiest piece to locate within the various series of Barclay Transport Toys. As with other pieces in the series, the metal axles are often seen with rust. Some exceptionally well-preserved pieces are still dull on the inside due to oxidation. The paint on the Classic Series pieces seems to have been generally well applied with full coverage and a reasonable resistance to the rigors of use. In contrast to the first two series, the cabs within the Third Series include several variations, which will be explained and illustrated below. Please remember that the dating is based on a combination of memory and deduction. These cabs pulled both the two-car and the four-car trailers. Since virtually no records from the Barclay Manufacturing Company exist, the exact dates of some of the variations may never be known.

Since the publication of *Barclay Toys*, two new colors have been identified, chocolate and forest green. In addition one new casting variety has been identified, C3.3.2. Each of these additions will be discussed below and are shown on the grid for the Third Series cabs.

Classic cab, side view

Classic cab, front view

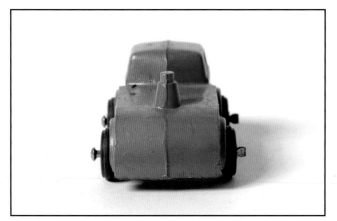

Classic cab, rear view

Classic cab, bottom view

Classic Cab Colors
(moss green shown on page 51)

Blue   *Light blue*   *Chocolate*   *Forest green*   *Light green*

Gray   *Orange*   *Pink*   *Red*   *Salmon*

C3.1.1 The Third Series was introduced in 1939 and produced continually until Barclay ceased toy production in April 1942 to manufacture metal components for the World War II war effort. While the design was completely new, the cab had many of the same characteristics of the earlier cabs including white, smooth, natural rubber wheels. Two characteristics that are often overlooked are open wheel-wells and a low hitch. Later specimens of this cab design have half-closed and then fully closed wheel-wells. While the open wheel-well design continued for a short time after production was resumed in 1945, the molds were apparently modified at this time and the hitch was raised. The adjustment of the hitch apparently was made to eliminate the tendency of the trailer to scrape the back portion of the cab when the trailer was connected to the low hitch variety.

While it is possible that a small number of this variation of the cab were produced after World War II, it is generally assumed that most of the cabs with white rubber wheels were produced before the 1942 shutdown. Natural rubber was in short supply early in the war and was gradually replaced by synthetic rubber soon after the war began. This is the most common version of the early Third Series cabs, but it is still difficult to find in a true mint state with no paint loss, shiny interior, and no rust on the axles.

It was previously thought that this variety only existed in two colors: red and light green. Since the publication of *Barclay Toys*, it is now known that examples of this cab in light blue also exist. The most common color is the light green. The light blue color is rare. On the inside, you will find the words, "Barclay"

and "Made in U.S.A.," identifying both the manufacturer and the country of origin. These identifiers are seen in all open wheel-well variations of this cab.

R3: Light Green ($10-15) ($20-25)
R4: Red ($15-20) ($25-35)
R7: Light Blue ($40-60) ($200-400)

Classic cabs (from bottom to top) C3.1.1, C3.1.3, C3.2.1, C3.2.2-Top View

C3.1.2 As the Third Series was introduced, a number of experiments appear to have taken place with the new transports. This cab is the same as the C3.1.1 cab; however, both the lights and the grill have been painted silver by the mask painting method. This treatment is seen on a number of other Barclay vehicles in the 1930s. This variation is believed to have appeared in 1939 or 1940, soon after the Third Series was introduced, is only known to exist in red, and is extremely scarce. Periodically, examples of this cab appear with hand painted ornamentation. It is generally assumed that any hand painted detail on these cabs occurred outside the factory.

R7: Red ($70-80) ($100-300)

Classic cab with mask painted lights and grill, C3.1.2

C3.1.3 This variation occurred just as production resumed in 1945 or 1946. The cab retains both the open wheel-well and the low hitch; however, the tires have changed to a smooth, black synthetic rubber material. This is a relatively scarce variation and appears to have been produced for only a short time prior to the redesign of the hitch. Since this toy is between fifty and sixty years old, finding this variation in a mint state is somewhat challenging. This variety is most commonly seen in red. Since the publication of *Barclay Toys*, this toy has been authenticated in orange, which is rare.

R4: Red ($10-20) ($30-60)
R7: Orange ($60-80) ($200-400)

C3.2.1 The change in the design of the hitch and the change in the tire to synthetic rubber appear to have occurred at about the same time. This variation retains the open wheel-well, but has the "high" hitch and black tires. It is assumed that production of this variation began at the same time or shortly after production resumed in 1945 and continued for several years. Given Barclay's tendency to overlap production

of different variations, it is possible that some pieces of the low hitch variety continued to be produced even as the high hitch varieties were being introduced. This variety is seen relatively often; however, true mint specimens are elusive. This variation was previously thought to come only in red; however, since the publication of *Barclay Toys*, examples have been authenticated in chocolate and salmon. Both the chocolate and salmon colors are rare.

R2: Red ($20-25) ($30-40)
R7: Chocolate, Salmon ($60-80) ($200-400)

C3.2.2 This variation has open wheel-wells, a high hitch, and white rubber tires. This variety was probably produced in the transition period when production resumed after World War II and reflects the desire to use up any remaining inventory of the white rubber tires. This variation is seen in red only and is scarce.

R4: Red ($15-20) ($30-60)

C3.3.1 (Identified in *Barclay Toys* as C3.3) This cab variety features black synthetic tires and a high hitch; however, the mold has been changed to create half-open or, depending upon your point of view, half-closed wheel-wells. It is not known whether this was done to simplify the manufacturing process or to strengthen the wheel assembly. In any case, this appears to be a relatively short-lived experiment and examples of this type are somewhat scarce. Reflecting continued reworking of the molds, the half-open wheel-well variety only has partial lettering of the manufacturer and country of origin. It is assumed that this type was produced around 1950, immediately before closing the wheel-well altogether. This variation exists in both red and light green with red being by far the most common.

R3: Red ($10-15) ($20-30)
R5: Light Green ($25-35) ($40-60)

Classic cab, half-open wheel-wells, C.3.3.1, top view

Classic cab, half-open wheel-wells, C.3.3.1, bottom view

Classic cabs (from top to bottom) C3.4.1, C3.4.2, C3.4.3, top view

C3.3.2 This cab is a variation of C3.3.1 with an additional reinforcement to the bar to which the rear axle is connected. It appears to be somewhat scarcer than C3.3.1 and, to date, only has been identified in red. It is safe to assume that this variation appeared shortly before the molds were again reworked and the half-closed wheel-wells were completely closed.

R4: Red ($15-20) ($20-25)

Classic cab with additional reinforcement bar, C.3.3.2

Classic cabs (from top to bottom) C3.4.1, C3.4.2, C3.4.3, bottom view

Classic Cab C3.4.1, moss green

C3.4.1 This is the final major type seen in the Third Series cab. This cab retains the high hitch and the smooth black synthetic tires; however, the wheel-wells are now completely closed. This is by far the most commonly seen Third Series cab. While most specimens show wear from play, mint specimens are relatively common. It is assumed that production of this variation began in the early 1950s and continued through the mid-1960s. Virtually all examples of this type are in red; however, green is occasionally encountered. In the late 1950s through 1965, a number of color variations were introduced for short periods. These include dark blue, light blue, gray, orange, and pink. Since the publication of *Barclay Toys*, and example of moss green has been authenticated. All of these colors are extremely scarce in all conditions.

R1: Red ($3-6) ($8-12)
R3: Green ($15-20) ($20-35)
R7: Dark Blue, Light Blue, Gray, Moss Green, Orange, and Pink ($60-80) ($200-400)

C3.4.2 This is another transitional variation. This cab is the same as the C3.4.1 cab with a high hitch and closed wheel-wells; however, the tires have the same ridge as is found on the tires on the Fourth or Modern Series cabs. Since the Modern Series cabs all have ridged tires, this variety suggests that production of the Third and Fourth Series cabs overlapped. This variation is normally found in red and is somewhat scarce. The moss green, gray, and salmon versions are extremely scarce. Since the publication of *Barclay Toys*, examples in blue, light blue, forest green, and orange have been authenticated. All of these additional colors are extremely scarce or rare.

R2: Red ($5-8) ($12-20)
R7: Blue, Light Blue, Forest Green, Moss Green,
*   Gray, Orange, and Salmon ($60-80) ($200-400)*

C3.4.3 The cab is exactly like the C3.4.1 type except that it has white rubber wheels. When *Barclay Toys* was published, there was no explanation for the existence of this cab; it was thought that white tires had been discontinued shortly after World War II. We now know that Barclay received a shipment of tires that mistakenly contained white tires rather than black tires. This occurred in the early to mid-1960s. Rather than return the white tires that were shipped in error, Barclay went ahead and used the white tires on two-car and four-car transport sets as well as certain Miniature Trucks and Cars. This variation appears periodically, but is scarce.

R7: Red ($30-50) ($65-85)

Classic Series Trailers

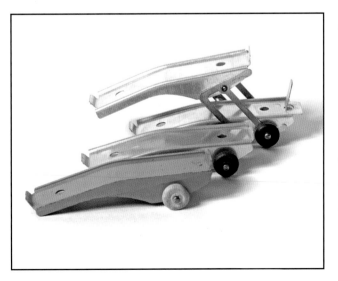

The Third or Classic Series introduced both new constructions for the trailers as well as the very popular four-car trailer. When first introduced in 1939, the Third Series continued the tradition of the First and Second Series and was only offered with a two-car trailer. In this version of the transport sets, the trailer was cast out of a lead alloy and painted in contrast to the use of stamped steel trailers that were produced for the First and Second Series. The same material and die-cast process was used for both the cab and the cars. In the case of the cast trailers, a mint specimen should be bright and shiny on the unpainted underside. The steel axles on a mint specimen should have no rust and again be shiny. Either at the time production resumed in 1945 or shortly thereafter, the composition and the construction of the trailer changed again to stamped, unpainted metal. Initially, the metal used was steel, but this was quickly changed to aluminum.

While there are a number of variations, virtually all of the stamped metal trailers have aluminum platforms with steel connectors on the four-car versions. There are several variations of this trailer; however, the basic design continued throughout the rest of the Third Series and through the Fourth Series. Mint specimens of the aluminum trailers are obtainable, but they are definitely less common than are used specimens. A mint trailer should have a mirror appearance and be free of scratches, rubs, and bends. The metal connectors, the rivets, and the axles should be free of rust and shiny. Dating is again based on a combination of memory and deduction. While it is believed that the dating is relatively accurate, virtually no records exist from Barclay Manufacturing Company and the exact dates of some of the variations may never be known. It also must be remembered that Barclay often overlapped production so some of the trailer variations may have been, and most likely were, produced simultaneously.

Classic Series Two-Car Trailers

Scarcity and pricing is listed in italics after the detailed description for each piece. Due to variations seen in the market, prices are listed in ranges for examples in C-8 (Very Good) and C-10 (Mint) conditions.

As an aid to the users of *Barclay Toys*, listings that appear in *Barclay Toys* are shown in a darker color without an "x." New variations are shown in a lighter color with an "x." Each piece in the sets will be discussed below.

Type	Ref.	Years	Characteristics	Colors				
				Unpainted	Blue-Light	Orange	Yellow	Red
Third or Classic Series Two-Car Trailers								
2T3.1.1	(BV11)	1939-42	Cast, white wheels, painted					x
2T3.1.2	(BV11)	1945-46	Cast, black wheels, painted			x	x	x
2T3.1.3	(BV11)	1945-46	Cast, black wheels, painted, reinforced tabs					
2T3.2.1	(BV11)(330) (BV75)(330)	1945-65	Aluminum, black weels				x	
2T3.2.2	(BV11)	1945-46	Aluminum, white wheels					
		1960-66		x				
2T3.2.3	(BV11)	1945-46	Copper plated steel, black wheels		x			
2T3.2.4	(BV11)	1945-46	Steel, Black Wheels					
2T3.3	(BV11)(330) (BV75)(330)	1965-70	Aluminum, Ridged Black Tires					

2T3.1.1 The Third Series was introduced in 1939 and produced continually until Barclay ceased toy production in April 1942. The design of the trailer differed from the first two series. First, this trailer was manufactured by the injection die-cast casting process using the same materials and processes used to manufacture the cabs and the cars. In contrast to the straight trailers of the earlier series, the trailer is bent in the middle, which brings the back of the trailer down to near ground level. The trailer is approximately three and one-quarter inches long. The top, sides, front tab, and rear tab were painted; however, the bottom of the trailer was not painted. On the underside, the words "BARCLAY" and "MADE IN USA" are included in the casting. Most of the cast trailers have smooth, white, natural rubber wheels suggesting that they were produced before production ceased in the spring of 1942. The most common color is blue followed by yellow and orange. Since the publication of *Barclay Toys*, this type of cast trailer has been authenticated in red, which is rare. For reasons that cannot be fully explained, the paint coverage on the blue version is typically much more complete than it is on the other colors. The yellow trailers, in particular, tend to have areas with less than complete paint coverage.

Two problems arose with respect to the construction of this trailer. First, there was a tendency for the trailer to split approximately at the bend in the trailer. Second, there was a significant likelihood that the tabs either would partially or completely break off. The problem with tab breakage was particularly acute with the orange trailers. Since these toys are now over sixty years old, it is not surprising that mint specimens are difficult to locate. This is particularly true for any color other than blue. The paint on a mint specimen will have a high sheen, the bare metal on the underside will be bright and shiny, and the axle will be free of rust and have a newer appearance. Given Barclay's tendency to use whatever parts were available, it is possible that a small number of these trailers were produced after World War II.

R3: Light Blue ($20-25) ($30-40)
R4: Orange, Yellow ($30-35) ($40-50)
R7: Red ($60-80) ($100-200)

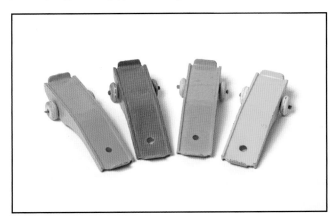

Classic two-car trailers, cast with white rubber tires

2T3.1.2 This variety of the cast trailer is the same as the 2T3.1.1 trailer; however, the tires are smooth, rounded, black synthetic rubber in place of the white natural rubber tires. It is presumed that this version of the trailer was produced at the time production resumed after World War II or very shortly thereafter.

The blue color of this trailer is scarce. Since the publication of *Barclay Toys*, this variety trailer has been authenticated in yellow and orange, which are both scarce, and red, which is a rare.

R4: Light Blue ($25-35) ($40-55)
R6: Yellow, Orange ($40-60) ($80-120)
R7: Red ($60-80) ($100-200)

Classic two-car trailers, cast with black rubber tires (yellow trailer is a 2T3.1.3)

2T3.1.3 This version of the cast trailer is the same as the 2T3.1.2 variety with black synthetic rubber tires. Barclay attempted to reinforce the front and back tabs by placing two extra bars on the upper side of each tab. While the reinforced tabs appear to have helped, the trailer is still seen with broken or partially broken tabs. The problem of spotty paint coverage of the yellow paint also exists with this variety. Since the stamped metal trailer was introduced shortly after production resumed, this variation of the cast trailer had to have had a relatively short life and is more difficult to locate than the version with white tires. As with the white tire version, true mint specimens are quite difficult to locate. This trailer is only seen in yellow.

R4: Yellow ($20-25) ($40-55)

2T3.2.1 Shortly after resuming production of the Transport Series toys in 1945, the cast trailer was abandoned. These new trailers were stamped aluminum and were normally unpainted. These trailers were made for Barclay by Heyco Products, Inc. ("Heyco"), which was located in Kenilworth, New Jersey. In contrast to the cast trailers, there is no indication of either the manufacturer or the country of origin. The platform is a single piece of aluminum bent in the middle, similar to the cast

trailers. This means that the back of the trailer rides close to the ground. There are tabs at each end, which are bent up to hold the cars on the trailer. The wheels are smooth, black, synthetic rubber. This trailer was used for the two-car transport set from 1945 until approximately 1965. Mint specimens are available and should have a bright, unused appearance with no scratches or marks. On a mint example, the steel axle should have no rust, the appearance should be shiny and new, and the tires should not show use.

Since the publication of *Barclay Toys*, a variation of this trailer has been authenticated. The variation is the exact same aluminum trailer, but it is painted yellow. It is not known exactly when these trailers were manufactured; however, it is assumed that they were produced in the 1940s or, perhaps, the early 1950s. The yellow version is quite scarce.

R1: Unpainted ($5-10) ($15-20)
R6: Yellow ($40-60) ($80-120)

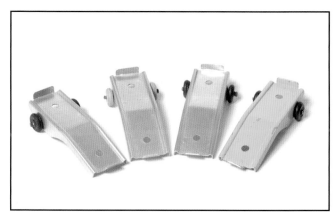

Classic Two-Car Trailers (left to right) 2T3.2.1, 2T3.2.2, and 2T3.3, all unpainted; 2T3.2.1 yellow

2T3.2.2 This version of the two-car trailer is the same as the 2T3.2.1 except that it has the smooth, round, white rubber tires used on the earlier trailers. Although indistinguishable, this trailer version was manufactured at two different times. It first appeared in 1945 or 1946 shortly after production restarted after World War II with the C3.2.2 cab. The second version of this trailer appeared in the 1960s with the C3.4.3 cab. Although the tires on the first version will appear to be discolored from age, even when mint, the tires on the second version, when mint, will appear to be virtually new. See example above.

R4: Unpainted, White Rubber Wheels ($20-25) ($40-55)

2T3.2.3 This version of the two-car trailer is the same as the 2T3.2.1 type except that the platforms are stamped from copper-plated steel. These trailers are typically seen with the older style Third Series cabs and they were manufactured sometime shortly after 1945 when Heyco purchased a company that specialized in copper-coated metals. Quite by accident, there was an inventory of copper-coated steel of the correct thickness and Heyco utilized this metal to create this version of the trailers. You can confirm the authenticity of these trailers by checking them with a magnet.

Since the publication of *Barclay Toys*, a variation of this trailer with a top surface painted blue has been authenticated. The plain copper-plated trailer is difficult to locate and virtually impossible to find in mint condition. The blue version of this trailer is rare in all conditions.

R6: Unpainted ($35-45) ($100-200)
R7: Blue ($75-100) ($125-250)

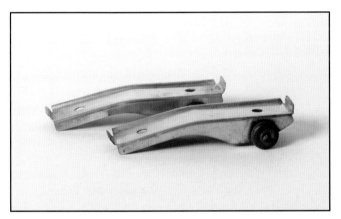

Classic two-car trailers (bottom to top) 2T3.2.3 copper-coated steel, 2T3.2.4 steel

2T3.2.4 This version of the two-car trailer is also the same as the 2T3.2.1 type except that both the platforms and the connectors are stamped from sheet steel. You can confirm the authenticity of these trailers by checking them with a magnet. We now know that these trailers were made very shortly after production resumed following the end of World War II. It is quite possible that they were the first version of the new metal trailers manufactured following the discontinuation of the cast trailers of the same design. Rucci has stated that the steel trailers were replaced with aluminum due to their extra weight.[24] Another factor that may or may not have been a consideration in ending the production of steel trailers was the fact that they tend to rust and discolor over time. Regardless

of the reason, Barclay ended the production of the steel trailers. Examples of these trailers are difficult to locate, particularly without rust, and extremely scarce in mint condition. See example above.

R6: Unpainted ($35-45) ($100-200)

2T3.3 This final version of the two-car trailer in the Third Series era is the same as the 2T3.2.1; however, the tires have a ridge in the middle of the tire where the tire touches the ground. The ridged tire is in contrast to the smooth round tires that had previously been used. The ridged tires were introduced on the Fourth Series cabs in early to mid-1960s; however, the C3.4.2 cab also has ridged tires. At least a small number of Third Series sets had the C3.4.2 cab and the 2T3.3 trailer. This trailer continued to be manufactured until 1969 or 1970 as part of all of the Fourth Series two-car sets. This trailer is available in mint and near-mint conditions; however, Fourth Series sets are seen far less frequently than sets of the Third Series. See example above.

R2: Unpainted ($5-10) ($15-20)

Classic Series Four-Car Trailers

Scarcity and pricing is listed in italics after the detailed description for each piece. Due to variations seen in the market, prices are listed in ranges for examples in C-8 (Very Good) and C-10 (Mint) conditions.

As an aid to the users of *Barclay Toys*, listings that appear in *Barclay Toys* are shown in a darker color without an "x." New variations are shown in a lighter color with an "x." Each piece in the sets will be discussed below.

4T3.1.1 Either at the time production resumed in 1945 or shortly thereafter, Barclay introduced its extremely popular four-car transport. These trailers were also made for Barclay by Heyco. In contrast to the cast trailers, there is no indication of either the manufacturer or the country of origin. This trailer has an upper and lower platform made from stamped aluminum. The platforms are connected with two connectors or riggers normally made from stamped galvanized steel. The steel connectors are attached to the upper platform with hollow brass rivets. An axle holding two smooth, rounded, black synthetic rubber tires is attached to the lower platform. The platform riggers are held to the lower platform by means of the axle.

Type	Ref.	Years	Characteristics	Colors
				Unpainted
Third or Classic Series Four-Car Trailers				
4T3.1.1	(BV157) (440)	1945-64	Aluminum, smooth black wheels, tab hole, separate steel or aluminum tab in place	
4T3.1.2	(BV157) (440)	1945-46	Same as 4T3.1.1, but smooth white tires	
		1960-66		x
4T3.1.3	(BV157) (440)	1945-46	Same as 4T3.1.1, but copper plated steel	
4T3.1.4	(BV157) (440)	1945-46	Same as 4T3.1.1, but steel	
4T3.1.5	(BV157) (440)	1960s	Aluminum, smooth black wheels, tab hole with lower tab unbent and scoring across the tab	
4T3.1.6	(BV157) (440)	1960s	Aluminum, smooth black wheels, tab hole on both lower and upper platform. No scoring.	
4T3.1.7	(BV157) (440)	1965-70	Same as 4T3.1.1, but ridged tires	
4T3.2.1.1	(BV157) (440) (BV107) (440)	1965-70	Aluminum, no tab hole, back tab bent up, ridged black tires	
4T3.2.1.2	(BV157) (440) (BV107) (440)	1965	Aluminum, no tab hole, back tab bent up, smooth black tires	x
4T3.2.2	(BV157) (440) (BV107) (440)	1965-70	Aluminum, no tab hole, back tab not bent up, ridged black tires	

Notes: (1) The variety listed as 4T3.1.6.1 in *Barclay Toys* most likely was not a product of the factory. This "variety" appears to have resulted from purchasers bending the back tabs up after having lost the small movable tab.
(2) Additional variety—4T3.2.2 axle with nubs at both ends.
(3) Additional variety—4T3.1.4 one steel and one aluminum platform.
(4) Additional variety—4T3.1.1 aluminum platforms with copper plated steel connectors.
(5) Additional variety–Four-Car Trailer with aluminum platforms and copper-steel connectors.

Each of the platforms is bent in the middle like the platform for the two-car transport. The upper platform has tabs bent up at each end to hold the cars on the platform. The lower platform has a tab bent up in front; however, in the back there is an unbent tab. The fact that the back tab is not bent up allows the cars to be rolled off the lower trailer. In order to keep the cars on the transport, there is a small hole at the back of the lower platform that holds a separate, detachable tab. This detachable tab is a very small piece made from either aluminum or steel. Since this piece is frequently lost, many trailers of this type have had the straight tab bent up by their owner in order to keep the cars on the trailer.

With variations, this was the basic design of the four-car trailer throughout the Third and Fourth Se-

ries. Mint specimens are available and should have a bright, unused appearance with no scratches or marks. The axle and the connectors are steel, should have no rust, and should have a shiny, new appearance. The black tires should not show use. This particular version of the trailer was produced continuously from 1945 through the mid-1960s, when a variation with ridged tires appeared.

R1: Unpainted ($25-35) ($40-55)

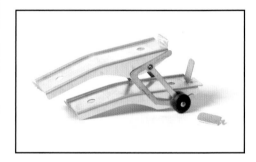

Classic four-car trailer with tab 4T3.1.1

4T3.1.2 This version of the four-car trailer is the same as the 4T3.1.1 trailer except that it has the smooth, round, white rubber tires used on the earlier trailers. Although indistinguishable, this trailer version was manufactured at two different times. It first appeared in 1945 or 1946 with the C3.2.2 cab, shortly after production restarted after World War II. The second version of this trailer appeared in the 1960s with the C3.4.3 cab. Although the tires on the earlier version of this trailer will appear to be discolored from age even when mint, the tires on the second version, when mint, will appear to be virtually new.

R5: Unpainted ($40-50) ($65-100)

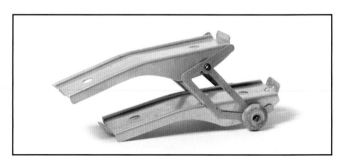

Classic four-car trailer, tab bent up, 4T3.1.2

4T3.1.3 This version of the four-car trailer is the same as the 4T3.1.1 trailer except that the platforms are stamped from copper-plated steel. These trailers are typically seen with the older style Third Series cabs and they were manufactured sometime shortly after 1945 when Heyco purchased a company that specialized in copper-coated metals. Quite by accident, there was an inventory of copper-coated steel of the correct thickness and Heyco utilized this metal to create this version of the trailers. You can confirm the authenticity of these trailers by checking them with a magnet. In most cases, the copper tab has been lost and the lower, back tab has been bent up to hold the cars on the lower platform of the trailer. The four-car copper-plated trailer is extremely difficult to locate and virtually impossible to find in mint condition, particularly with its original copper tab.

R6/R7: Unpainted ($50-65) ($150-250)

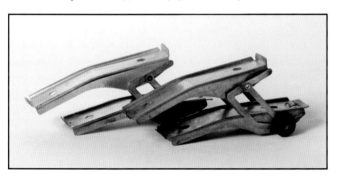

Classic four-car trailers (bottom to top) 4T3.1.3–copper-covered steel, 4T3.1.4–steel

4T3.1.4 This version of the four-car trailer is also the same as the 4T3.2.1 except that both the platforms and the connectors are stamped from sheet steel. When you pick up this trailer, it is noticeably heavier than the aluminum version. You can confirm the authenticity of these trailers by checking them with a magnet. We now know that these trailers were made very shortly after production resumed following the end of World War II. It is almost certain that these trailers were the first version of the four-car trailers. As previously noted, Rucci has stated that the steel trailers were replaced with aluminum due to their extra weight. Another factor that may or may not have been a consideration in ending the production of steel trailers was the fact that they tend to rust and discolor over time. Regardless of the reason Barclay ended the production of the steel trailers, they are difficult to locate and extremely scarce in mint condition. See example above.

R6: Unpainted ($45-65) ($100-150)

4T3.1.5 This variation of the basic four-car trailer is similar to the 4T3.1.1 variety. It has the hole on the lower platform for the detachable tab; however, the straight tab that extends from the platform was scored with the intention that the customer could then bend the tab up. It is not clear whether the detachable tab was included in these sets or not. We know that the basic 4T3.1.1 trailer continued into the earlier years of the blister pack packaging; therefore, it is assumed that the scored-tab trailers were manufactured in the early 1960s. This version of the trailer is available; however, it is clearly scarcer than most versions of the four-car trailer.

R4: Unpainted ($25-35) ($45-75)

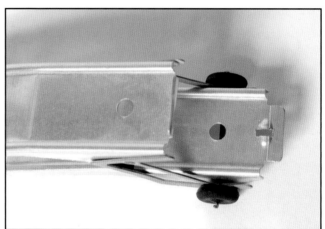

Classic four-car trailer 4T3.1.5

4T3.1.6 This variation of the four-car trailer is similar to the 4T3.1.1 variety. There is a hole on the lower platform for the detachable tab; however, there is no scoring, there is no detachable tab, and there is a tab hole on the upper platform. This variation also occurred in the early 1960s.

R2: Unpainted ($25-35) ($45-75)

Classic four-car trailer 4T3.1.6

4T3.1.7 This variation is the same as the 4T3.1.1 except that the tires are the ridged variety seen on the later versions of the trailer as well as on the Fourth Series cabs. This variation is somewhat scarce and may have been manufactured simultaneously with the 4T3.2.1 and/or 4T3.2.2 trailers.

R5: Unpainted ($25-35) ($50-70)

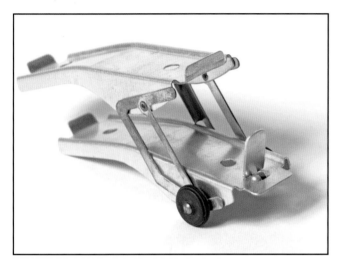

Classic four-car trailer 4T3.1.7

4T3.2.1.1 This type of the four-car trailer is the same as the 4T3.1.1 except that the tab hole for the detachable tab has been removed and the tab extending from the back of the lower platform was bent up. The tires are ridged. When the tab was bent at the factory, the crease will be very straight, very tight to the platform, and at the same angle as the upper trailer. The 4T3.2.2 trailers frequently had their back bent up by their owners. Typically, the

Classic trailers (left to right) 4T3.2.2, 4T3.2.1.1, 4T3.2.1.2

inexactness of the bend is obvious; however, they are sometimes confused with the 4T3.2.1.1 trailers.

At least a small number of sets containing this variation of the four-car trailer were issued with the Third Series cabs; however, this trailer is primarily seen as part of the Fourth Series trailer sets. This variation appeared at the very end of the Third Series; therefore, they date from 1964 or 1965 through 1969 or 1970. This trailer variation appears to have been produced both at the beginning of the Fourth Series as well as nearer the end. The 4T3.2.2 trailer, to be discussed in a moment, was definitely produced between 1965 and 1970. It is certainly possible that the 4T3.2.1.1 trailer was produced simultaneously with the 4T3.2.2 variation. These trailers overlapped the Third and Fourth Series cars. Sets from the early to mid-1960s contained various combinations of the Third and Fourth series cars.

R3: Unpainted ($20-30) ($40-50)

4T3.2.1.2 This variation of the four-car trailer is exactly the same as the 4T3.2.1.1 trailer except that the wheels are of the smooth black variety of the earlier trailers. In reality, this is a transitional variety where the new version of the trailer is fitted with the older tires. This variety is reasonably scarce and has been authenticated subsequent to the publication of *Barclay Toys*. See example above.

R6: Unpainted ($40-50) ($60-70)

4T3.2.2 This variation of the four-car trailer is the same as the 4T3.2.1.1 trailer except that the tab extending from the back of the lower platform is not bent. Owners frequently bent the tab up; however, any attempt to bend the tab detracts from the value of the piece. As noted, this variation is generally seen in sets that can be dated during the middle of the 1963–1970 period. It may have been produced exclusively for a period of time or simultaneously with the 4T..2.1.1. variety. It appears that this variation of the four-car trailer was only used with the Fourth Series cabs and cars. While this variation is available, it is seen less frequently than its companion 4T3.2.1.1 trailer. See example above.

R4: Unpainted ($25-35) ($45-75)

A variation of this variety exists with a nub at both ends of the axle.

Classic Series Cars

Like the cars in the First and Second Series, the cars in the Third or Classic Series come in two varieties, sedans and coupes. All of the cars were cast using the injection die-cast casting method. Normally, the one-piece cast body was spray-painted and the metal wheels were attached by means of a steel axle. As will be explained, very early in the production of this series of cars, Barclay apparently experimented with painting the cars after the axles were attached. This appears to have been a very short-lived experiment. The axle is a pin with a nub at one end and a crimp at the other end. These cars have open side windows and you can expect to see a minor amount of paint splashed on the inside.

The Classic Series design was introduced in 1939 and was produced continuously until approximately 1965. The Fourth Series cars or "Shoebox" cars were introduced in the very late 1950s or the early 1960s and were produced simultaneously with the Third Series cars for several years. Unlike the earlier cars, the Third Series cars come in a number of distinct variations and a substantial number of colors, which changed over time. In respect to the colors, this book identifies the major variations of color. Barclay did not scientifically mix their paints and you will find slight shade and tint variations throughout the series. While it is expected that mint specimens will be free from chips, it is not unusual to see a mint specimen with chips received while being manufactured, packed, or shipped.

There has been some debate as to the number of car castings created by each mold with some writers and collectors suggesting two castings were created in each mold while others maintain that four castings were created in each mold. Rucci answered this question when he stated that four castings of the Classic Series cars were created in each mold.[25]

Given the very high volume at which these toys were produced, it is obvious that several molds were most likely used simultaneously. Since production of the Classic sedans was very high and a number of variations exist, it is assumed that molds producing different variations were in use at the same time during different periods of production.

Classic Series Sedans

Scarcity and pricing is listed in italics after the detailed description for each piece. Due to variations seen in the market, prices are listed in ranges for examples in C-8 (Very Good) and C-10 (Mint) conditions.

As an aid to the users of *Barclay Toys*, listings that appear in *Barclay Toys* are shown in a darker color without an "x." New variations are shown in a lighter color with an "x." Each piece in the sets will be discussed below.

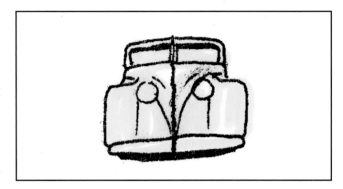

Drawing of plain sedan by Robert E. Wagner

S3.1.1 Plain Sedan As seen in the accompanying pictures, this car is cast with a plain grill, open wheel-wells, unpainted metal wheels, and two door handles. The car has the appearance of a 1939 Buick. This variation was first produced in 1939 and production continued until the 1950s, when the wheel-wells were closed. This variation is the most available of the earlier Third Series sedans; however, mint specimens of this earlier type are more difficult to locate than the later variations with closed wheel-wells. Certain colors are quite scarce, particularly in mint condition. Mint specimens should have complete and vibrant paint, the inside of the casting and the wheels should be bright and shiny, and the axle should be free from rust and have a silvery appearance.

Classic sedans, open and closed wheel-wells

Type	Years	Characteristics	Colors																					
Third or Classic Sedans (BV11 or 157) (440 or 330)			Blue	Blue-Lt.	Blue-Steel	Brown-Light	Camel	Chocolate	Clay	Flesh	Gold	Gray	Green-Aqua	Green-Forest	Green-Lt.	Green-Moss	Orange	Pink	Red	Salmon	Silver	Tan	Yellow	Yellow-Lemon
Plain Sedans																								
S3.1.1	1939-50s	Cast, plain grill, open wheel-wells, unpainted metal wheels, two door handles; perhaps '39 Buick																						
S3.1.2	1939	Same as 3.1.1 except painted wheels	x																					
S3.1.3	1950s-65	Same as 3.1.1 except closed wheel-wells			x					x			x											
S3.1.4.1	1957-65	Same as 3.1.1 except gold-colored wheels																						
S3.1.4.2	1957-65	Same as 3.1.3 except gold-colored wheels					x			x											x			
S3.1.5	1965	Same as 3.1.3 except dull, cleated rubber tires	x															x						
Parking Light Sedan																								
S3.2.1	1939	Cast, plain grill, open wheel-wells, unpainted metal wheels, sq. parking light left front, die-cut left back, two door handles, dipping wind shield, flat headlights	x																					
S3.2.2	1939-50s	Same as 3.2.1 except painted wheels																					x	
S3.2.3	1950s-65	Same as 3.2.1 except closed wheel-wells							x	x	x				x									
S3.2.4	1965	Same as 3.2.3 except dull, cleated rubber tires																						
Grill Bars Sedan																								
S3.3.1	1950s-65	Cast, vertical grill, closed wheel-wells, metal wheels, four door handles, partial left front parking light, rounded trunk							x	x					x									
S3.3.2	1950s-65	Same as S3.3.1 except gold-colored wheels					x																	

Notes: (1) Although a number of classic sedans repainted black exist, to date no genuine example has been found.
(2) Examples of S3.2.3 (red) exist with a small hole in the hood. These were part of the older versions of the game, U-Drive-IT.

Additional Varieties (Examples of Cars Painted Multiple Colors Can Be Found in the Appendix)
(1) S3.1.3 Double painted. Light blue over orange.
(2) S3.1.2 Double painted. Lt. green example painted solid green inside.
(3) S3.1.2 Double painted. Blue example painted yellow inside and over painted blue on the outside.
(4) S3.1.1 Solid yellow on inside.
(5) S3.1.2 Orange with 5 cent sticker.

The most common colors in the open wheel-well variety of the plain sedan are light green and orange. These colors were offered throughout the production of this variation. The remaining colors are not rare, but definitely scarce.

R2: Light Green, Orange ($10-15) ($20-25)
R3: Light Blue, Blue, Forest Green, and Yellow ($15-20) ($25-30)

Classic open wheel-well sedans S3.1.1 (plain) and S3.2.1 (parking light)

S3.1.2 Plain Sedan This variation is the same as the S3.1.1 except that the casting was painted after the wheels were attached, resulting in wheels that are painted the same color as the body. It is almost certain that these cars were produced in 1939 or 1940 and they are extremely scarce in all colors. They should not be confused with cars that were painted later outside of the factory. Since *Barclay Toys* was published, an example of a blue sedan in this variety has been authenticated.

R6: All Colors ($25-30) ($40-80)

Classic sedans with wheels painted S3.1.2 (plain) and S3.2.2 (parking light)

S3.1.3 Plain Sedan This variation is the same as the S3.1.1 sedan except that the wheel-wells have been closed. This toy was produced from the 1950s until the end of the Third Series in the mid-1960s. This is clearly the most available of the Third Series sedans; however, certain colors are quite scarce, particularly in mint condition.

Classic sedan, side view

Classic sedan, front view

Classic sedan, rear view

Since the publication of *Barclay Toys*, three additional colors of this variation have been authenticated. These new colors are steel blue, flesh, and aqua green. It is reasonable to assume that the flesh color variety was produced in the early to mid-1960s. The steel blue and aqua green varieties are transitional colors that were used on cars of both the Third and Fourth Series.

R1: Light Green and Orange ($8) ($10-20)
R2: Light Blue, Blue, Camel, Forest Green, Red, and Silver ($10-12) ($15-25)
R3: Pink, Tan, and Yellow ($15-18) ($22-32)
R6: Clay, Gray, Salmon, Flesh, Steel Blue, Aqua Green ($40-60) ($80-100)
R7/10: Chocolate, Moss Green (Light and Dark), Salmon, Lemon Yellow ($60-80) ($100-200)

Classic sedans with closed wheel-wells S3.1.3

S3.1.4.1 and S3.1.4.2 Plain Sedan–Gold Wheels These variations are the same as the S3.1.1 and S3.1.3 Plain Sedans; however, the silver colored metal wheels are replaced with gold colored wheels. It is not absolutely certain when these cars were produced, but it appears to be in the transition period when the Third and Fourth Series cars were being produced together. This "gold wheel" variation is often found in a mixture of Third and Fourth Series cars with gold colored wheels placing production of this variation in the early to mid-1960s.

Classic sedans with gold wheels S3.1.4.1 and S3.1.4.2

Since the publication of *Barclay Toys*, three new colors of S3.1.4.2 have been authenticated: light brown, clay, and silver. All colors of the gold wheel variation are reasonably scarce and difficult to locate.

R6: All Colors except Light Brown Flesh, Clay, and Silver ($25-35) ($40-70)
R7: Light Brown, Flesh, Clay, and Silver ($40-50) ($ 60-100)

S3.1.5 Plain Sedan This variation is also the same as the S3.1.3 sedan; however, the wheels are the dull rubber wheels with cleats found on the Fourth Series cars that were manufactured beginning approximately 1965. This transitional variety was most likely produced just as production of the Third Series cars ceased. This variety is rare in all colors and very difficult to locate. Since the publication of *Barclay Toys*, two additional colors have been authenticated, blue and red.

R7: All Colors ($40-50) ($60-100)

Classic sedans with rubber wheels S3.1.5

Drawing of parking light sedan by Robert E. Wagner

S3.2.1 Parking Light Sedan This variation is similar to the plain sedan. The piece has a plain grill, open wheel-wells, unpainted metal wheels, and two door handles. The design resembles a 1939 Buick. The parking light sedan has two distinctive features, a small square parking light on the left front fender and a die cut on the left back fender. For some collectors, the most distinctive element of this variety is the straight headlights found on this variety in contrast to the rounded headlights found on the plain sedans. Since the wheel-well is open, this variation was produced in the earlier years of the production of the Third Series. Whether it was produced at the very start of production is not clear. Because there is a distinct contrast between this car and the plain sedan, it is assumed that this variety was produced from separate molds.

In general, this variation is scarcer than the plain sedans, particularly in mint condition, and more difficult to locate than the later variation of parking light sedans with closed wheel-wells. Since the publication of *Barclay Toys*, an example of this variation in blue has been authenticated. The most common colors are light green and orange. The yellow and blue sedans are scarce. See examples on previous page.

R3: Light Green and Orange ($18-22) ($30-40)
R5: Blue and Yellow ($25-35) ($45-65)

S3.2.2 Parking Light Sedan This version of the parking light sedan is exactly the same as the S3.2.1; however, this early version was painted after the wheels were attached producing a car with wheels painted exactly the same color as the car. As previously noted, this variation was almost certainly produced in 1939 or 1940 and may have been an experiment. In any case, these cars are rare in all colors and should not be confused with cars that were painted outside the Barclay factory by a third party. Since the publication of *Barclay Toys*, an example of this variation in yellow has been authenticated.

R7: All Colors ($40-50) ($60-100)

S3.2.3 Parking Light Sedan This variation of the parking light sedan is the same as the S3.2.1 except that the wheel-wells are closed. Production of this type began in the early to mid-1950s and continued into the 1960s. While this variation is the most common of the parking light sedans, it is definitely more difficult to locate than the plain sedan and in certain colors is extremely scarce. The most common colors are light green and orange. Since the publication of

Barclay Toys, this variety has been authenticated in chocolate, flesh, and gold. Of these newly identified colors, chocolate and flesh are very scarce and gold is extremely rare.

R3: Light Green and Orange ($12-15) ($20-25)
R5: Light Blue, Blue, Camel, Pink, Red, Silver, and Yellow ($25-30) ($40-55)
R7: Chocolate, Flesh, Moss Green, Gray, and Salmon ($50-60) ($80-110)
R7/10: Clay and Gold ($80-100) ($130-250)

Parking light sedan, side view

Parking light sedan, front view with parking light on left front wheel-well

Parking light sedan, rear view with horizontal line on left rear wheel-well

Parking light dedans with closed wheel-wells S3.2.3

S3.2.4 Parking Light Sedan This variation is also the same as the S3.2.1 sedan; however, the wheels are the dull rubber wheels with cleats found on the Fourth Series cars beginning in the mid-1960s. This transitional variety was most likely produced just as production of the Third Series cars ceased. This variety is rare and very difficult to locate.

R7: Light Green ($40-50) ($70-100)

S3.3.1 Grill Bars Sedan This type of sedan clearly differs from other variations. Since it has closed wheel-wells, it is assumed that production began sometime in or after the early to mid-1950s. Production continued into the 1960s. The car is similar to the plain sedan; however, it has three very distinct features

Drawing of grill bars sedan by Robert E. Wagner

and a fourth more subtle difference. First, on each side of the front grill, this sedan has three vertical grill bars. Second, in contrast to the other sedans in the Third Series, this version has four door handles. Third, it has a small parking light on the left front fender. Fourth, the body of this sedan is slightly narrower than either the plain or parking light sedans. While the grill bars sedan can be located, it is definitely more difficult to find than either the plain sedan or the parking light sedan.

Grill bars sedan, side view showing two door handles

Grill bars sedan, front view showing grill bars

Grill bars sedan, rear view

Since the publication of *Barclay Toys*, three additional colors of this variety have been authenticated, chocolate, clay, and forest green. The only colors encountered with any frequency are light green and orange. All other colors vary from very scarce to extremely rare.

R3: Light Green and Orange ($20-25) ($30-35)
R5: Light Blue, Blue, Camel, Pink, Red, Silver, and Yellow ($30-35) ($45-60)
R7: Chocolate, Clay, Moss Green, Gray, and Salmon ($55-65) ($85-130)
R7/10: Forest Green ($75-85) ($100-200)

Grill bars sedans S3.3.1

Grill bars sedan S3.3.1, forest green

S3.3.2 Grill Bars Sedan–Gold Wheels This variety is the same as S3.3.1 except that it has gold-colored wheels.

R7: Camel $40-50) ($ 60-100)

Classic Series Coupes

Scarcity and pricing is listed in italics after the detailed description for each piece. Due to variations seen in the market, prices are listed in ranges for examples in C-8 (Very Good) and C-10 (Mint) conditions.

As an aid to the users of *Barclay Toys*, listings that appear in *Barclay Toys* are shown in a darker

color without an "x." New variations are shown in a lighter color with an "x." Each piece in the sets will be discussed below.

CO3.1.1 Plain Coupe As seen in the accompanying pictures, this car is cast with a full grill, wide body, open wheel-wells, and unpainted wheels. This variety has the appearance of a 1939 Plymouth. This variety was first produced in 1939 and production continued until the 1950s, when the wheel-wells were closed. This variety is the most available of the earlier Third Series coupes; however, mint specimens of this earlier type are more difficult to locate than the later variation with closed wheel-wells. Certain colors are quite scarce, particularly in mint condition. Mint specimens should have complete and vibrant paint. The inside of the casting and the wheels should be bright and shiny. The axle should be free from rust and should have a silvery appearance. Blue and red are the most common colors. Other colors are scarce. Yellow is extremely rare.

Drawing of plain coupe by Robert E. Wagner

Classic coupe, open and closed wheel-wells

Type	Years	Characteristics	Colors																								
Third or Classic Coupes (BV11 or 157) (440 or 330)			Blue	Blue-Lt.	Blue-Steel	Brown	Camel	Clay	Cream	Flesh	Gray	Gold	Green-Aqua	Green-Forest	Green-Lt.	Green-Moss	Khaki	Lilac	Orange	Orange-Burnt	Pink	Red	Salmon	Silver	Tan	Turquoise	Yellow	Yellow-Lemon
Plain Coupes																											
CO3.1.1	1939-50s	Cast, wide body, open wheel-wells, unpainted metal wheels, full grill, smooth cast, wide body; perhaps '39 Plymouth																										
CO3.1.2	1939	Same as 3.1.1 except painted wheels	x																									
CO3.1.3	1950s-65	Same as 3.1.1 except closed wheel-wells			x								x	x				x		x						x		
CO3.1.4	1957-65	Same as 3.1.3 except gold-colored wheels																										
CO3.1.5	1965	Same as 3.1.3 except cleated rubber tires						x				x		x	x													
Crooked-Line Coupe																											
CO3.2.1	1950s-65	Cast, narrow body, closed wheel-wells, metal wheels, crooked line on right grill, tapered backend; perhaps '37 Willys or '37 Studebaker																										
CO3.2.2	1957-65	Same as 3.2.1 except gold wheels																										
No-Line Coupe																											
CO3.3	1950s-65	Cast, Mid-Width Body, Closed Wheel-Wells, Metal Wheels, Headlight and Three Grill Bars on Left Side, No Headlight and One Grill Bar on Right Side, Later Version had no Headlight or Grill on Left Side, Rounded Backend															x											

Notes: (1) Although a number of classic coupes repainted black exist, to date no genuine example has been found.

(2) Examples of CO3.1.3 (red, blue), CO3.2.1 (red), and CO3.3 (red) exist with a small hole in the hood. These were part of the older versions of the game, U-Drive-It.

Additional Varieties (Examples of Cars Painted Multiple Colors Can Be Found in the Appendix)

(1) CO3.1.3 Double painted. Light green over pink.

(2) CO3.3 Double painted. Blue over red-solid blue wheels.

(3) CO3.1.2 Blue with painted wheels and front axles crimped on both ends.

Classic coupe, open wheel-well CO3.1.1

R2: Blue and Red ($12-15) ($18-22)
R3: Light Blue ($14-18) ($22-25)
R4: Light Green ($18-22) ($26-35)
R5: Forest Green ($25-30) ($35-45)
R7/10: Yellow ($125-150) ($200-500)

CO3.1.2 Plain Coupe This variation is exactly like the CO3.1.1 except that the casting was painted before the wheels were attached resulting in wheels that are painted the same color as the body. It is almost certain that these cars were produced in 1939 or 1940. These cars are extremely scarce in all colors and they should not be confused with cars that were painted later outside of the factory by a third party. Since the publication of *Barclay Toys*, the blue color in this variety has been authenticated. This variety is very scarce in all colors.

R6: All Colors ($25-30) ($40-80)

lilac, burnt orange, and turquoise. All of these additional colors are very scarce to extremely rare.

R1: Blue and Red ($8-9) ($10-20)
R2: Light Blue ($12-15) ($18-25)
R3: Forest Green, Light Green, Orange, Pink, and Silver ($13-16) ($20-30)
R5: Cream, Salmon, Tan, and Lemon Yellow ($23-28) ($35-45)
R6: Steel Blue, Clay, Aqua Green, and Gray ($40-60) ($80-100)
R7/10: Brown, Gold, Moss Green, Lilac, Burnt Orange, and Turquoise ($60-80) ($100-200)

Classic coupe, painted wheels CO3.1.2

Classic plain coupe, side view

CO3.1.3 Plain Coupe This variation is the same as the CO3.1.1 coupe except that the wheel-wells have been closed. It was produced from the early 1950s until the end of the Third Series. This is clearly the most available of the Third Series coupes; however, certain of the colors are scarce to extremely rare, particularly in mint condition. Since the publication of *Barclay Toys*, six additional colors in this variation have been authenticated, steel blue, gold, aqua green,

Classic plain coupe, front view   *Classic plain coupe, rear view*

Classic coupe, plain with closed wheel-wells CO3.1.3

CO3.1.4 Plain Coupe This variation is the same as the CO3.1.3 coupe; however, the silver-colored metal wheels were replaced with gold-colored wheels. It is not certain when these cars were produced, but it was first seen in the transition period when the Third and Fourth Series cars were being produced together. The "gold wheel" variation is often found with a mixture of Third and Fourth Series cars with gold colored wheels. This would place production of this variation in the late 1950s to the mid-1960s, most likely near the end of this period. This variation is reasonably scarce and difficult to locate. The flesh color is extremely rare.

R6: All Colors except Flesh ($25-35) ($40-70)
R7–10: Flesh ($60-80) ($100-200)

Classic coupe with gold wheels CO3.1.4 and CO3.2.2

CO3.1.5 Plain Coupe This variation is also the same as the CO3.1.3 coupe; however, the metal wheels are now the dull rubber wheels with cleats found on the Fourth Series cars beginning approximately 1965 or 1966. This is another transitional variety produced just as production of the Third Series cars ceased. Since the publication of *Barclay Toys*, four additional colors of this variation have been identified: clay, gold, forest green, and light green. This variety is extremely scarce and very difficult to locate in all colors and extremely rare in certain colors.

R7: All Colors except Clay and Gold ($40-50) ($60-100)
R7/10: Clay and Gold ($80-100) ($130-250)

Classic coupe with rubber tires CO3.1.5

Drawing of crooked-line coupe by Robert E. Wagner

CO3.2.1 Crooked-Line Coupe On first glance, this variation is similar to the plain coupe; however, on closer inspection, it is clearly from a different mold. The body is distinctly narrower than the plain coupe and has a crooked-line cast into the right side of the grill. Aside from the narrow body, this variety can be distinguished from the no-line variety by the way the rear portion of the car peaks in the middle and then tapers down toward each side in contrast to the rounded rear end of the no-line variety. Some believe that this car resembles either a 1937 Willys or a 1937 Studebaker. Since the wheel-well is closed, this variation was first produced in the 1950s. This variety is available; however, it is definitely scarcer than the plain coupe and, in some colors, it is very scarce. The most common colors are blue, pink, and red. All other colors are very scarce to rare.

R3: Blue, Pink, and Red ($18-22) ($30-40)
R5: Light Blue, Light Green, Orange, and Salmon ($25-35) ($45-65)
R7: Moss Green and Gray ($50-60) ($80-110)
R7/10: Brown ($80-100) ($130-250)

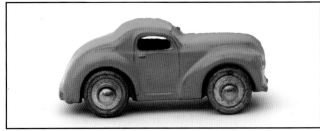

Classic crooked-Line coupe, side view

Classic crooked-line coupe, front view

Classic crooked-line coupe, rear view

Classic crooked-line coupe

Drawing of no-line coupe by Robert E. Wagner

CO3.2.2 Crooked-Line Coupe This version of the crooked-line coupe is the same as the CO3.2.1; however, the silver-colored metal wheels were replaced with gold-colored wheels. It is not certain when these cars were produced, but they were first seen in the transition period when the Third and Fourth Series cars were being produced together. The "gold wheel" variation is often found with a mixture of Third and Fourth Series cars with gold-colored wheels placing production of this variation in the early to mid-1960s. This variation is very scarce and difficult to locate. See example above at CO3.1.4.

R7: All Colors ($40-50) ($60-100)

CO3.3 No-Line Coupe This type of coupe is clearly distinct from the other variations. Since it has closed wheel-wells, it is assumed that production began in the early 1950s and continued into the 1960s. This car has a wider body than the crooked-line coupe, but a slightly more narrow body than the plain coupe; a headlight and three grill bars on the left side; and no headlight and one grill bar on the right side. A later version has no headlight or grill on either side. The easiest way to differentiate the no-line coupe from the crooked-line coupe is that the rear portion of the no-line coupe is rounded in contrast to the crooked-line coupe, where the rear portion of the car peaks in the middle and then tapers to each side. While the no-line coupe can be found, it is definitely

more difficult to find than the plain coupe or the crooked-line coupe. Since the publication of *Barclay Toys*, a khaki color version of this variety has been authenticated. The khaki color is rare.

R3: Blue and Red ($15-20) ($25-30)
R5: Light Blue, Camel, Light Green, Orange, Pink, Salmon, ($25-30) ($40-55)
R7: Moss Green, and Gray ($50-60) ($80-110)
R7/10: Brown and Khaki ($80-100) ($130-250)

Classic no-line coupe, side view

Classic no-line coupe, front view   *Classic no-line coupe, rear view*

Classic no-line coupe CO3.3

Classic Series Original Sets

Original sets are made up of pieces of similar age and condition. In general, a matched original set is more difficult to locate than a set that combines pieces from multiple sources, which may vary in age and condition. A two-car set consists of a cab, trailer, sedan, and coupe. Most four-car sets were sold with a cab, trailer, two sedans, and two coupes. Perhaps as early as the late 1950s and certainly in the 1960s, some four-car sets were sold with varying combinations of sedans and coupes. One set might have three sedans and one coupe, while the next set might have three coupes and one sedan. The modern cars from the Fourth Series were produced simultaneously with the cars of the Third Series. For a period of time,

sets were sold with a mixture of classic and modern cars. The pricing found below assumes sets with only classic cars.

Below is listed the correct combinations for the various classic sets. While Barclay may have mixed various pieces when they were available, these are the standard combinations by cab type. Pricing is for a set with the most common pieces.

C3.1.1 or C3.1.2 with 2T3.1.1 White tires, open wheel-well cab with painted white-wheeled trailer and open wheel-well cars.

R3: Matched Set ($45-70) ($75-95)

Classic two-car sets with open wheel-wells, white tires, and cast trailers

C3.1.3 with 2T3.1.2 or 2T3.1.3 Black wheels, open wheel-well cab with painted, black-wheeled trailer and open wheel-well cars.

R4: Matched Set ($50-75) ($85-100)

Classic two-car sets with open wheel-wells, black tires, and cast trailers

C3.2.1 with 2T3.2.1, 2T3.2.3, 2T3.2.4, 4T3.1.1, 4T3.1.3, 4T3.1.4, 4T3.1.5, or 4T3.1.6 Black wheels, high hitch, open wheel-well cabs with trailers of the period and open wheel-well cars.

R3: Matched Two-Car Set ($40-50) ($55-75)
R5: Matched Four-Car Set in Box (Mint Only) ($135-200)

Classic sets with high hitch and open wheel-wells including a C3.2.2 set

Classic sets with high hitch and open wheel-wells

C3.2.2 or C3.4.3 with 2T3.2.2 or 4T3.1.2 White-wheeled, high hitch, open wheel-well (C3.2.2) or closed wheel-well (C3.4.3) cabs with corresponding trailers.

R6: Matched Two-Car Set ($55-65) ($85-110)
R6: Matched Two-Car Set in Blister Pack (Mint Only) ($120-140)
R6: Matched Four-Car Set ($80-95) ($120-130)
R6: Matched Four-Car Set in Blister Pack (Mint Only) ($160-250)

Two C3.4.3 mint sets in blister packs

C3.3.1, C3.3.2, or C3.4.1 with 2T3.2.1, 2T3.2.3, 2T3.2.4, 4T3.1.1, 4T3.1.3, 4T3.1.4, 4T3.1.5, or 4T3.1.6 Half open or closed wheel-well cab with period trailers and closed wheel-well cars.

R2: Matched Two-Car Set ($40-50) ($55-65)
R5: Matched Two-Car Set in Blister Pack (Mint Only) ($70-85)
R2: Matched Four-Car Set ($85-110) ($100-120)
R5: Matched Four-Car Set in Box (Mint Only) ($135-190)
R5: Matched Four-Car Set in Blister Pack (Mint Only) ($125-160)

Classic mint set in blister pack

Classic mint set in blister pack with rare lemon-yellow coupe

Classic C3.3.1, C3.3.2, or C3.4.1 sets with one C3.4.2 set

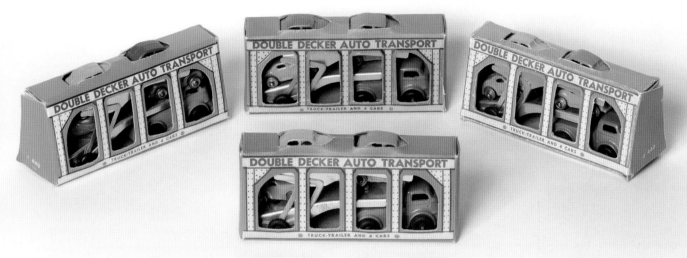

Classic mint sets in box

Classic C3.3.1, C3.3.2, or C3.4.1 sets

Classic C3.3.1, C3.3.2, or C3.4.1 sets with one C3.4.2 cab

C3.4.1 with 4T3.2.1.2 Later variety trailer with smooth tires and closed wheel-well cars.

R6: Matched Four-Car Set ($95-120) ($140-240)

C3.4.2 with 2T3.3, 4T3.1.7, 4T3.2.1.1, or 4T3.2.2 Ridged tired cabs and trailers with closed wheel-well cars.

R2: Matched Two-Car Set ($45-55) ($60-70)
R5: Matched Two-Car Set in Blister Pack (Mint Only) ($75-80)
R2: Matched Four-Car Set ($80-95) ($100-120)
R5: Matched Four-Car Set in Blister Pack (Mint Only) ($125-160)

Classic C3.4.2 sets

Classic C3.4.2 set sold with cars having black rubber tires

Various combinations of Classic and Modern Series cars exist in blister packs with seven (7) cars to the set. Packs with all classic cars command the highest prices.

R5: Seven Cars in a Blister Pack–More Common Colors (Mint Only) ($85-130)
R7/10: Seven Cars in a Blister Pack–Rare Colors (Mint Only) ($250-600)

Classic cars in blister pack

Classic cars in blister pack

Classic cars in blister pack with numerous rare colors

Classic cars in blister pack

Mixed Classic and Modern cars in blister pack

Classic Series: Other Characteristics, Packaging, and Availability

The Classic Series is the most widely recognized and the most widely collected of the four Barclay Transport Toys ranges. The Classic Series includes a tremendous number of variations as well as the most common and the rarest pieces found in the various series. Since the cars were sold individually as well as part of the sets, there are many more cars than there are cabs and trailers. For reasons that are not clear, there also appear to be more cabs than there are trailers.

While many Classic Series pieces come to the collectible toy market, original sets are relatively scarce. Many of the sets that are offered are, in fact, mismatched combinations of cabs, trailers, and cars that simply were never sold together. While the earlier open wheel-well varieties are seldom distinguished in the market, many of these pieces are much more difficult to find than are the later varieties. As collectors become more aware of the variations, these earlier varieties will undoubtedly gain the interest that they deserve.

As has been indicated, this series was sold as individual cars, sets of cars, two-car trailer sets, and four-car trailer sets. As far as it is known, the four-car trailer sets were first sold as a boxed set. At least some of the earlier two-car sets were sold attached to a flat piece of cardboard, but it is not known whether this packaging method was consistently used or not. The cars were sold during the 1950s as individual pieces without packaging and were probably shipped in bulk. Beginning in the late 1950s or early 1960s, the cars, two-car trailer sets, and four-car trailer sets began to be sold in blister packs. Throughout the life of the Third Series, the most common color combination in the four-car sets was a green and an orange sedan paired with a blue and a red coupe.

While many pieces of the Third Series are available in the collectors' market, the pieces most frequently encountered are the more common varieties and colors in grades less than C-10. There are numerous varieties within this series that are very difficult to find and that range from scarce to extremely rare.

Fourth
or Modern Series

The Fourth or Modern Series of Barclay Transport Toys was the final chapter in this extended line of toys. The cars and the cabs are distinctly different from those of the Third Series. Even though this series is not as old as the Third Series, the cars and transports from Third Series are seen much more frequently than those of the Fourth Series. Since none of the pieces in the Modern Series are identified by either manufacturer or country of origin, they are often attributed to other manufacturers in error. The transition from the Third or Classic Series to the Modern Series actually took place over several years. The Modern Series cars, which are also called Shoebox cars, were introduced either at the very end of the 1950s or the very early 1960s. These cars were produced simultaneously with the Classic Series cars until the mid-1960s.

According to Rucci, the design of the Modern Series cab was completed in 1959 and was put into production in the early 1960s.[26] The modern cabs continued to be produced until Barclay ceased production in 1971. The Fourth Series had both two-car and four-car transport sets and was sold in sets of the cab, transport, and matching cars as well as in sets of cars only. A limited number of cars were sold individually. In contrast to the Third Series, there are a limited number of casting variations; however, there are a number of variations in terms of the materials used and substantial variations of color. This section of the book will systematically discuss and illustrate each of the known varieties.

Modern Series Colors

Initially, the cars in the Modern Series were produced simultaneously with the cars of the Classic Series and used the same colors. With minor changes, these colors continued throughout most of the production period for the Modern Series. In contrast to the colors found in the Classic Series, the colors are consistent and you see relatively few shade variations.

In the last two or three years before Barclay ceased operations, the color range was substantially expanded to include new, bright metallic and neon colors. During this period, most of the traditional colors continued to be produced. Many of the colors in this final version of the Fourth Series are quite difficult to locate.

The identification grids for the modern cars are divided into two sections. Except where noted, all of the colors are illustrated under Section 1 below. The additional colors found in the grids for Section 2 are illustrated next.

Modern Series Colors–Section 1
See example of moss green in classic colors. See examples of gold, green metallic, green neon, orange neon, and red neon with Section 2 modern colors below. Chocolate metallic is not pictured.

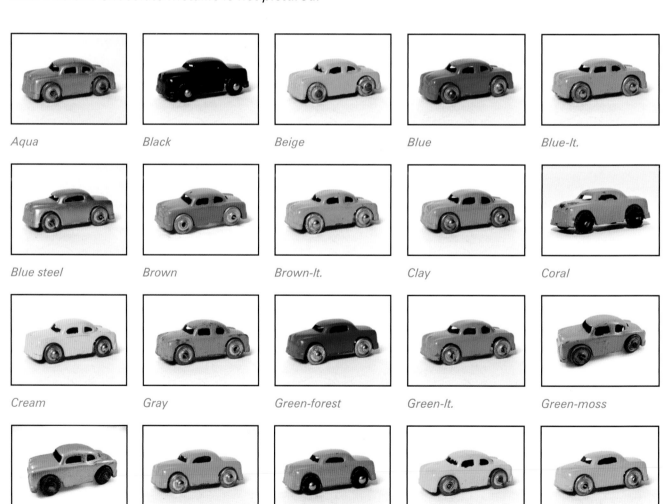

Aqua	Black	Beige	Blue	Blue-lt.
Blue steel	Brown	Brown-lt.	Clay	Coral
Cream	Gray	Green-forest	Green-lt.	Green-moss
Magenta	Orange	Orange-burnt	Pink	Pink-bright

Red

Salmon

Silver

Tan

White

Yellow

Yellow-lemon

Modern Series Colors–Section 2

Blue-metallic

Blue-neon

Cinnamon-metallic

Copper

Gold

Green-metallic

Green-neon

Maroon-neon

Olive-metallic

Orange-neon

Orange red-neon

Pink-neon

Purple-metallic

Purple-neon

Red-metallic

Red-neon

Violet

Yellow lemon-neon

Modern Series Cabs

Scarcity and pricing is listed in italics after the detailed description for each piece. Due to variations seen in the market, prices are listed in ranges for examples in C-8 (Very Good) and C-10 (Mint) conditions.

As an aid to the users of *Barclay Toys*, listings that appear in *Barclay Toys* are shown in a darker color without an "x." New variations are shown in a lighter color with an "x." Each piece in the sets will be discussed below.

According to Rucci, the Fourth Series cab is a modern cab-over engine design patterned after the 1958 Ford cab-over engine (COE) C-Series, medium-duty truck. The original design was completed in 1959; however, it did not go into production until 1960 or 1961. Unlike most of the miniature Barclay toys, this toy has a specific scale, 1/124.[27]

The cab is almost exactly two and one-quarter inches in length, one and one-eighth inches in width at its widest point, and one and one-quarter inches in height. The profile is definitely higher than the Third Series cabs; however, this cab pulls the same trailers as the Third Series cabs. As with the previous series, this cab was cast by forcing hot metal into a steel mold under pressure using the injection die-casting method. The casting was then spray-painted and the axles and wheels were attached. The cab

has open windows; therefore, it should have at least some traces of the paint on the inside. There is no identification on the casting.

Although the Modern Series cab was the last cab to be made, it is more difficult to locate than the cabs from the Classic Series, particularly in pristine, mint condition. Generally, the paint on the modern cabs covers very well; however, there are often paint chips on the more pronounced edges of the cab including pieces that are near mint. The inside of the cab should be shiny and the axles should be rust free on a mint specimen. The modern cab was introduced in the 1960s after the modern cars were introduced. Except for one minor variation with respect to the wheels and differences in color, the modern cab continued to be produced until production ended in 1971.

Type	Ref.	Years	Characteristics	Colors											
				Blue	Green-Forest	Green-Lt.	Orange	Orange-Red Neon	Pink-Neon	Red	Red-Metallic	Salmon	Yellow	Yellow-Neon	Yellow- Lemon-Neon
Fourth or Modern Series Cabs															
C4.1	(BV75 or 107) (330 or 440)	1960s	Cast, black wheels, '58 Ford cab—over engine truck	x	x			x	x	x	x		x	x	
C4.2	(BV75 or 107) (330 or 440)	1970-71	Cast, black wheels with white sidewalls; '63 Ford				x								x

Notes: (1) C4.2 May exist or may not exist in either light blue or light blue neon.
(2) In *Barclay Toys*, the yellow color was identified as "hot-yellow."

C4.1 The Fourth Series or Modern Series cab pulls both the two-car and four-car trailers. While the basic construction of the cab is the same as the Classic Series cab, the wheels are the synthetic rubber with a ridge running around the middle of the tire. These tires are the same as the tires on the last version of the Classic Series cab. Virtually all examples of this cab are painted red; however, specimens of a number other colors exist. At the time *Barclay Toys* was written, the only other colors that had been identified were dark blue, orange, and salmon. Since *Barclay Toys* was published, a number of additional colors have been authenticated including forest green, light green, metallic red, yellow, neon yellow, orange-red neon, and pink neon. Of the colors other than red, the dark blue is the most commonly seen, but it is still scarce. The remaining non-red colors are all rare.

As previously indicated, this version of the Modern Series cab was first produced in the early 1960s and continued to be produced until 1969 or 1970. Given Barclay's tendency to overlap both series and variations, it is very possible that this variation was produced until Barclay closed in 1971.

Modern Cab, side view

Modern cab, front view

Modern cab, back view

Modern cab, bottom view

Modern Cabs with Black Tires

R1: Red ($5-8) ($12-15)
R5: Dark Blue ($20-25) ($40-60)
R6: Orange ($35-45) ($50-80)
R7: Forest Green, Light Green, Metallic Red, Salmon, Yellow, Neon Yellow, Orange-Red Neon, Pink Neon ($50-60) ($80-150)

Blue

Forrest Green

Light green

Metallic Red

Orange

Red

Yellow

C4.2 This variation of the Modern Series cab was produced just before Barclay's closure. The first production probably took place in 1969 or 1970 and it was produced until Barclay ceased production in 1971. This cab is exactly the same as the C4.1 cab except that the black, ridged wheels have a white circle painted around the outside of the tire to give the wheel the appearance of a whitewall. We do not know the logic for having a whitewall on a truck. In addition to the colors of red and dark blue, forest green, orange-red neon, and pink neon were identified in *Barclay Toys*. Since *Barclay Toys* was published, two additional colors, orange, and lemon-yellow neon, have been authenticated. All cabs with whitewall wheels are scarce and many of the colors are extremely scarce.

Modern Cabs with Whitewall Tires

R6/7: Red, Dark Blue ($50-60) ($70-100)
R7/10: All Other Colors ($60-70) ($90-175)

Blue

Forest green

Orange

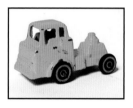

Orange-red neon

Pink neon

Red

Lemon-yellow neon

Modern Series Trailers

Until the whitewall version of the trailer was introduced in 1969 or 1970, the Modern Series used the trailers from the last years of the Classic Series. Specifically, the two-car transport sets used the 2T3.3 trailer with the ridged tires and the four-car transport sets used either the 4T3.2.1.1 or the 4T3.2.2 trailer. The Modern Series four-car set was introduced in the mid-1960s. For reasons that cannot be explained, the 4T3.2.1.1 trailer with the bent-up lower back tab seems to have been the norm both in the earlier years and in the final years of production. The 4T3.2.2 with the straight, unbent tab appears to have been produced between these two periods. It is also quite possible and probably likely that both varieties were produced simultaneously.

Modern Series Two-Car Trailers

Scarcity and pricing is listed in italics after the detailed description for each piece. Due to variations seen in the market, prices are listed in ranges for examples in C-8 (Very Good) and C-10 (Mint) conditions.

Type	Ref.	Years	Characteristics	Colors
Fourth or Modern Series Two-Car Trailers				Unpainted
2T4.1	(BV75) (330)	1965-70	Same as 2T3.3	
2T4.2	(BV75) (330)	1970-71	Same as 2T3.3 with white sidewalls	

Modern Series two-car trailers

2T4.1 This trailer is the same as the 2T3.3 trailer.

R2: Unpainted ($5-10) ($15-20)

2T4.2 This trailer is the same as the 2T3.3 trailer except that it has whitewall tires as discussed in the previous section. All trailers with whitewall tires are quite scarce.

R6/7: Unpainted ($20-30) ($40-50)

Modern Series Four-Car Trailers

Scarcity and pricing is listed in italics after the detailed description for each piece. Due to variations seen in the market, prices are listed in ranges for examples in C-8 (Very Good) and C-10 (Mint) conditions.

4T4.1 This trailer is the same as the 4T3.2.1.1 trailer.

R3: Unpainted ($20-30) ($40-50)

4T4.2 This trailer is the same as the 4T3.2.2 trailer.

R4: Unpainted ($25-35) ($45-75)

4T4.3 This trailer is the same as the 4T3.2.2 trailer, except that it has white walls. Trailers of this type are quite scarce.

R6: Unpainted ($35-45) ($50-100)

Type	Ref.	Years	Characteristics	Colors
Fourth or Modern Series Four-Car Trailers				Unpainted
4T4.1	(BV107) (440)	1965-70	Same as 4T3.2.1.1	
4T4.2	(BV107) (440)	1965-70	Same as 4T3.2.2	
4T4.3	(BV107) (440)	1970-71	Same as 4T3.2.1 with white sidewalls	

Modern Series four-car trailers

Modern Series Cars

Production of the Fourth or Modern Series cars began in either the late 1950s or very early 1960s. The cars of this series are known as Shoebox cars due to their shape. While the designs are decidedly more modern than the cars in the Classic Series, they also are much less detailed. The Shoebox cars were made in two styles, a coupe and a sedan. Some collectors suggest that they were perhaps modeled after the 1951 Packard; however, Rucci states that the cars were not modeled after any existing vehicle, the design was generic.[28] Both the sedans and the coupes are approximately one and nine-sixteenths inches long.

The construction of the Modern Series cars was similar to the cars in the previous series; the cast body of the car was made by injecting molten metal into a steel die-cast mold. The completed casting was then ejected from the mold by a series of ejector pins. After the casting was created, the cars were spray-painted and finally the steel axles were inserted and the wheels were attached. Until the mid-1960s, when the Modern Series sets began to regularly appear, the Shoebox cars were produced simultaneously with the Classic Series cars. They were frequently found in the various blister packs of this era, typically mixed with cars from the Classic Series. At least a few of the Modern Series cars were sold individually by retailers in a similar manner to the cars in the Classic Series.

As with all Barclay vehicles of this period, mint specimens should not have chips, should be bright and shiny on the inside, should be free of rust on the axles, and the axles should have minimal discoloration. Since these cars have open windows, there should be some paint splashed on the inside having come through the windows as the car was painted. There are a number of different varieties of Fourth Series cars. Variations resulted from changes in the molds, changes in the tires, and numerous variations of color. There is no manufacturer or country of origin identified; therefore, Shoebox cars are often misattributed to other manufacturers.

One unique characteristic of the Shoebox car is a number from one to eight on the inside of the roof of each car. This number identifies the position of a specific casting within the mold. Each mold produced eight cars, thus, the numbers of one through eight. In terms of scarcity, cars in true mint state, particularly those of the later varieties, are more difficult to find than one might assume due to the tendency of the cars to easily chip and the ebbing popularity of Barclay products as the 1960s progressed.

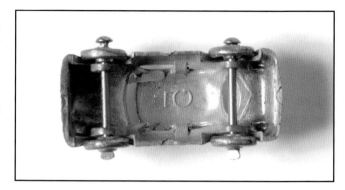

Modern sedan with mold position number

The most common cars are the first type with metal wheels. The varieties produced after 1965 are generally more difficult to locate and some colors and some styles are extremely difficult to find. This last statement is particularly true of the final style produced for a short period immediately before Barclay's shutdown. It should be noted that the quality of the cars gradually deteriorated through the latter part of the 1960s and on into 1970 and 1971.

Modern car wheel types (top to bottom): metal, cleated, large smooth, small smooth, single-piece wheels and axle

Note on Scarcity and Pricing of all Modern Series Cars: In general, the collectors' market has not recognized the relative scarcity of the Modern Series cars. The steel-wheeled variation is the most common variety. Throughout the series, the most common colors are blue, light green, orange, and red. The author believes that the color listings are relatively complete; however, there is the distinct possibility that additional colors exist within some of the type variations. Scarcity and pricing are listed in italics after the detailed description for each piece. Due to variations seen in the market, prices are listed in ranges for examples in C-8 (Very Good) and C-10 (Mint) conditions.

Modern Series Sedans: Section 1

Scarcity and pricing is listed in italics after the detailed description for each piece. Due to variations seen in the market, prices are listed in ranges for examples in C-8 (Very Good) and C-10 (Mint) conditions.

As an aid to the users of *Barclay Toys*, listings that appear in *Barclay Toys* are shown in a darker color without an "x." New variations are shown in a lighter color with an "x." Each piece in the sets will be discussed below.

Type	Years	Characteristics	Colors																										
Fourth or Modern Series Sedans (BV75 or 107) (440, 330, or 331)			Aqua	Black	Beige	Blue	Blue-Lt.	Blue Steel	Brown	Brown-Lt.	Chocolate-Metallic	Clay	Cream	Gray	Green-Forest	Green-Lt.	Green-Moss	Magenta	Orange	Orange-Neon	Pink	Pink-Bright	Red	Salmon	Silver	Tan	White	Yellow	Yellow-Lemon
S4.1.1	1957-65	Cast, metal wheels and axles, marked 1-8, open back window, eyelet axle holder; perhaps '51 Packard	x	x	x			x	x	x							x							x					
S4.1.2	1960-65	Same as S4.1.1 except gold wheels			x	x															x			x					
S4.2.1.1	1965-70	Same as S4.1.1 except with cleated rubber or plastic vinyl tires, metal axles make from pins crimped at one end, forked or eyelet wheel assembly, open back window													x			x								x			
S4.2.1.2	1965-70	Same as S4.2.1.1 except closed back window		x																	x				x				
S4.2.2.1	1966-70	Same as S4.2.1.1 except axle nub at both ends																							x				
S4.2.2.2	1966-70	Same as S4.2.1.2 except axle nub at both ends																							x				
S4.2.3	1966-70	Same as S4.2.1.2 except with small smooth rubber tires, metal axle made from pin crimped at one end, forked axle holders, closed back wndow		x											x								x		x				

Notes: (1) Examples of Cars Painted Multiple Colors Can Be Found in the Appendix.

S4.1.1 This modern sedan has metal wheels and axles, the numbers one through eight marked on the inside of its roof, an open-back window, and eyelet axle holders. This type was most likely first produced in the late 1950s or early 1960s and its production continued until the mid-1960s. This is the oldest and most common Shoebox car, although certain colors are relatively scarce. An interesting aspect of this sedan is that it was produced simultaneously with the Classic Series sedan and the sedans of the two series were often mixed together in car and trailer sets as well as in seven-car blister packs. This practice continued until production of the classic cabs and cars ceased in the mid-1960s. As far as is known, this version of the Shoebox car was not used on the Modern Series trailer sets.

Since the publication of *Barclay Toys*, several additional colors of this first version of the Shoebox car have been authenticated. These colors include aqua, black, beige, steel blue, brown, light brown, moss green, and salmon. All of these additional colors are scarce to rare.

R1: Blue, Light Green, Orange, and Red ($3-4) ($5-6)
R2/R4: Lt. Blue, Forest Green, Pink, Bright Pink, Silver, Tan, Lemon Yellow ($5-6) ($8-15)
R6: Clay and Gray ($15-25) ($30-50)
R7/8: Aqua, Black, Beige, Steel Blue, Brown, Lt. Brown, Cream, Moss Green, Salmon ($20-30) ($35-70)

Modern sedan, side view   *Modern sedan, front view*

Modern sedan, rear view   *Modern sedan, bottom view*

Alternative wheel assembly (top to bottom): forked and eyelet

Modern sedans S4.1.1

S4.1.2 This variation is the same as S4.1.1 except that it has gold-colored metal wheels rather than the more common silver-colored metal wheels. Since this variety is often seen with the gold-wheeled variety of the Third Series cars, it is assumed that these cars were produced in the first half of the 1960s, when both types were being produced simultaneously. This variety is reasonably scarce. In addition to the colors previously identified, several additional colors have been identified since the publication of *Barclay Toys*. These additional colors include beige, light blue, orange, and salmon.

R6/7: All Colors ($20-25) ($30-70)

Modern sedans with gold wheels S4.1.2

S4.2.1.1 This is the second type of Shoebox car. The body of the car is essentially the same as the S4.1.1 type; however, the wheels are made from either a dull, synthetic rubber or plastic vinyl with cleats. The two varieties of wheels are difficult to differentiate; however, the rubber variety tends to be more flexible and appears to be dull when compared to the plastic variety. In contrast, the plastic wheels are relatively stiff and tend to have a shiny appearance. There are two varieties of the wheel assembly. The more common version has a forked axle holder. A second version has the eyelet axle holder used on the S4.1.1 variety. The axle is steel made from a metal pin with a nub at one end and a crimp at the other end. The back window is open. Rucci explained that the decision to use a forked axle holder rather than the eyelet axle holder was made in order to simplify the production process.[29]

This version of the Shoebox car appears to have been made from the mid-1960s until the final version was introduced around 1969 or 1970. While available,

this variety is not nearly as common as the earlier cars with metal wheels and is challenging to collect in its various sub-varieties. Since the publication of *Barclay Toys*, gray, magenta, and white examples of this variety have been authenticated.

R2/R4: All Colors Except Gray, Magenta, and White ($5-8) ($10-20)
R6/7: Gray, Magenta, and White ($20-30) ($35-70)

S4.2.1.2 This variation of the Shoebox car is the same as the S4.2.1.1 car; however, it has a closed rear window. As previously noted, it is not known whether the closed rear window variation was the result of a faulty manufacturing process or was produced from molds that were slightly different. This variation is more difficult to locate than the open-window variety. Since the publication of *Barclay Toys*, the colors black, orange, and silver have been authenticated for this variety.

R2/R4: All Colors ($5-8) ($10-20)

Modern sedans S4.2.1.2

S4.2.2.1 This variation is the same as the S4.2.1.1 with an open rear window; however, the axle has a nub at both ends. It is not known when this variety was produced, but it was during the 1966 to 1970 period. It is distinctly possible that this variation was produced simultaneously with other variations and it is relatively difficult to locate. Since the publication of *Barclay Toys*, the color silver has been authenticated in this variety. The double-nub variety in the various miniature toy ranges was the result of complaints that the crimped end of the axles presented a danger to children.

R2/R4: All Colors ($5-8) ($10-20)

Modern sedan S4.2.1.1

Modern sedans S4.2.2.1 and S4.2.2.2

S4.2.2.2 This variation is the same as the S4.2.1.2 with a closed rear window; however, the axle has a nub at both ends. Since the publication of *Barclay Toys*, the color silver has been authenticated in this variety. See example above.

R2/R4: All Colors (($5-8) ($10-20)

S4.2.3 This variation of the Shoebox car is the same as the S4.2.1.1 except that the wheels have a small, smooth synthetic rubber tire. The car has a steel axle made from a pin with a nub at one end and a crimp at the other end, forked axle holders, and a closed back window. It is not clear when this variation was produced; however, it would have been sometime between 1966 and 1970. It is distinctly possible that this variation was produced simultaneously with other variations. Since the publication of *Barclay Toys*, several additional colors have been authenticated for this variety. Additional colors include black, forest green, red, salmon, and silver. This variety of the Modern car is relatively difficult to locate.

R5/6: All Colors ($10-15) ($20-30)

Modern sedans S4.2.3

Modern Series Sedans: Section 2

Scarcity and pricing is listed in italics after the detailed description for each piece. Due to variations seen in the market, prices are listed in ranges for examples in C-8 (Very Good) and C-10 (Mint) conditions.

As an aid to the users of *Barclay Toys*, listings that appear in *Barclay Toys* are shown in a darker color without an "x." New variations are shown in a lighter color with an "x." Each piece in the sets will be discussed below.

S4.3.1 This final variation of the modern sedan retains the basic shape of the Shoebox cars; however, the wheels and the axle are now a single piece of molded plastic. The plastic component is simply pushed into the forked holder. From the standpoint of playability, the design is unsatisfactory. The wheels move with difficulty, if at all, and there is a tendency for the plastic piece to pop out of the holder. The finish of this variety of car shows a general decline in the quality of the casting and the application of the paint.

Modern sedan, Series 2, with single-piece axle and wheel assembly

Type	Years	Characteristics	Colors																									
S4.3 Fourth or Modern Series Sedans (BV75 or 107) (330, 440, or 331)			Black	Blue	Blue-Metallic	Blue-Neon	Cinnamon-Metallic	Copper	Gold	Green-Forest	Green-Metallic	Green-Neon	Maroon	Olive-Metallic	Orange	Orange-Neon	Orange-Red Neon	Pink-Neon	Purple-Neon	Red	Red-Metallic	Red-Neon	Silver	Tan	Violet	White	Yellow	Yellow Lemon-Neon	Yellow-Lemon
S4.3.1	1970-71	Cast, plastic wheels, plastic axles						x						x															
S4.3.2	1970-71	Same as S4.3.1 with flower power label																											
S4.3.3	1970-71	Same as S4.3.1 with small, round number label on top of car														x						x						x	
S4.3.4	1970-71	Black paint over gold paint	x																										

The most distinguishing characteristic of this variety is a substantial expansion of the colors to include a number of hot or neon colors. This variety of car was probably introduced in 1969 or 1970 and continued until Barclay ceased operations in 1971. Since the publication of *Barclay Toys*, two additional colors, copper and metallic olive, have been authenticated in this series. Although available, this type is not seen as frequently as one might expect and is very to extremely scarce in many of the colors.

R3/R7: All Colors ($4-25) ($6-50)

Modern sedans S4.3.1

S4.3.2 This variety is exactly the same as S4.3.1 except that a Flower Power label has been placed on the top of the car. This same label can be seen on a number of Barclay products manufactured just prior to the closure of the company. This variety is very scarce.

R6/7: All Colors ($15-25) ($35-55)

Modern sedans with Flower Power and round number labels S4.3.2 and S4.3.3

S4.3.3 This variety is exactly the same as S4.3.1 except that a small, round number label has been placed on the top of the car. This variety is very scarce.

R6/7: All Colors ($15-25) ($35-55)

S4.3.4 This variety is extremely unusual. The car was first painted gold and then partially coated black to create a two-toned swirl effect. Barclay Cars included a picture of this variety, but it was thought that the car shown was an experiment or an accident. Since the publication of *Barclay Toys*, other examples of this variety have been located leading to the conclusion that this variety was an intentional creation of the Barclay factory. This variety is very scarce.

R7: Black over Gold ($30-35) ($60-70)

Modern sedan S4.3.3

Modern Series Coupes: Section 1

Scarcity and pricing is listed in italics after the detailed description for each piece. Due to variations seen in the market, prices are listed in ranges for examples in C-8 (Very Good) and C-10 (Mint) conditions.

As an aid to the users of *Barclay Toys*, listings that appear in *Barclay Toys* are shown in a darker color without an "x." New variations are shown in a lighter color with an "x." Each piece in the sets will be discussed below.

CO4.1.1 This Shoebox coupe has metal wheels and axles, has numbers one through eight cast on the inside of its roof indicating the location of each casting in the mold, has an open back window, and has eyelet axle holders. This type of car was most likely first produced in the late 1950s and its production continued until the mid-1960s. This is the oldest and most common Modern Series coupe, although certain colors are very scarce.

This coupe was produced simultaneously with the cars from the later years of the Classic Series. Cars from the two series were often mixed together in the car and trailer sets of the late 1950s and the

Type	Years	Characteristics	Aqua	Black	Blue	Blue-Lt.	Blue-Steel	Clay	Coral	Cream	Gray	Green-Forest	Green-Lt.	Green-Metallic	Green-Neon	Gold	Orange	Orange-Burnt	Orange-Neon	Pink	Pink-Bright	Red	Red-Neon	Salmon	Silver	Tan	Yellow	Yellow-Lemon
Fourth or Modern Series Coupes (BV75 or 107) (440, 330, or 331)																												
CO4.1.1	1957-65	Cast, metal wheels and axles, marked 1-8, open back window, eyelet axle holder; perhaps '51 Packard.		x						x	x																	
CO4.1.2	1957-65	Same as CO4.1.1 except closed back window																										
CO4.1.3	1960-65	Same as CO4.1.1 except gold wheels																		x	x	x		x				
CO4.2.1	1965-70	Same as CO4.1.1 except with cleated rubber or vinyl plastic tires, metal axle made from pin crimped at one end, forked or eyelet wheel assembly, closed back window						x	x										x									
CO4.2.2	1966-70	Same as CO4.2.1 except axle nub at both ends													x													
CO4.2.3	1966-70	Same as CO4.2.1 except with small smooth rubber tires, metal axle made from pin crimped at one end, forked axle holders, closed back window		x	x							x									x			x	x			
CO4.2.4	1966-70	Same as CO4.2.1 except large smooth plastic tires															x				x						x	

Notes: (1) CO4.1.1 Blue over red with solid wheels.
(2) CO4.1.1 Orange with solid orange wheel painted over gold wheels.

Modern coupe, side view

Modern coupe, front view

Modern coupe, rear view

Modern coupe, bottom view

first half of the 1960s. As far as is known, this version of the Shoebox car was not used on the Modern Series trailer sets introduced in the mid-1960s. Since the publication of *Barclay Toys*, three additional colors have been authenticated in this series. These additional colors are black, cream, and gray.

R1: Blue, Light Green, Orange, and Red ($3-4) ($5-6)
R2/R4: Light Blue, Forest Green, Pink, Bright Pink, Silver, Tan, Lemon Yellow ($5-6) ($8-15)
R6: Black, Cream, and Salmon ($15-25) ($30-50)
R7/8: Aqua, Clay, Gray, and Steel Blue ($20-30) ($35-70)

Modern coupes CO4.1.1

CO4.1.2 This variation is the same as CO4.1.1 variety except that it has a closed back window. It is assumed that it was produced during the same period as the C4.1.1. It is not known whether the closed-window varieties were created due to a flawed production process or whether they simply represent a variation in one or more of multiple molds. This variety is more difficult to locate than the open-window variety.

R2/R4: All Colors except Clay ($5-6) ($8-15)
R6: Clay ($15-25) ($30-50)

Modern coupes CO4.1.2

CO4.1.3 This variation is the same as CO4.1.1 except that it has gold colored metal wheels rather than the more common silver colored metal wheels. This variety is often seen with the gold-wheeled variety of the Third Series cars; therefore, it is assumed that these cars were produced in the first half of the 1960s, when both varieties were produced simultaneously. This variety is very scarce. Since the publication of

Barclay Toys, four additional colors of this variety have been authenticated. These additional colors are pink, bright pink, red, and salmon.

R6: All Colors except Bright Pink, and Salmon ($20-25) ($30-70)
R7: Bright Pink and Salmon ($30-35) ($40-80)

Modern coupes CO4.1.3

CO4.2.1 This is the second type of Shoebox car. The body of the car is essentially the same as the CO4.1.2 type; however, the wheels are made from either a dull, synthetic rubber with cleats or plastic vinyl with cleats. The two wheel varieties are difficult to differentiate; however, the rubber variety tends to be more flexible and appears dull when compared to the plastic variety. In contrast, the plastic wheels are relatively stiff and tend to have a shiny appearance.

There are two varieties of the wheel assembly. The more common version has a forked axle holder. A second version has the eyelet axle holder used on the CO4.1.1 variety. The axle is steel and is made from a metal pin with a nub at one end and a crimp at the other end. The back window is closed. This version of the Shoebox car appears to have been made from about 1965 until the final version was introduced around 1969 or 1970. While available, this variety is not nearly as common as the earlier cars with metal wheels. Since the publication of *Barclay Toys*, three additional colors, clay, coral, and orange neon, have been authenticated in this variety.

R2/R4: All Colors Except Those Listed as R6/7 ($5-8) ($10-20)
R6/7: Steel Blue, Clay, Gray, Gold, Burnt Orange, Orange Neon, and Red Neon ($20-30) ($35-70)
R7–10 Coral ($35-45) ($50-95)

Modern coupes CO4.2.1

CO4.2.2 This variation is the same as the CO4.2.1 with a closed back window; however, the axle has a nub at both ends. It is not known when this variety was produced, but it was during the 1966 to 1970 period. It is distinctly possible that this variation was produced simultaneously with other variations and it is relatively difficult to locate. Since the publication of *Barclay Toys*, a green neon example of this variety has been authenticated.

R2/R4: All Colors ($5-8) ($10-20)

Modern coupes CO4.2.2

CO4.2.3 This variation of the Shoebox car is the same as the CO4.2.1 except the wheels have a small, smooth synthetic rubber tire. The car has a steel axle made from a metal pin with a nub at one end and a crimp at the other end, forked axle holders, and an open back window. It is not clear when this variation was produced; however, it was sometime between 1966 and 1970. It is distinctly possible that this variation was produced simultaneously with other variations. As compared to some of the other non-steel wheeled varieties of the Shoebox cars, this variation is relatively difficult to locate. Since the publication of *Barclay Toys*, several additional colors of this variety have been authenticated. These additional colors are black, blue, forest green, red, salmon, and silver.

R5/6: All Colors ($10-15) ($20-30)

Modern coupes CO4.2.3

CO4.2.4 This variety of the Modern coupe is the same as CO4.2.1 except that the cars have large, smooth

black plastic tires. This variety has been discovered subsequent to the publication of *Barclay Toys* and it is quite scarce.

R6/7: All Colors ($20-25) ($35-45)

Modern coupes CO4.2.4

Modern Series Coupes: Section 2

Scarcity and pricing is listed in italics after the detailed description for each piece. Due to variations seen in the market, prices are listed in ranges for examples in C-8 (Very Good) and C-10 (Mint) conditions.

As an aid to the users of *Barclay Toys*, listings that appear in *Barclay Toys* are shown in a darker color without an "x." New variations are shown in a lighter color with an "x." Each piece in the sets will be discussed below.

CO4.3 This final variation of the Barclay transport cars retains the same basic shape as all Shoebox cars; however, the wheels and axle are now a single piece of molded plastic. The plastic component is simply pushed into the forked holder. From the standpoint of playability, the design is unsatisfactory. The wheels move with difficulty, if it all, and there is a tendency for the plastic piece to pop out. This variety also shows the general decline in the quality of the casting process as well as in the application of the paint.

The most distinguishing characteristic of this variety is a substantial expansion of the colors used on the cars, which include a number of hot or neon colors. This type of car was probably introduced in 1969 or 1970 and continued until Barclay ceased operations in 1971. Although available, this type is not seen as frequently as one might expect and is very to extremely scarce in many of the colors. Since

Type	Years	Characteristics	Colors																									
			Black	Blue	Blue-Metallic	Copper	Gold	Green-Forest	Green-Metallic	Green-Neon	Maroon	Orange	Orange-Burnt	Orange-Red	Orange-Red Neon	Pink-Neon	Purple-Metallic	Purple-Neon	Red	Red-Neon	Red-Metallic	Silver	Tan	White	Yellow	Yellow-Lemon	Yellow-Lemon-Neon
CO4.3 Fourth of Modern Series Coupes (BV75 or 107) (330, 440, or 331)																												
CO4.3	1970-71	Cast, plastic wheels and axles								x			x					x					x			x	

Notes: (1) Additional variations: C4.3.1–black over gold and black over yellow.

the publication of *Barclay Toys*, several additional colors in this variety have been authenticated. These additional colors include green neon, burnt orange, purple neon, tan, and lemon yellow.

R3/7: All Colors ($4-25) ($6-50)

Modern coupes, Series 2, CO4.3

Modern Series Original Sets

Original sets are made up of pieces of similar age and condition. As far as is known, the Modern Cab was only sold with the ridged-wheel trailers and with various sets of plastic- or rubber-wheeled cars. In general, the trailer sets always contained a cab, trailer, and either two or four cars. Normally, the two-car trailer sets had a sedan and a coupe, while the four-car trailer sets had two sedans and two coupes. Today, pieces from the Modern Series are often mixed with pieces from the Classic Series in ways that simply never existed. The correct combinations are listed below, however, one note of caution relates to the cabs and trailers with white sidewalls. The sets in blister packs that have been located all include white sidewalls on both the cab and the trailer. It is possible, however, that some

of the white sidewall pieces were sold with a plain sidewall companion piece. Pricing is for a set with the more common pieces; however, sets with whitewall tires are scarce to rare in every color combination.

C4.1 with 2T4.1, 4T4.1, or 4T4.2 Ridged-wheel cabs and trailers with matching Modern Series plastic- or rubber-wheeled cars.

R2: Matched Two-Car Set ($45-55) ($60-70)
R5: Matched Two-Car Set in Blister Pack (Mint Only) ($75-80)
R3: Matched Four-Car Set ($80-95) ($100-120)
R5: Matched Four-Car Set in Blister Pack (Mint Only) ($125-160)

Modern four-car sets

Modern two-car sets

Modern two-car sets

Modern four-car sets

C4.2 with 2T4.2 or 4T4.3 Trailers and a combination of Modern Series plastic- or rubber-wheeled cars.

R6/7: Matched Two-Car Set ($90-100) ($120-130)
R6/7: Matched Two-Car Set in Blister Park (Mint Only) ($140-170)
R6/7: Matched Four-Car Set ($110-120) ($140-200)
R6/7: Matched Four-Car Set in Blister Pack (Mint Only) ($170-300)
R7/10: Matched Four-Car Set in Blister Pack with Extra Car (Mint Only) ($200-400)

Modern four-car sets

Modern two-car sets

Modern four-car sets

Modern Series cars in blister packs with five (5), seven (7), or ten (10) cars to the pack. Prices vary depending on the rarity of the colors and variations included. Packs with a number of rare colors or with exceptional condition of the blister pack may sell for higher prices.

R5: Seven Cars in a Blister Pack (Mint Only) ($85-$130)
R6/7: Five Cars in a Blister Pack (Mint Only) ($85-$130)
R6/7: Ten Cars in a Blister Pack (Mint Only) ($140-$200)

Modern seven-car package

Modern five-car package

Modern ten-car package

Modern Series: Other Characteristics, Packaging, and Availability

The Modern Series was the last of the four major types of Barclay Transports Toys. While it does not include as many extreme rarities found in the Classic Series, overall it is clearly not as common as the Classic Series. Since the cars were sold individually as well as part of sets, there are more cars than there are cabs and trailers. As is the case with the Classic Series, there also appear to be more cabs than there are trailers. While the color variations of each type that are known are identified, there is every expectation that additional colors exist within certain type variations.

Except for a few cars that may have been sold individually and those early metal-wheeled modern cars that were mixed into the last of the boxed Classic Series sets, all of the Modern Series pieces were sold as part of blister pack sets. Different types of blister packs had sets of cars, two-car trailer sets, or four-car trailer sets. As with the Classic Series, the most common color combination in the early four-car sets was a green and an orange sedan paired with a blue and a red coupe.

While many pieces of the Fourth Series are available in the collectors' market, the pieces most frequently encountered are the more common varieties and colors in grades less than C-10. There are numerous varieties within this series that are very difficult to find that range from scarce to rare. Given their tendency for chipping, locating mint specimens of Shoebox cars is often challenging.

Detailed Catalog

Miniature Trucks Range

Background

The Miniature Trucks range was first sold in the late 1950s and components of this range were produced until Barclay ceased operations in 1971. Over the course of its production, eleven distinct types of trucks were produced, although at no time were all eleven produced simultaneously. Each truck type has two components. The first component is a single-piece cab and undercarriage. With the exception of the semi-trailer trucks, the second component was the body, which was permanently attached to the cab component. In the case of the semi-trailer trucks, the trailer includes a vertical peg that fits into a hole on the undercarriage of the cab. Castings for all components of the Miniature Trucks were made by the die-cast method by injecting molten metal under pressure into steel molds.

Dating of this series requires a special note. Various authors have stated that Goldsmith claimed credit for introducing the plastic blister packaging. Since to the best of our knowledge, the Miniature Trucks and Miniature Cars were only sold in blister packs and since Goldsmith did not join the company until 1961, this would suggest that these two ranges were not introduced until the early 1960s. Based upon the information provided by Rucci, it is now clear that the blister packaging was introduced before Goldstein arrived.[30] This and other observations form a compelling view that the Miniature Trucks and Miniature Cars ranges were introduced in the late 1950s.

While there are slight variations, the various types of Miniature Trucks are approximately two inches in length with the exception of the semi-trailer trucks, which are approximately three inches in length. As a consequence of their size, the Miniature Trucks are sometimes referred to as "two-inch" trucks.

Aside from the variations between the types of trucks, the individual examples can vary with respect to the casting of the cab, the cab color, the casting of the body, the color of the body or trailer, the wheel material, the type of wheels, and the labels. Each of these variations will be explained before moving to the detailed description of the various types of trucks.

Castings of the Cab and Undercarriage Component

In the Miniature Trucks range, there are four distinct castings of the cab and undercarriage component. As shown below, the earliest cabs in the Miniature Trucks range had no side bars and wheels were attached through an eyelet assembly similar to that found on the Transport Toys range cars and cabs in the 1950s and earlier 1960s. This initial casting is only found on the earliest examples of the Miniature Trucks. In either the late 1950s or the early 1960s, the Miniature Trucks' cab molds were reworked and the two side bars were added; however, the eyelet wheel assembly was retained. As you will note in the detailed listings, this mold was used for a relatively short period. In the very early 1960s, the cab molds were again altered to eliminate the eyelet wheel assembly and replace it with a forked wheel assembly. The forked assemble was used to eliminate the need to drill the holes required for the eyelet wheel assembly.

Castings: Truck Cab and Undercarriage Component

1.1   50s Cab, No Side Bars, Triangular or Round Wheel Assembly-Eyelet Holes for Wheel Attachment

1.2   50S Cab, Side Bars, Triangular or Round Wheel Assembly-Eyelet Holes for Wheel Attachment

1.3   50s Cab, Side Bars, Triangular or Round Rear Wheel Assembly-Forked Arrangement for Wheel Attachment

2   60s Cab, Side Bars, Triangular Wheel Assembly-Forked Arrangement for Wheel Attachment

Cab castings 1.1, 1.2, 1.3 (Left to Right)

The final variation of the cab casting was the modern cab found on the trucks in the final three or four years of production. This cab style is clearly a miniature of the larger modern cabs in the Transport Toys range, which was based on the 1958 Ford cab-over engine (COE), C-Series medium-duty truck. While the modern cab in the Transport Toys range was first produced in the early 1960s, the smaller version of that design found in the Miniature Trucks range was more likely introduced no earlier than the mid-1960s. Many of various types of trucks with the modern cab are very difficult to locate and are either scarce to extremely rare.

Wheel Material and Type

The material used on the wheels of the Miniature Trucks includes metal, plastic, and plastic with whitewalls. These wheel types are listed below:

> **Wheel Materials**
> Metal
> Plastic
> Plastic-W=Plastic Whitewall

Within the plastic wheel category, there are numerous variations in terms of size, color, and physical appearance:

> **Wheel Type**
> Plastic-Small Smooth=SS
> Plastic-Small Cleated=SC
> Plastic-Large Black Smooth=LS
> Plastic-Extra Large Black Smooth=ELBS
> Plastic-Extra Large White Smooth=ELWS
> Plastic-Extra Large Ridged=ELR

With respect to dating, the metal wheels were the earliest type of wheels found on the Miniature Trucks. The small metal wheels on these early vehicles are the same wheels used on the Transport Toys cars from the early 1930s until the mid-1960s. The metal wheels were succeeded by plastic wheels with the small, smooth wheels being the earliest variety. These same small, smooth wheels are found on a very small number of the Transport Toys cars from the 1960s. The most common of the plastic wheels found on the Miniature Trucks are the small, cleated wheels. These are the

From left to right: metal wheels, plastic wheels, plastic whitewall wheels

From left to right: SS wheels, SC wheels, LS wheels

From left to right: ELR wheels, ELWS wheels, ESBS wheels

same wheels found on the Transport Toys cars in the mid-1960s. In the last several years of production of the Miniature Trucks, the wheels were the large, black, smooth variety. The final and rarest type of wheels used for the Miniature Trucks were the large, black, smooth variety with whitewalls. As will be noted in the detailed descriptions, the three extra-large wheels were only used on the small dump trucks.

In regard to the Miniature Trucks with plastic wheels, the detailed grids show all of the variations that have been noted. The most common plastic wheel type is the small, cleated wheel, which was also used on the modern transport cars. If the particular variety was produced in the earlier periods of this series, examples should exist with the small smooth plastic wheels. Likewise, if a particular variety was produced in the mid-1960s or later, examples should exist with the large, black, smooth wheels. Undoubtedly, there do exist additional plastic wheel types for any number of the variations listed in the detailed grids.

Other Characteristics of the Miniature Trucks

As has been noted, the Miniature Trucks can vary in a number of ways. Differences in the cab castings and wheels have been discussed above. Other variations occur in the body castings, the cab color, the body or trailer color, and the logos.

The colors used on the Miniature Trucks, both on the cabs as well as the bodies and trailers, are the same colors utilized on the Transport Toys and the civilian figures. This range was first produced in the late 1950s and, on a selected basis, continued until Barclay closed. During this period, the colors that were used tended to be stable with less color variation

than existed in the earlier years of the Barclay transport range. The only real exception to this observation appears to be yellow. Although both yellow and lemon yellow were used on various pieces, the yellow does vary in terms of tint and intensity. In the final two or three years, neon colors appeared on various varieties of the Miniature Trucks. As is the case for other miniature vehicles sold by Barclay, neon examples are scarce and many varieties are rare.

Aside from vehicle type, castings, wheel types, and colors, other major variations relate to logos. The earliest trucks in this series did not have logos; however, logos began to appear on many of the trucks shortly after the range was introduced. In some cases, the logos are generic, such as the "Cola" logos on some of the early bottle delivery trucks. Most of the logos relate to specific products or services such as "Pepsi," "Hertz," or "Railway Express." Other logos combine symbols with words such as the "Shell" logo. Another variation is the milk truck, which used the picture of "Elsie" cow and the word "Milk" to represent Borden's Milk. It must be noted that a number of the trucks in this range had no logos at all, including the dump trucks, the refuse trucks, and the moving vans.

Just prior to the time that Barclay ceased production, most of the neon-painted trucks had no labels or had only generic labels such as the various Flower Power labels that were used on a few of the Transport Series cars. Variation of labels also exists with respect to a number of the brands represented. These variations will be noted in the detailed grids and accompanying discussion, many of which are quite rare.

In the past, it has been suggested that Barclay may not have had permission to use the labels that represented a specific company. Rucci stated that this was not the case and that Barclay did obtain specific authorization to utilize the logos that appear on its Miniature Trucks.[31]

Bottle Delivery Trucks

Scarcity and pricing is listed in italics after the detailed description for each piece. Due to variations seen in the market, prices are listed in ranges for examples in C-8 (Very Good) and C-10 (Mint) conditions.

Type	Description	Cab Casting	Cab Color	Body Casting	Body Color	Wheel Mat.	Type	Logo—Side/Top
Bottle Delivery Truck								
MT1.1.1	Traditional cab, bottle del. body	1.2	Green		Red	Metal	—	None
MT1.1.2	Traditional cab, bottle del. body	1.2	Aqua		Red	Metal	—	None
MT1.1.3	Traditional cab, bottle del. body	1.2	Red		Red	Metal	—	None
MT1.1.4	Traditional cab, bottle del. body	1.2	Blue		White	Metal	—	None
MT1.2.1	Traditional cab, bottle del. body	1.2	Blue		White	Metal	—	Cola
MT1.2.2	Traditional cab, bottle del. body	1.2	Blue		White	Plastic	SC	Cola
MT1.3.1	Traditional cab, bottle del. body	1.3	Yellow		Yellow	Plastic	SS, LS	Coca-Cola
MT1.3.2	Traditional cab, bottle del. body	1.3	Yellow		Yellow	Plastic-W	LS	Coca-Cola
MT1.3.3	Traditional cab, bottle del. body	2	Yellow		Yellow	Plastic	LS	Coca-Cola
MT1.4	Traditional cab, bottle del. body	1.2	Blue		White	Metal	—	Pepsi-Small
MT1.5.1	Traditional cab, bottle del. body	1.3	Blue		White	Plastic	SC, LS, SS	Pepsi
MT1.5.2	Traditional cab, bottle del. body	1.3	Red		White	Plastic	SC	Pepsi
MT1.6	Traditional cab, bottle del. body	1.3	Cream		Cream	Plastic	SS, LS	YooHoo
MT1.7	Modern cab, bottle del. body	2	Yellow-Lemon		Yellow-Lemon	Plastic-W	LS	None
MT1.8	Modern cab, bottle del. body	2	Yellow		Yellow	Plastic-W	LS	Coca-Cola likely

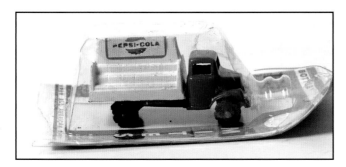

Bottle delivery truck MOC

MT1.1.1-MT1.1.4 Early Bottle Delivery Trucks–No Labels This group of trucks represents the earliest of the bottle delivery trucks. The wheels are metal and they do not have labels. By far the most common variety is the green cab and red body combination. The other combinations are difficult to locate.

R2/3: Green-Red ($10-12) ($15-20)
R6/7: All Other Colors ($20-30) ($40-50)

Early bottle delivery trucks MT1.1.1-MT1.1.4

MT1.2.1-MT1.2.2 Cola Delivery Trucks This variety was one of the first Miniature Trucks with a logo, although the logo was generic. Once Barclay began using established brands on the logo, this variety ceased to be produced. Both versions of this variety are seen from time to time, but they are not that common.

R5: All Types ($18-25) ($30-40)

Cola delivery trucks MT1.2.1 and MT1.2.2

MT1.3.1-MT1.3.3 Coca-Cola Delivery Trucks These trucks carry the official Coca-Cola logo and are collected by Coca-Cola and beverage product collectors in addition to Barclay collectors. All Coca-Cola trucks are scarce and the MT1.3.2 version with white side-walls and the MT1.3.3 version with a modern cab are rare. Of the black plastic wheel varieties, the "LS" wheel version is the more common.

R6: Black Plastic Wheels ($($20-30) ($40-50)
R7/10: Traditional Cab with White Side-Walls ($60-70)
($90-150)
R7/10: Modern Cab ($60-70) ($90-150)

Coca-Cola delivery trucks MT1.3.1 and MT1.3.2

MT1.4 Pepsi Cola Delivery Trucks with Small Logos These were the earliest trucks with a Pepsi logo. Note the metal wheels. In contrast with the later Pepsi trucks, which are relatively common, these trucks have the smaller logo and are very rare.

R7/10: Small Pepsi Cola Logo ($30-40) ($70-130)

Pepsi Cola delivery truck, small logo MT1.4

MT1.5.1-MT1.5.2 Pepsi Cola Delivery Trucks with Large Logos These varieties are the more common trucks with the Pepsi logo. In their standard variation with a blue cab and a white body, Pepsi trucks are some of the more common types of the Miniature Trucks. In contrast, the version of these trucks with a red cab is rare.

R2/3: Blue Cab ($10-12) ($15-20)
R7/8: Red Cab ($30-40) ($50-100)

Pepsi Cola delivery trucks, large logo MT1.5.1 and MT1.5.2

MT1.6 Yoo-Hoo Delivery Truck This variety carries the Yoo-Hoo logo, which is a regional beverage in the Mid-Atlantic region of the United States. Perhaps because of its regional nature, this is generally a more difficult variety to locate than its more common competitors, such as Coca-Cola and Pepsi.

R5: Yoo-Hoo ($18-25) ($30-40)

Yoo-Hoo delivery truck MT1.6

MT1.7 Modern Cab This distinctive variety is a product of the final days of Barclay. The only color located to date is lemon yellow, which is rare. There is no logo.

R7/8: Modern Cab ($30-40) ($50-100)

Delivery truck with Modern cab MT1.7

MT1.8 Bottle Truck Modern Cab 2, Coca-Cola yellow, plastic LS wheels, label residue. Most likely the toy had a Coca-Cola Label.

R7/10: Modern Cab MT1.8 ($60-70) ($90-150)

Modern bottle delivery truck MT1.8

Box Vans

Although all box vans are listed as "MT2," there are, in fact several variations of these trucks. The detailed listing grid will be shown separately for the various types of box vans.

Box Vans: Front of Box Cut-Out

Scarcity and pricing is listed in italics after the detailed description for each piece. Due to variations seen in the market, prices are listed in ranges for examples in C-8 (Very Good) and C-10 (Mint) conditions.

Box Van-Front of Box Cut-Out						Wheel		Logo–
Type	Description	Cab Casting	Cab Color	Body Casting	Body Color	Mat.	Type	Side/Top
MT2.1.1	Traditional cab, body with front cut-out, flat sides	1.1	Red	1	Aluminum	Metal	—	—
MT2.1.2	Traditional cab, body with front cut-out, flat sides	1.1	White	1	White	Metal	—	—

MT2.1.1-MT2.1.2 Box Vans–Front of Box Cut-Out
These are the earliest version of the box van. Among other features, the cab casting is the very first casting (1.1) with metal wheels. The differentiating feature of this variety is the fact that the undercarriage of the cab has a hump where the front of the body must be attached. As a consequence, the front of the body must have a cut-out in order to properly be attached. The red cab version is relatively common; however, it is more difficult to locate in mint condition. The white cab version is rare.

R2/3: Red Cab ($10-12) ($15-20)
R7/8: White Cab ($30-40) ($50-100)

Box van, front of box cut-out, MT2.1.1 and MT2.1.2

Box Vans: Square Box, Ribbed Sides

Scarcity and pricing is listed in italics after the detailed description for each piece. Due to variations seen in the market, prices are listed in ranges for examples in C-8 (Very Good) and C-10 (Mint) conditions.

Box Van—Square Box, Ribbed Sides								
Type	**Description**	**Cab Casting**	**Cab Color**	**Body Casting**	**Body Color**	**Wheel**		**Logo— Side/ Top**
						Mat.	**Type**	
MT2.2.1	Traditional cab, square body, ribbed sides	1.2	Red	2	Aluminum	Metal	—	None
MT2.2.2	Same as 2.2.1	1.2	Green	2	Aluminum	Metal	—	None
MT2.3.1	Same as 2.2.1	1.2	Green	2	Aluminum	Metal	—	Hertz— Yellow On Black
MT2.3.2	Same as 2.2.1	1.2	Green	2	Aluminum	Plastic	SC	Hertz— Yellow On Black
MT2.3.3	Same as 2.2.1	1.2	Yellow	2	Yellow	Plastic	SC	Hertz— Black On Yellow

MT2.2.1-MT2.3.3 These varieties of the box van are still very early in the evolution of the Miniature Trucks, but they do include changes to both the cab and the body casting. The hump on the carriage portion of the cab casting has been eliminated. As a consequence, the body casting is now squared without the cut-out, but the body retains the ribbed sides that existed in the prior version of the body casting. The initial versions of this variety have no logos; however the later three versions have Hertz logos. With respect to the logos, the yellow-on-black Hertz logo was the earliest version of this logo and is very scarce. The final version of this variety, MT2.3.3, has the more common black on yellow Hertz logo.

R2: MT2.2.1 Red Cab ($7-8) ($10-12)
R2/3: MT2.2.2 Green Cab; MT2.3.3 Yellow Cab ($10-12) ($15-20)
R7/8: MT2.3.1, MT2.3.2 Yellow on Black Hertz Label ($30-40) ($50-100)
R7/8: MT2.3.3 Yellow Cab and Body ($30-40) ($50-100)

Box Van, square box, Hertz yellow-on-black label MT2.3.2

Box van, square box, no label, MT2.2.1 and MT2.2.2

Box Van, square box, Hertz labels, MT2.3.2 and MT2.3.3

Box Vans: Square Box, Flat Sides

Scarcity and pricing is listed in italics after the detailed description for each piece. Due to variations seen in the market, prices are listed in ranges for examples in C-8 (Very Good) and C-10 (Mint) conditions.

| **Box Van-Square Box, Flat Sides** | | | | | | **Wheel** | | **Logo–Side/Top** |
Type	**Description**	**Cab Casting**	**Cab Color**	**Body Casting**	**Body Color**	**Mat.**	**Type**	
MT2.3.1	Traditional cab	1.3	Red	3	Aluminum	Plastic	SC, SS, LS	A&P
MT2.3.2	Modern cab	2	Red	3	Aluminum	Plastic	LS	A&P
MT2.3.3	Modern cab	2	Red-Metallic	3	Aluminum	Plastic	LS	A&P
MT2.4.1	Traditional cab	1.2	Blue	3	Aluminum	Metal	-	Avis–4 sides
MT2.4.2	Traditional cab	1.3	Blue	3	Aluminum	Plastic	LS	Avis–4 sides
MT2.4.3	Traditional cab	1.3	Blue	3	Aluminum	Plastic	SS	Avis–6 sides
MT2.4.4	Modern cab	2	Blue	3	Aluminum	Plastic	LS	Avis–6 sides
MT2.4.5	Modern cab	2	Red	3	Aluminum	Plastic	LS	Avis–6 sides
MT2.4.6	Modern cab	2	Blue	3	Aluminum	Plastic	LS	Avis–4 sides
MT2.5.1	Traditional cab	1.3	Green	3	Aluminum	Plastic	SC	Hertz
MT2.5.2	Traditional cab	1.3	Orange	3	Aluminum	Plastic	LS	Hertz
MT2.5.3	Traditional cab	1.3	Red	3	Aluminum	Plastic	SC	Hertz
MT2.5.4	Traditional cab	1.3	Yellow	3	Aluminum	Plastic	SC, LS	Hertz
MT2.5.5	Modern cab	2	Yellow	3	Aluminum	Plastic	LS	Hertz
MT2.5.6	Modern cab	2	Yellow	3	Aluminum	Plastic-W	LS	Hertz
MT2.6.1	Traditional cab	1.3	Military	3	Military	Plastic	SS, LS	Large Army/large star
MT2.6.2	Modern cab	2	Military	3	Military	Plastic	LS	As Above
MT2.7	Traditional cab	1.3	White	3	White	Plastic	SC	Stuart
MT2.8.1	Traditional cab	1.3	Cream	3	Aluminum	Plastic	SC, SS, LS	U-Haul
MT2.8.2	Modern cab, square body	2	Cream	3	Aluminum	Plastic	LS	U-Haul
MT2.9	Modern cab	2	White	3	White	Plastic	LS	None
MT2.10	Traditional cab	1.2	Blue	3	Blue	Plastic	SC	None

Box vans MOC

Box vans MOC

All of the box vans listed in this section, have the square box body of the previous variety, but have flat rather than ribbed sides.

MT2.3.1-MT2.3.3 A&P Refrigeration Box Vans Box vans with the A&P Refrigeration logo are relatively difficult to locate. Examples with the traditional cab are by far the most common, while any example of this type with the modern cab is very scarce.

R5: Red Traditional Cab ($18-25) ($30-40)
R7: Modern Red Cab ($25-30) ($60-100)
R7/8: Modern Metallic Red Cab ($30-40) ($50-100)

A&P label, side view

A&P label, rear view

A&P box vans MT2.3.1-MT2.3.3

MT2.4.1-MT2.4.5 Avis Box Vans Examples of box vans with Avis logos are found periodically; however, their scarcity varies depending upon the cab color and the type of design on the label. Cabs with the Avis label are not nearly as common as those with the Hertz label. The earliest version of the Avis box van has the early 1.2 cab casting and metal wheels. Its most distinguishing characteristic, however, is the fact that it has a four-sided logo. The four-sided logo is repeated in the second variation of the Avis box van. The most common variation of this variety is the traditional cab with the six-sided logo. As is the case with virtually all of the Miniature Trucks, versions of the Avis box van with the modern cab are very scarce. A rather surprising development is the location of a modern box van with a four-sided Avis logo.

R4: MT2.4.3 Blue Traditional Cab, 6-Sided Label ($12-15) ($20-25)
R6: Traditional Cab Versions with 4-Sided Label ($25-35) ($40-80)
R7/8: Modern Cab Versions with 6-Sided Label ($30-40) ($50-100)
R7/10: Modern Cab Version with 4-Sided Label ($60-70) ($90-150)

Avis 4-Sided Label, rear view

Avis 4-sided label, side view

Avis 6-sided label, rear view

Avis box vans MT2.4.1-MT2.4.3

Avis 6-sided label, side view

Avis box vans MT2.4.4-MT2.4.6

MT2.5.1-MT2.5.6 Hertz Box Vans The Hertz box vans are one of the most common Miniature Trucks. That being said, certain versions of the variety are difficult to locate. The most common version of the Hertz box vans have a green traditional cab. The second most common version have a yellow traditional cab. Hertz box vans with orange or red traditional cabs are rare as are both examples with the modern cab.

R2: *Traditional Green Cab ($7-8) ($10-12)*
R2/3: *Traditional Yellow Cab ($10-12) ($15-20)*
R6: *Modern Yellow Cab ($25-35) ($40-80)*
R7/8: *Modern Yellow Cab with Whitewall Tires ($30-40) ($50-100)*
R7/10: *Traditional Red or Orange Cab ($60-70) ($90-150)*

Hertz box vans MT2.5.1-MT2.5.4

Hertz box vans MT2.5.5 and MT2.5.6

MT2.6.1-MT2.6.2 Military Box Vans The box vans with military labels are somewhat more common than other varieties of the box van with respect to vehicles having both traditional and modern cabs. The labels on this variety are the large army and large star varieties in contrast to the small army and small star labels found on other Miniature Trucks and Cars with the military paint color and labels.

R2/3: *Traditional Military Cab ($10-12) ($15-20)*
R5: *Modern Military Cab ($18-25) ($30-40)*

MT2.6.1 and MT2.6.2

MT2.7 Stuart Box Vans The Stuart In-Fra-Red Sandwich box vans come in only one variety and are difficult to locate. Unlike the other company logos used by Barclay, this company appears to have been a much smaller enterprise. As far as can be determined, Stuart ceased doing business sometime in the 1980s.

R6: *Traditional Cab ($25-35) ($40-80)*

Stuart box van MT2.7

MT2.8.1-MT2.8.2 U-Haul Box Vans U-Haul box vans are relatively scarce in all varieties and are particularly scarce in the version with the modern cab. As with most of the company logos used by Barclay, U-Haul was a national company whose logo would be recognized in all parts of the United States.

R5: *U-Haul Traditional Cab ($18-25) ($30-40)*
R7/8: *U-Haul Modern Cab ($30-40) ($50-100)*

U-Haul box vans MT2.8.1 and MT2.8.2

U-Haul label, side view

U-Haul label, rear view

MT2.9 White Modern Box Vans This example of the box van was manufactured as Barclay was rapidly moving toward closing. This variety is all white and has no labels. While it is possible that this variety once had labels, it is very unlikely given the time period when it was manufactured. This variety is rare.

R7/10: White Box Van ($60-70) ($90-150)

MT2.10 Box Van All Blue Given the cab type, this box van was one of the earliest vans of this type. it is very rare.

R7-10: All Blue Box Van ($60-70) ($90-150)

Box van with Modern cab MT2.9

Box van MT2.10, all blue

Canvas-Covered Transports

The canvas-covered transports come in two different body castings—a wide-body version and a narrow-body version. This variety was produced in two finishes, either a Red Cross or a military finish. It was manufactured in one casting or another from the initial introduction of the Miniature Trucks until near the time that Barclay ceased production in 1971.

Canvas-Covered Transports: Wide-Body and Narrow-Body

Scarcity and pricing is listed in italics after the detailed description for each piece. Due to variations seen in the market, prices are listed in ranges for examples in C-8 (Very Good) and C-10 (Mint) conditions.

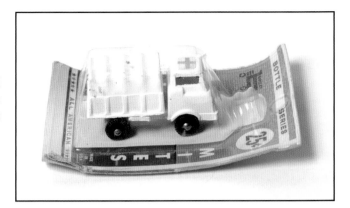

Canvas-covered truck MOC

Military finish: small army-small star, large army-large star

Canvas Covered Transport								
Type	**Description**	**Cab Casting**	**Cab Color**	**Body Casting**	**Body Color**	**Wheel**		**Logo–Side/Top**
						Mat.	**Type**	
Wide Body								
MT3.1.1	Traditional cab, wide body	1.1	White	1	White	Metal	—	Red Cross–painted
MT3.1.2	Traditional cab, wide body	1.1	White	1	White	Metal	—	Red Cross–label
MT3.1.3	Traditional cab, wide body	1.1	Military	1	Military	Metal	—	None
Narrow Body								**(Only Labels Below)**
MT3.2.1	Traditional cab, narrow body	1.2	White	2	White	Metal	—	Red Cross
MT3.2.2	Traditional cab, narrow body	1.3	White	2	White	Plastic	SS, SC, LS	Red Cross
MT3.2.3	Modern cab, narrow body	2	White	2	White	Plastic	LS	Red Cross
MT3.3.1	Traditional cab, narrow body	1.2	Military	2	Military	Metal	—	None
MT3.3.2	Traditional cab, narrow body	1.2	Military	2	Military	Plastic	SC	Small Army–small star
MT3.3.3	Traditional cab, narrow body	1.3	Military	2	Military	Plastic	LS	None
MT3.3.4	Traditional cab, narrow body	1.3	Military	2	Military	Plastic	SS, SC	Large Army–large star
MT3.3.5	Modern cab, narrow body	2	Military	2	Military	Plastic	LS	Large Army–large star or none

MT3.1.1-MT3.1.3 Canvas-Covered Transports–Wide-Body As indicated, all of the canvas-covered transports are either the Red Cross or military versions. The first version, MT3.1.1, is distinctive in that the Red Cross marking on its roof was painted. This is the only example within the Miniature Trucks range where a logo was painted rather than created with a label. The more common version, MT3.1.2, of the wide-body canvas-covered transport retains the Red Cross; however, the logo is created by the use of a label. The military version of the wide-body casting does not have labels. Examples of both of these vehicles are scarce.

R3: MT3.1.2 Red Cross Painted ($12-14) ($18-22)
R5: MT3.1.3 Military No Labels ($18-25) ($30-40)
R6: MT3.1.1 Red Cross Painted ($25-35) ($40-80)

Red Cross trucks MT3.1.1 and MT3.1.2

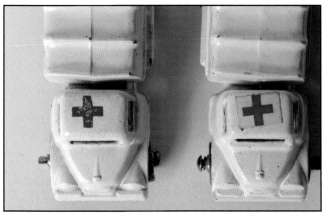

Red Cross markings: painted and label (left to right)

MT3.2.1-MT3.2.3 Red Cross Transports–Narrow-Body As reflected in the grid, there are three versions of the Red Cross narrow-body transports. By far the most common variety is MT3.2.2, which has a 1.3 cab casting and is found with multiple wheel varieties. The MT3.2.1 variety is relatively difficult to locate and, as is the case for all types of the Miniature Trucks, the modern cab version of this variety is quite scarce.

R2/3: MT3.2.2 Cab Casting 1.3 ($10-12) ($15-20)
R6: MT3.2.1 Cab Casting 1.2 ($25-35) ($40-80)
R7/8: MT3.2.3 Modern Cab ($30-40) ($50-100)

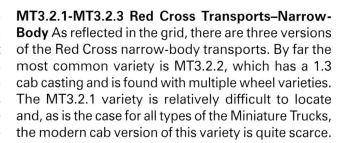

Red Cross narrow-bodies MT3.2.2 and MT3.2.3

Canvas-covered truck, military finish
MT3.1.3

MT3.3.1–MT3.3.5 Military Transports–Narrow-Body

As was the case with the Red Cross version of this variety, versions with the 1.2 cab casting are relatively difficult to locate. The most common version with the military finish is the MT3.3.4 variety. The MT3.3.3 type most likely was produced later in the production run of this variety because it has the larger wheels, which was the last type of wheel used before the cab was changed to the modern cab. While this variety exists in unopened blister packs, it is difficult to authenticate outside a blister pack because it is exactly the same vehicle as its companion toy with labels. As is the case universally, the version with the modern cab is quite scarce.

Military narrow-body MT3.3.1 and MT3.3.3

R2/3: MT3.3.4 Cab Casting 1.3 ($10-12) ($15-20)
R5: MT3.3.3 If Authenticated ($18-25) ($30-40)
R6: Examples with Cab Casting 1.2 ($25-35) ($40-80)
R7/8: Modern Cab ($30-40) ($50-100)

Military narrow-bodies, Modern cabs MT3.3.5

Military narrow-body MT3.3.2 and MT3.3.4

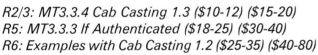

Illustration of narrow- and wide-bodies, small and large stars

Dump Trucks

Dump Trucks: Long Body

Scarcity and pricing is listed in italics after the detailed description for each piece. Due to variations seen in the market, prices are listed in ranges for examples in C-8 (Very Good) and C-10 (Mint) conditions.

Type	Description	Cab Casting	Cab Color	Body Casting	Body Color	Wheel		Logo– Side/Top
						Mat.	Type	
MT4.1.1	Traditional cab, long body	1.1	Red		Blue	Metal	—	None
MT4.1.2	Traditional cab, long body	1.1	Red		Blue-Lt.	Metal	—	None
MT4.1.3	Traditional cab, long body	1.1	Red		Blue-Steel	Metal	—	None
MT4.1.4	Traditional cab, long body	1.1	Red		Blue	Plastic	SC	None
MT4.2.1	Traditional cab, long body	1.2	Red		Blue	Metal	—	None
MT4.2.2	Traditional cab, long body	1.2	Blue-Lt.		Blue-Lt.	Metal	—	None
MT4.3.1	Traditional cab, long body	1.3	Red		Yellow	Plastic	LS	None
MT4.3.2	Traditional cab, long body	1.3	Red		Blue	Plastic	SC LS	None

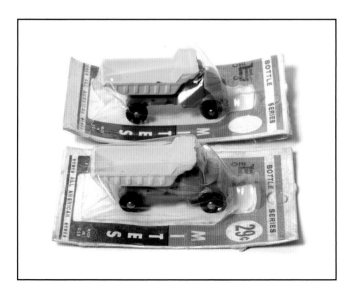

Dump trucks MOC

MT4.1.1–MT4.3.2 Dump Trucks–Long Body In contrast to the other varieties of vehicles in the Miniature Trucks range, the dump trucks with a long body remained relatively consistent throughout their production run with the exception of cab casting and color variations. This dump truck is approximately two and three-sixteenth inches long, has a moveable dump, and has no logos. Production of this toy ended sometime in the mid-1960s. Two varieties of this two are scarce to rare, MT4.1.3 with a steel blue dump and the all blue MT4.2.2.

R2/4: All Varieties Except Those Listed Below ($10-18) ($15-30)
R6: MT4.1.3 Blue Steel Dump ($25-35) ($40-80)
R7/10: MT4.2.2 Lt. Blue Cab and Dump ($60-70) ($90-150)

Dump trucks MT4.1.1-MT4.1.4

Dump truck MT4.2.1

Dump trucks MT4.3.1 and MT4.3.2

Dump Trucks: Small

The small dump trucks exists in two versions. The first version has a narrow undercarriage with a narrow dump component. The configuration of the first version is such that the dump rests at an angle when stationery with the back of the dump at the highest point. The second version of the small dump trucks has a wide undercarriage and a wide dump component. In contrast to the first version of this vehicle, the dump on this version is horizontal when stationery. In both cases, the dump is movable and there are two sizes of wheels. In the grid below, the material of the wheels are identified. The type column only relates to plastic wheels. There are no labels on any of these vehicles.

The first variation is somewhat more difficult to locate than the second variation, particularly in mint

condition. As will be noted, certain colors are clearly more difficult to locate than others. As with the longer dump trucks, production of this toy ended in the mid-1960s. The casting variations are shown below:

Casting variations, side view

> **Castings Variations: Small Dump: Undercarriage Component**
> 1–Narrow Body Attachment
> 2–Wide Body Attachment

Casting variations, rear view

> **Casting Variations: Small Dump: Dump Component**
> 1–Narrow Dump Attachment
> 2–Wide Dump Attachment

Scarcity and pricing is listed in italics after the detailed description for each piece. Due to variations seen in the market, prices are listed in ranges for examples in C-8 (Very Good) and C-10 (Mint) conditions.

Casting variations, undersides

Dump Truck: Small Dump								
Type	**Description**	**Cab Casting**	**Cab Color**	**Body Casting**	**Body/ Dump Color**	**Wheel**		**Logo– Side/ Top**
						Mat.	**Type**	
MT5.1.1	Narrow undercarriage, dump	1	Blue	1	Orange	Met/Pla	ELBS	None
MT5.1.2	Narrow undercarriage, dump	1	Blue	1	Yellow-Lemon	Met/Pla	ELBS	None
MT5.1.3	Narrow undercarriage, dump	1	Lt. Blue	1	Cream	Met/Pla	ELBS	None
MT5.1.4	Narrow undercarriage, dump	1	Lt. Blue	1	Yellow	Met/Pla	ELBS	None
MT5.1.5	Narrow undercarriage, dump	1	Mint	1	Orange	Met/Pla	ELBS	None
MT5.1.6	Narrow undercarriage, dump	1	Lt. Blue	1	Red	Met/Pla	ELBS	None
MT5.2.1	Wide undercarriage, dump	2	Mint	2	Orange	Met-Pla	ELR	None
MT5.2.2	Wide undercarriage, dump	2	Mint	2	Orange	Met-Pla	ELWS	None
MT5.2.3	Wide undercarriage, dump	2	Black	2	Yellow	Plastic	ELR, LS	None
MT5.2.4	Wide undercarriage, dump	2	Blue	2	Orange	Plastic	ELR, SC	None
MT5.2.5	Wide undercarriage, dump	2	Blue	2	Yellow	Plastic	ELR, LS	None
MT5.2.6	Wide undercarriage, dump	2	Green	2	Orange	Plastic	ELR, SC	None
MT5.2.7	Wide undercarriage, dump	2	Green	2	Yellow	Plastic	ELR, LS	None

Notes: Met/Pla=Metal/Plastic

Small dump truck MOC

MT5.1.1–MT5.1.6 Small Dump Trucks–Narrow Components The small dump trucks with narrow components were the earlier version of this vehicle. The only differences in these six vehicles are the color combinations of the cabs and the bodies. All of the colors can be located; however, certain color combinations are clearly more difficult to locate than others. In general, mint examples of the small dump trucks with narrow castings are more difficult to locate than those with the wide castings.

R2/4: Blue-Orange, Blue-Lemon Yellow, Lt. Blue-Yellow, Mint-Orange ($10-18) ($15-30)
R5: Lt. Blue-Cream, Lt. Blue Red ($18-25) ($30-40)

MT5.2.1–MT5.2.7 Small Dump Trucks–Wide Components
The small dump trucks with wide components were produced in the later years of this vehicle's production run. The only differences between the various varieties are the wheel types and the colors. All of the colors can be located; however, certain color combinations are clearly more difficult to locate than others.

R2/4: All Color Combination Except Black-Yellow and Green-Yellow ($10-18) ($15-30)
R5: Black-Yellow and Green-Yellow ($18-25) ($30-40)

Small dump truck second castings MT5.2.1-MT5.2.3 and MT5.2.5-MT5.2.7

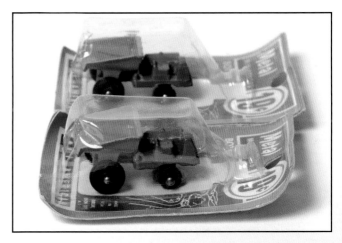

Small dump truck second castings MT5.2.4 and MT5.2.6

Small dump truck first castings MT5.1.1-MT5.1.6

Flatbed Log Carriers

This variety of the Miniature Trucks is actually just a flatbed truck; however, it was always sold with three wooden logs. The trucks itself themselves are slightly less than two inches long. The logs are cut from quarter-inch dowels and are slightly less than one and one-quarter inches long. The logs stick out over the back of the truck bed. The flatbed log carriers differ with respect to the cab variety, color combinations, and wheel types. There were no logos applied to this variety.

Scarcity and pricing is listed in italics after the detailed description for each piece. Due to variations seen in the market, prices are listed in ranges for examples in C-8 (Very Good) and C-10 (Mint) conditions.

Flatbed-Log Carrier								
Type	Description	Cab Casting	Cab Color	Body Casting	Body/ Dump Color	Wheel		Logo– Side/ Top
						Mat.	Type	
MT6.1	Traditional cab, flatbed body	1.2	Red		Blue	Metal	—	None
MT6.2.1	Traditional cab, flatbed body	1.3	Red		Green	Plastic	SS, SC, LS	None
MT6.2.2	Traditional cab, flatbed body	1.3	Red		Red	Plastic	SC, LS	None
MT6.2.3	Traditional cab, flatbed body	1.3	Yellow		Yellow	Plastic	LS	None
MT6.3.1	Modern cab, flatbed body	2	Red		Green	Plastic	LS	None
MT6.3.2	Modern cab, flatbed body	2	Red		Red	Plastic	LS	None
MT6.3.3	Modern cab, flatbed body	2	Red		Green	Plastic-W	LS	None

MT6.1 Flatbed Log Carriers–Metal Wheels These early log carriers have metal wheels and the cab casting is 1.2. This variety is distinctive in that the body color is blue and is difficult to locate, particularly in mint condition.

R6: Flatbed Log Carrier–Red/Blue ($25-35) ($40-80)

Flatbed trucks with logs MT6.1-MT6.2.3

Flatbed trucks without logs MT6.1-MT6.2.3

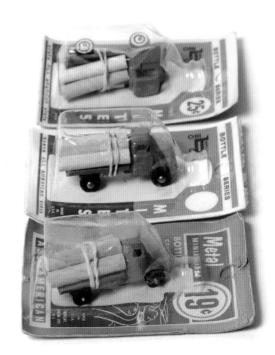

Flatbed trucks MOC

MT6.2.1–MT6.2.3 Flatbed Log Carriers with 1.3 Cab Castings By far the most common variety of flatbed trucks is the red cab with green body variety, MT6.2.1. The red cab with red body combination is seen, but is clearly more difficult to locate than the red/green combination. The all-yellow version is rare.

R2: Red Cab/Green Body ($7-8) ($10-12)
R5: All-Red ($18-25) ($30-40)
R7/8: All-Yellow ($30-40) ($50-100)

MT6.3.1-MT6.3.3 Flatbed Log Carriers-Modern Cabs All versions of the flatbed trucks with the modern cab are scarce. Both the all-red version and the red/green version with whitewall tires are rare.

R6: Red/Green with Modern Cab ($25-35) ($40-80)
R7/8: Red/Red Version, Red/Green–Whitewall Tires:
   Both with Modern Cabs ($30-40) ($50-100)

Flatbed truck with Modern cab MT6.3.1

Moving Vans

This variety of the Miniature Trucks was one of the first introduced and one of the first to be dropped from this range. The toy is slightly less than two inches long. There was only one casting variety for the cab and one casting variety for the body. While you may occasionally see this truck with a logo, no examples of this truck with a logo have been authenticated as being produced by Barclay.

Scarcity and pricing is listed in italics after the detailed description for each piece. Due to variations seen in the market, prices are listed in ranges for examples in C-8 (Very Good) and C-10 (Mint) conditions.

Moving Van						Wheel		Logo—
Type	Description	Cab Casting	Cab Color	Body Casting	Body/ Dump Color	Mat.	Type	Side/ Top
MT7.1.1	Traditional cab, moving van	1.1	Green		Red	Metal		None
MT7.1.2	Traditional cab, moving van	1.1	Green-Lt		Red	Metal		None
MT7.1.3	Traditional cab, moving van	1.1	Green		Green	Metal		None
MT7.1.4	Traditional cab, moving van	1.1	Red		Red	Metal		None

MT7.1.1-MT7.1.4 Moving Vans All four color combinations of this vehicle are seen from time to time; however the green/red and the light green/red combinations are by far the most common. The all-green and all-red combinations are more difficult to locate.

R2/4: Green/Red, Light Green/Red ($10-18) ($15-30)
R6: All-Green, All-Red ($25-35) ($40-80)

Moving vans MT7.1.1-MT7.1.4

Open Bed Trucks

This variety of the Miniature Trucks was produced for almost the entire period that this range was produced. This variety is almost exactly two inches long. With the exception of the cabs, the castings never varied. The recently discovered first version of the open bed truck used the 1.2 cab casting. The final versions were in the neon colors with whitewall tires. Although examples of this variety are seen, it appears to be one of the least frequently encountered of the Miniature Trucks.

Scarcity and pricing is listed in italics after the detailed description for each piece. Due to variations seen in the market, prices are listed in ranges for examples in C-8 (Very Good) and C-10 (Mint) conditions.

Open Bed								
Type	**Description**	**Cab Casting**	**Cab Color**	**Body Casting**	**Body/ Dump Color**	**Wheel**		**Logo– Side/Top**
						Mat.	**Type**	
MT8.1.1	Traditional cab, open bed body	1.2	Red		Red	Metal	—	None
MT8.2.1	Traditional cab, open bed body	1.3	Green		Red	Plastic	SC	None
MT8.2.2	Traditional cab, open bed body	1.3	Yellow		Yellow	Plastic	LS	None
MT8.3.1	Traditional cab, open bed body	1.3	Military		Military	Plastic	SC, LS	Large Army/ large star or large Army/ small star
MT8.3.2	Modern cab, open bed body	2	Military		Military	Plastic	LS	Large Army/ star
MT8.4.1	Traditional cab, open bed body	1.3	Yellow		Yellow	Plastic	LS	Euclid
MT8.4.2	Modern cab, open bed body	2	Yellow		Yellow	Plastic	LS	Euclid
MT8.5.1	Modern cab, open bed body	2	Lemon Yellow		Lemon Yellow	Plastic-W	LS	Flower Power
MT8.5.2	Modern cab, open bed body	2	Red-Orange Neon		Red-Orange Neon	Plastic-W	LS	Flower Power
MT8.5.3	Modern cab, open bed body	2	Red-Neon		Red-Neon	Plastic-W	LS	Flower Power

MTI.1.1 All-Red Version with Metal Wheels This initial version of the open bed truck uses the 1.2 cab casting, has both a red cab and a red body, and metal wheels. This early version is rare.

R7/8: Traditional Cab, All-Red ($30-40) ($50-100)

Open-bed truck, all red

Open-bed truck, all red

MT8.2.1-MT8.2.2 Traditional Cabs–No Labels These variations are seen periodically, but are not common. Authentication of the all-yellow version can only be guaranteed when it is in an unopened blister pack because it is exactly the same as the MT8.4.1 version with the Euclid label, which is the most common variety of this toy. The Euclid label always appears on the right side of the truck.

R5: Traditional Cabs, No Labels ($18-25) ($30-40)

Open-bed truck, no label MT8.2.1

Open-bed truck with and without Euclid label

MT8.3.1-MT8.3.2 Military Versions The military versions of this toy appear to be relatively less popular as compared to the other versions of this vehicle. As is generally the case, the military version with the modern cab is difficult to locate.

R4: Traditional Cab–Military Version ($12-15) ($20-25)
R6: Modern Cab–Military Version ($25-35) ($40-80)

Open-bed trucks with military finish MT8.3.1 and MT8.3.2

MT8.4.1-MT8.4.2 Euclid Label The most common version of the open bed trucks is MT8.4.1 with the Euclid logo. Since the cab is the 1.3 casting and the wheels are the "LS" variety, it is assumed that this variety was primarily sold in the mid-1960s. As one would expect, this version with a modern cab is scarce. The small, round Euclid label is located on the body of the truck near the passenger door. The

Open-bed trucks with Euclid label MT8.4.1 and MT8.4.2

Euclid Road Machinery Company manufactured heavy equipment for earthmoving, especially heavy dump trucks. In the 1950s, it was purchased by General Motors.

R2/3: Traditional Cab–Euclid Label ($10-12) ($15-20)
R6: Modern Cab–Euclid Label ($25-35) ($40-80)

Open-back truck, Modern cabs and Flower Power labels MT8.5.1 and MT8.5.2

MT8.5.1-MT8.5.3 Modern Cabs-Flower Power Label
This final version of the open bed trucks has a modern cab and a Flower Power label. Since these examples have whitewall tires and two of the three are in neon colors, it is safe to assume that these trucks were manufactured in the period shortly before Barclay ceased doing business. All three varieties are scarce to rare.

R6/7: Modern Cab–Lemon Yellow ($30-35) ($40-80)
R7/10: Modern Cab–Red Orange Neon, Red Neon ($60-70) ($90-150)

Open-back truck, Modern cabs MT8.4.2, MT8.5.2, MT8.5.3

Refuse Trucks

This variety of the Miniature Trucks was one of the first varieties produced and apparently was one of the first varieties discontinued. The truck is almost exactly two inches in length and has the 1.1 cab casting with metal wheels. No labels were ever applied to this variety.

The interesting aspect of this variety is how often it is confused with the tank truck or simply referred to as a second version of the tank truck. The refuse trucks are based upon a classic design of some older refuse trucks with a line of bins on each side of the body. Bins could be opened separately and the refuse then thrown into the specific bin. When you compare the bodies of the tank trucks and the refuse trucks, you will note that they are completely different.

Scarcity and pricing is listed in italics after the detailed description for each piece. Due to variations seen in the market, prices are listed in ranges for examples in C-8 (Very Good) and C-10 (Mint) conditions.

Refuse						Wheel		
Type	Description	Cab Casting	Cab Color	Body Casting	Body/ Dump Color	Mat.	Type	Logo– Side/ Top
MT9.1.1	Traditional cab, refuse carrier	1.1	Red		Blue	Metal		None
MT9.1.2	Traditional cab, refuse carrier	1.1	Red		Lt. Blue	Metal		None

MT9.1.1-MT91.2 Refuse Trucks There are only two variations of these trucks and the only difference is the color of the body. Of the two, the blue version is the most common; however, the light blue version can normally be located.

R2/3: Red Cab, Blue Body ($10-12) ($15-20)
R4: Red Cab, Light Blue Body ($12-15) ($20-25)

Refuse trucks MT9.1.1 and MT9.1.2

Semi-Trailer Trucks

This is one of the most interesting varieties of the Miniature Trucks range. The earliest versions of the semi-trailer trucks have a 1.2 cab casting, which suggests that they were produced very early in the production run of the Miniature Trucks. The final versions of the variety have whitewall tires and many have neon colored components, which suggests that these semi-trailer trucks were made until Barclay closed in 1971.

The challenging aspect of this variety is the fact that the cabs and trailers can easily be mixed together in combinations that were never sold by Barclay. Although many variations are listed in the detailed grid, only those combinations that have been found in unopened blister packs or have been seen so frequently that it can be safely assumed to be an original combination are listed. Particularly in the months prior to the date Barclay ceased production, any number of trailer sets were sold

in a wide variety of cab and trailer combinations. As more sets in blister packs are discovered, there is a high probability that additional trailer set combinations will be identified.

In contrast to some of the other varieties in the Miniature Trucks range, logos seemed to have been very important from the earliest days of this variety. The order of the various trailer sets shown on the grid is organized by label; however, multiple label designs were used for some companies. The trailer sets are almost exactly three inches long. The cab and the trailers are connected by means of a peg extending vertically from the trailer that fits into a hole on the back of the undercarriage of the cab. In addition to various castings of the cabs used in these sets, there are two distinct castings for the trailers. The most common casting has forked axle holders; however, the first casting has eyelet axle holders. The two versions are noted below:

Castings: Trailer

1–Eyelet Axle Holder

2–Forked Axle Holder

Alternative trailer castings

Determining rarity and pricing for the trailer sets is challenging. It is clear that the very early sets are very difficult to find. There are also any number of rare sets with unusual logos as well as the sets sold just as Barclay was preparing to close. As a consequence, pricing is given in relatively large pricing bands for certain groups of trucks.

Given the size of the grid for this variety, the grid is broken into two parts.

Semi-Trailer Trucks: Part 1

Semi-Trailer Sets Group 1: Axle Holder on Trailer-Either Eyelet or Forked								
Type	**Description**	**Cab Casting**	**Cab Color**	**Body Casting**	**Body/ Dump Color**	**Wheel**		**Logo— Side/Top**
						Mat.	**Type**	
MT10.1	Traditional cab, eyelet	1.2	Lemon Yellow	1	Yellow-Lemon	Plastic	SC	None
MT10.2	Traditional cab, eyelet	1.2	Red	1	Aluminum	Metal	-	Barclay
MT10.3.1	Traditional cab, forked	1.3	Orange	2	Orange	Plastic	SS, SC	Allied
MT10.3.2	Traditional cab, forked	2	Orange	2	Orange	Plastic	LS	Allied
MT10.3.3	Traditional cab, forked	2	Orange	2	Orange	Plastic-W	LS	Allied
MT10.3.4	Traditional cab, forked	2	Orange-Neon	2	Orange	Plastic-W	LS	Allied
MT10.3.5	Traditional cab, forked	2	Orange-Red Neon	2	Orange	Plastic-W	LS	Allied
MT10.3.6	Traditional cab, forked	2	Red-Neon	2	Orange	Plastic-W	LS	Allied
MT10.3.7	Traditional cab, forked	2	Green-Neon	2	Orange	Plastic-W	LS	Allied
MT10.3.8	Traditional cab, forked	2	Pink-Neon	2	Orange	Plastic-W	LS	Allied
MT10.3.9	Traditional cab, forked	2	Lemon-Neon	2	Orange	Plastic-W	LS	Allied
MT10.4.1	Traditional cab, eyelet	1.2	Black	1	Aluminum	Plastic	SC	Hertz
MT10.4.2	Modern cab, forked	2	Orange-Red Neon	2	Yellow	Plastic-W	LS	Hertz
MT10.4.3	Modern cab, forked	2	Lemon Yellow	2	Yellow	Plastic-W	LS	Hertz
MT10.4.4	Modern cab, forked	2	Lemon Yellow	2	Aluminum	Plastic-W	LS	Hertz
MT10.4.5	Modern cab, forked	2	Orange	2	Yellow	Plastic-W	LS	Hertz
MT10.4.6	Modern cab, forked	2	Pink-Neon	2	Yellow	Plastic-W	LS	Hertz
MT10.5.1	Traditional Cab, Forked	1.3	Red	2	Green	Plastic	SS, LS	Railway Exp.
MT10.5.2	Traditional Cab, Forked	1.3	Yellow	2	Green	Plastic	SC	Railway Exp.
MT10.5.3	Modern cab, forked	2	Red	2	Green	Plastic	LS	Railway Exp.
MT10.5.4	Modern cab, forked	2	Red	2	Green	Plastic-W	LS	Railway Exp.
MT10.5.5	Modern cab, forked	2	Red-Neon	2	Green	Plastic-W	LS	Railway Exp.
MT10.5.6	Modern cab, forked	2	Orange-Red Neon	2	Green	Plastic-W	LS	Railway Exp.
MT10.5.7	Modern cab, forked	2	Yellow Neon	2	Green	Plastic-W	LS	Railway Exp.
MT10.5.8	Modern cab, forked	2	Pink Neon	2	Green	Plastic-W	LS	Railway Exp.
MT10.5.9	Modern cab, forked	2	Orange Neon	2	Green	Plastic-W	LS	Railway Exp.
MT10.5.10	Modern cab, forked	2	Metallic Red	2	Green	Plastic	LS	Railway Exp.

Note: (1) Railway Exp.=Railway Express

Scarcity and pricing is listed in italics after the detailed description for each piece. Due to variations seen in the market, prices are listed in ranges for examples in C-8 (Very Good) and C-10 (Mint) conditions.

MT10.1 Early Semi-Trailer Set This early trailer set has a 1.2 cab casting, a 1 trailer casting, plastic wheels, and no labels. It is rare.

R7/10: Lemon Yellow Cab and Trailer ($60-70) ($90-150)

MT10.2 Barclay Semi-Trailer Set This trailer set is, perhaps, the rarest of all the Barclay trailer sets. The cab is the early 1.2 casting and the trailer is the 1 casting. The wheels are metal and the trailer is unpainted with a Barclay label.

R7/10: Barclay Label ($90-150) ($300-700)

Early semi-trailer set MT10.1

Barclay semi-trailer label, left side

Barclay semi-trailer label, right side

Barclay semi-trailer set MT10.2

MT10.3.1–MT10.3.9 Allied Sets The Allied Van Lines trailer sets first appeared with the traditional 1.3 cab; however, most of the various set combinations have a modern cab and trailer with whitewall tires. The most common varieties are MT10.3.1-MT10.3.3 with both the cab and the trailer in the Allied's traditional orange color. The varieties identified as MT10.3.4-MT10.3.9 appeared in the final year or two before Barclay closed and are generally difficult to locate. It is certainly possible that additional cab and trailer combinations exist from the period just prior to the closure of Barclay.

Allied semi MOC

R5: MT10.3.1–MT10.3.3 Allied Orange Cab and Trailer ($18-25) ($30-40)
R6/7: MT10.3.4–MT10.3.9 Allied Mixed Colors ($30-35) ($40-80)

Allied sets, mixed colors

Allied label, side view

Allied label, front view

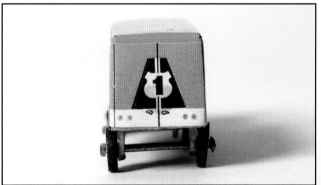

Allied label, rear view

Allied sets in traditional colors

MT10.4.1–MT10.4.6 Hertz Sets While the Hertz label is very common with respect to box vans, it was used very infrequently with regard to the semi-trailer sets. The initial Hertz trailer set appeared in an early three truck blister pack set and is extremely rare. The other four sets with the Hertz label have whitewall tires and, therefore, appeared shortly before Barclay closed. All are very difficult to locate.

R7/10: Hertz Sets with Whitewall Tires ($60-70) ($90-150)
R7/10: Early Hertz Set, MT10.4.1 ($70-120) ($200-300)

Hertz semi MOC

Hertz labels, large and small "Truck Rental"

Hertz semi, MT10.4.6

Hertz labels, small "Truck Rental" and red taillights

Hertz labels, large "Truck Rental" and yellow taillights

Hertz sets MT10.4.3-MT10.4.5

MT10.5.1–MT10.5.10 Railway Express Sets The earliest trailer sets with the Railway Express logo used the traditional 1.3 cab. The standard cab color is red; however, these earlier sets exist with a yellow cab. The most common variety of the Railway Express sets with the modern cab has a red cab; however, a number of varieties with the modern cab exist with whitewall tires suggesting they were sold in the last year or two of Barclay's existence. As is the case with the Allied Moving Company sets, it is certainly possible that additional cab and trailer combinations exist from the final years of production.

Railway Express semi MOC

Railway Express sets with traditional red cabs

R5: MT10.5.1–MT10.5.3 Railway Express Sets ($18-25) ($30-40)
R6/7: MT10.5.4–MT10.5.9 Railway Express Sets with Whitewalls ($30-35) ($40-80)
R7/10: Railway Express Semi MT10.5.10 ($60-70) ($90-150)

Railway Express label, front view

Railway Express label, side view

Railway Express label, rear view

Railway Express Semi MT10.5.10

Railway Express sets with mixed color cabs

Semi-Trailer Trucks – Part 2

Scarcity and pricing is listed in italics after the detailed description for each piece. Due to variations seen in the market, prices are listed in ranges for examples in C-8 (Very Good) and C-10 (Mint) conditions.

Semi-Trailer Sets Group 2: Axle Holder on Trailer-Either Eyelet or Forked								
Type	**Description**	**Cab Casting**	**Cab Color**	**Body Casting**	**Body/ Dump Color**	**Wheel**		**Logo– Side/Top**
						Mat.	**Type**	
MT10.6.1	Traditional cab, eyelet	1.2	Red	1	Blue	Metal	—	U.S. Mail
MT10.6.2	Traditional cab, forked	1.3	Red	2	Blue	Plastic	SC, LS, SS	U.S. Mail
MT10.6.3	Traditional cab, forked	1.3	Blue	2	Blue	Plastic	SC	U.S. Mail
MT10.6.4	Traditional cab, forked	1.3	Pale Red	2	Blue	Plastic	LS	U.S. Mail
MT10.6.5	Modern cab, forked	2	Red	2	Blue	Plastic	LS	U.S. Mail
MT10.6.6	Modern cab, forked	2	Red	2	Blue	Plastic-W	LS	U.S. Mail
MT10.6.7	Modern cab, forked	2	Pink-Neon	2	Blue	Plastic-W	LS	U.S. Mail
MT10.6.8	Modern cab, forked	2	Red-Neon	2	Blue	Plastic-W	LS	U.S. Mail
MT10.6.9	Modern cab, forked	2	Orange-Red Neon	2	Blue	Plastic-W	LS	U.S. Mail– Four Sides
MT10.6.10	Modern cab, forked	2	Yellow-Neon	2	Blue	Plastic-W	LS	U.S. Mail– Four Sides
MT10.7.1	Traditional cab, eyelet	1.2	Red	1	Aluminum	Metal	—	Woolworth
MT10.7.2	Traditional cab, eyelet	1.2	Red	1	Blue	Metal	—	Woolworth
MT10.7.3	Traditional cab, eyelet	1.2	Aqua	1	Blue	Metal	—	Woolworth
MT10.7.4	Traditional cab, forked	1.3	Red	2	Green	Metal	—	Woolworth
MT10.7.5	Traditional cab, forked	1.3	Red	2	Green	Plastic	SC	Woolworth
MT10.7.6	Traditional cab, forked	1.3	Green	2	Green	Plastic	SC	Woolworth
MT10.8.1	Traditional cab, forked	1.3	Pink-Neon	2	Pink-Neon	Plastic-W	LS	Flower Power
MT10.8.2	Modern cab, forked	2	Blue	2	White	Plastic	LS	None
MT10.8.3	Modern cab, forked	2	Green-Neon	2	Pink-Neon	Plastic	LS	None
MT10.8.4	Modern cab, forked	2	Pink-Neon	2	Pink-Neon	Plastic-W	LS	None
MT10.9	Modern cab, forked	2	Unknown	2	Aluminum	Plastic-W	LS	U-Haul

Notes: (1) Various pieces have double-nub axle.
(2) MOC examples exist with a mixture of white-wall and plain wheels.
(3) MOC examples exist with different wheels on the trailer and cab in the same set.

MT10.6.1–MT10.6.10 U.S. Mail Sets While the U.S. Mail trailer sets tend to be the most common variety of semi-trailer sets, several variations are very scarce to rare. The first trailer set with the U.S. Mail logo, MT6.1, is one of the first vehicles in the Miniature Trucks range and has a 1.2 cab casting as well as metal wheels. This variation is seen from time to time, but is difficult to locate. The most common of the U.S. Mail sets is the MT10.6.2 with a red 1.3 Traditional cab, plastic wheels of various types, and a three-sided logo.

Versions with the 1.3 traditional cab in colors other than red are very scarce. The U.S. Mail trailer sets with a modern cab and plain plastic wheels are relatively common; however sets with a modern cab and whitewall tires are difficult to locate. Of special note are MT10.6.9 and MT10.6.10, which have the rare four-sided logo in contrast to the three-sided logo used on all other U.S. Mail trailer sets.

R2/3: MT10.6.2 Traditional Red Cab ($10-12) ($15-20)
R5: MT10.6.5 Modern Red Cab, Plain Plastic Wheels ($18-25) ($30-40)
R6/10: All Other U.S. Mail Trailer Sets ($30-70) ($40-150)

U.S. Mail semi-trailers MOC

U.S. Mail set MT10.6.1

U.S. Mail set MT10.6.2-MT10.6.4

U.S. Mail set MT10.6.5

U.S. Mail set MT10.6.6-MT10.6.8

U.S. Mail label, three sides, side view

U.S. Mail Label, three sides, front view

U.S. Mail set MT10.6.9 and MT10.6.10

U.S. Mail label, four sides, side view

U.S. Mail label, four sides, front view

U.S. Mail label, four sides, rear view

MT10.7.1–MT10.7.6 Woolworth Sets For many years the Woolworth five-and-dime stores were Barclay's largest customer; however the Woolworth trailer sets are among the more difficult to locate and some are very rare. MT10.7.1, MT10.7.2, and MT10.7.3 have the 1.2 traditional cabs and were among the first Barclay trailer sets. The trailers are either plain aluminum or blue and all are rare. Though scarce, MT10.7.5 is the most common Woolworth trailer set. All other varieties are very scarce to extremely rare.

R5: MT10.7.5 Traditional 1.3 Green Trailer ($18-25) ($30-40)
R6/7: MT10.7.4 and MT10.7.6 ($30-35) ($40-80)
R7/10: 1.2 Cabs, Aluminum or Blue #1 Trailers ($60-70) ($90-150)

Woolworth set MT10.7.5 and MT10.7.6

Woolworth set MT10.7.1

Woolworth label, front view

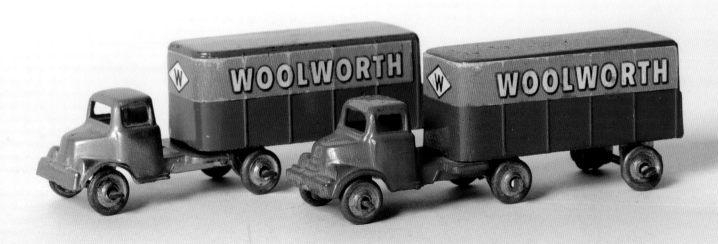

Woolworth set MT10.7.3 and MT10.7.4

MT10.8.1–MT10.8.4 Flower Power Trailers Sets or Sets without Logos In the months before Barclay ceased production, a number of trailer sets were manufactured and sold with only the generic Flower Power logo or without any logo. All of these sets are rare.

R7/8: All Varieties ($30-40) ($50-100)

Flower Power label on top MT10.8.1

Sets without labels MT10.8.3 and MT10.8.4

Set without label MT10.8.2

MT10.9 U-Haul Semi Modern cab 2 (color uncertain), trailer 2, plastic wheels–W LS, 3-sided U-Haul label. This variety is very rare.

R8/10: U-Haul semi ($100-150) ($200-400)

U-Haul semi MT10.9

Tank Trucks

The tank trucks were not one of the first Miniature Trucks, but the initial version was produced soon after these vehicles first appeared and this variety continued to be produced until Barclay ceased its production in 1971. The tank trucks are slightly less than two inches in length and consist of two components, a cab with an undercarriage and the tank body. The early tank trucks had no logos; however most examples do have various logos. In the final

year or two prior to the time Barclay closed, the tank trucks were painted in neon colors, had whitewall wheels, and either generic Flower Power labels or lacked labels entirely.

Scarcity and pricing is listed in italics after the detailed description for each piece. Due to variations seen in the market, prices are listed in ranges for examples in C-8 (Very Good) and C-10 (Mint) conditions.

Tank Truck								
Type	**Description**	**Cab Casting**	**Cab Color**	**Body Casting**	**Body/Dump Color**	**Wheel**		**Logo— Side/Top**
						Mat.	**Type**	
MT11.1	Traditional cab, tank truck	1.2	Red		Blue	Metal	—	None
MT11.2.1	Traditional cab, tank truck	1.3	Red		Aqua	Plastic	SC	None
MT11.2.2	Traditional cab, tank truck	1.3	Green		Green	Plastic	LS	None
MT11.3.1	Traditional cab, tank truck	1.2	Military		Military	Metal	—	None
MT11.3.2	Traditional cab, tank truck	1.3	Military		Military	Plastic	SS, SC	Large Army/ large star
MT11.3.3	Traditional cab, tank truck	1.3	Military		Military	Plastic	SC	Small Army/ large star
MT11.4.1	Traditional cab, tank truck	1.3	White		White	Plastic	LS	Elsie
MT11.4.2	Traditional cab, tank truck	1.3	Yellow		Yellow	Plastic	LS	Elsie
MT11.5.1	Traditional cab, tank truck	1.3	Yellow		Yellow	Plastic	SS, LS	Shell
MT11.5.2	Modern cab, tank truck	2	Yellow		Yellow	Plastic	LS	Shell
								Sinclair Logo
MT11.6.1	Traditional cab, tank truck	1.3	Green		Green	Plastic	SC	White 1-piece
MT11.6.2	Traditional cab, tank truck	1.3	Green		Green	Plastic	SS, LS	White 2-piece
MT11.6.3	Traditional cab, tank truck	1.3	Green		Green	Plastic	SC	Brown 1-piece
MT11.6.4	Modern cab, tank truck	2	Red		Green	Plastic	LS	Brown 1-piece
MT11.6.5	Modern cab, tank truck	2	Green		Green	Plastic	LS	White 2-piece
MT11.7.1	Traditional cab, tank truck	1.3	Blue		Silver	Plastic	LS, SS	Sunoco
MT11.7.2	Modern cab, tank truck	2	Blue		Gray	Plastic	LS	Sunoco
MT11.8.1	Modern cab, tank truck	2	Red-Neon		Red-Neon	Plastic-W	LS	Flower Power
MT11.8.2	Modern cab, tank truck	2	Orange-Neon		Orange-Neon	Plastic-W	LS	Flower Power
MT11.8.3	Modern cab, tank truck	2	Green-Neon		Green-Neon	Plastic-W	LS	None
MT11.8.4	Modern cab, tank truck	2	Red-Neon		Yellow-Neon	Plastic-W	LS	Flower Power

Notes: (1) MT11.2 in solid yellow and solid white without labels may have been manufactured and sold by Barclay.

Tank truck MOC

Tank truck MOC

MT11 Early Tank Trucks, Metal Wheels, No Logo
These very early tank trucks are notable because
they feature the 1.2 cab casting, metal wheels, and
no logo. They are found from time to time, but are
relatively scarce.

R5: Red Cab, Blue Body ($18-25) ($30-40)

Early tank truck with 1.2 cab MT11.1

MT11.2.1–MT11.2.2 Cab-1.3, No Logos These versions of the tank trucks have the 1.3 traditional cab and a body without a logo. Of the two varieties, the all-green version is the more common. While it is clear that the green version was sold without logos, collectors must be aware that the tank trucks with the Sinclair logo have exactly the same cab and body as the version without logos. As noted on the grid, Barclay may have sold the tank truck in all-yellow and all-white versions without logos; however, this has yet to be confirmed. Examples of these latter varieties are pictured in the Appendix.

R4: Green Cab, Green Body ($12-15) ($20-25)
R5: Red Cab, Aqua Body ($18-25) ($30-40)

Early tank trucks, no logo, 1.3 cabs MT11.2.1 and MT11.2.2

MT11.3.1–MT11.3.3 Military The initial variety in the military version is similar to the MT11.1 version, a 1.2 Cab casting with metal wheels and no labels. The remaining two varieties differ only with respect to wheel types and logos.

R4: MT11.3.1–No Logos ($12-15) ($20-25)
R5: Military Versions with Logos ($18-25) ($30-40)

MT11.4.1–MT11.4.2 Milk Carriers with Elsie the Cow This version of the tank truck was only produced with the Traditional 1.3 cab and large smooth tires, which suggests that its time in production was somewhat limited. The label includes the word "Milk" with an Elsie the Cow logo, which was the logo used at this time by Borden's Milk. When this toy was manufactured, the Borden Company was one of the largest dairies in the United States. The traditional white cab and body is scarce and the yellow cab and body is rare. This tank truck is collected by collectors of Barclay miniature toys as well as collectors of Borden memorabilia.

R6: White Cab and White Body ($25-35) ($40-80)
R7/10: Yellow Cab and Yellow Body ($60-70) ($90-150)

Borden Milk Elsie tank trucks MT11.4.1 and MT11.4.2

Elsie label (on both sides of tank)

Military tank trucks MT11.3.1 and MT11.3.2

MT11.5.1–MT11.5.2 Shell Oil The Shell Oil (Royal Dutch Shell) tank trucks are seen periodically, but are perhaps the scarcest of the various oil company tank trucks. The trucks with a 1.3 body are by far the most common of the Shell trucks. Shell trucks with a modern cab are rare.

Sinclair Oil tank trucks MT11.6.1-MT11.6.3

R5: Traditional Cab, Shell Logo ($18-25) ($30-40)
R7/10: Modern Cab, Shell Logo ($60-70) ($90-150)

Shell Oil tank trucks MT11.5.1 and MT11.5.2

Sinclair Oil tank trucks MT11.6.4 and MT11.6.5 with correct label

Shell Oil label (on both sides of tank)

Sinclair Oil tank truck MT11.6.5

MT11.6.1–MT11.6.5 Sinclair Oil Of the oil company tank trucks, Sinclair seems to be somewhat more common; however, the existence of multiple types of logos complicates any generalization concerning this variety. There are three distinct labels used on the Sinclair tank trucks: 1) red on white on a green background, one piece; 2) red on white on a green background, two pieces; and 3) red on brown on a green background, one piece. Of the five versions of this variety, three have the traditional cab and two have the modern cab. Examples with the modern cab are rare.

R5: Traditional Cab, Various Sinclair Logos ($18-25) ($30-40)
R7/10: Modern Cab, Sinclair Logos ($60-70) ($90-150)

Sinclair label types; traditional cabs

MT11.7.1–MT11.7.2 Sunoco Oil The Sunoco tank trucks periodically appear. The version with a traditional cab is somewhat more common than some other versions of the tank truck, but the version with a modern cab is rare.

R5: Traditional Cab, Sunoco Logo ($18-25) ($30-40)
R7/10: Modern Cab, Sunoco Logo ($60-70) ($90-150)

Sunoco Oil tank trucks MT11.7.1 and MT11.7.2

MT11.8.1–MT11.8.4 Neon Tank Trucks The neon tank trucks appeared shortly before Barclay closed. Of these, the only one that is found with any frequency is the version with a red neon cab and red neon body. The other versions are extremely rare. The neon tank trucks have either a generic Flower Power logo or no logo and all have whitewall tires.

R6: Red Neon Cab and Body ($25-35) ($40-80)
R7/10: Other Neon Varieties ($60-70) ($90-150)

Tank trucks, neon, right side MT11.8.1-MT11.8.3

Tank trucks, neon MT11.8.4

Tank trucks, neon, left side MT11.8.1-MT11.8.3

Blister Packs Containing Multiple
Miniature Trucks and Miniature Cars

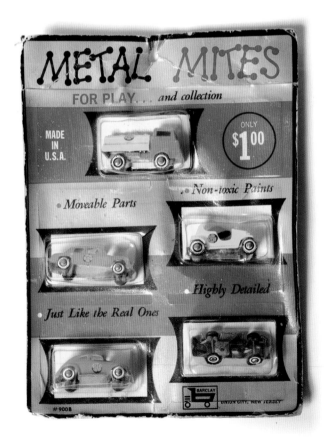

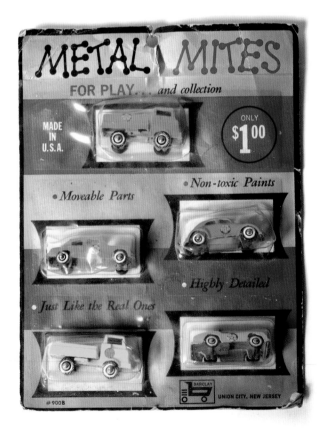

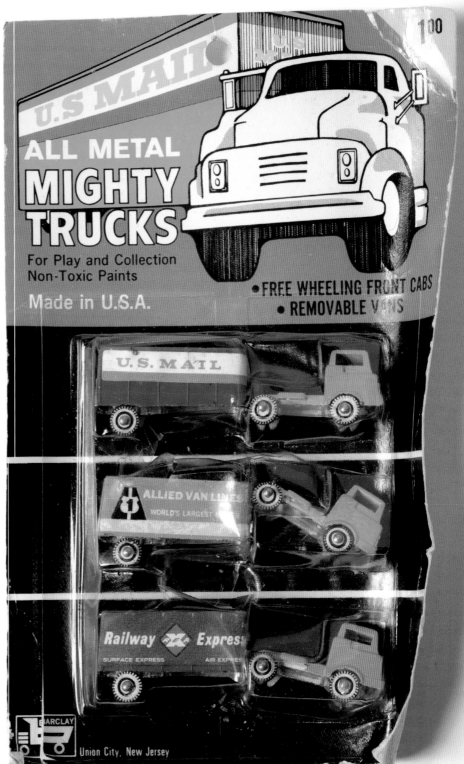

Detailed Catalog

Miniature Cars Range

Background

The Miniature Cars and the Miniature Trucks ranges were first introduced at approximately the same time in the late 1950s. Certain components of the Miniature Cars range were produced until Barclay closed in 1971. The Miniature Cars range consists of five types of vehicles; however, there are numerous casting, color, and labeling variations. The five major series of cars are antique cars, racers, sedans, sports cars, and Volkswagen Beetles. In contrast to the Miniature Trucks range, where most of the various types of trucks used a common cab, each of the five vehicle types in the Miniature Cars range, are completely different from the other vehicle types in the range.

Wheel Material and Wheel Type

The materials used for the wheels of the Miniature Cars include metal, plastic, and plastic with whitewalls. The codes used in the grids and commentaries are noted below:

Wheel Material:

Metal

Plastic

Plastic-W=Plastic Whitewall

Within the various types of wheels, there are numerous variations in terms of size, color, and physical appearance:

Wheel Type:

Metal Gold=MG

Metal Silver=MS

Metal—Spokes Gold=SPG

Metal—Spokes Silver=SPS

Plastic—Small Smooth=SS

Plastic—Small Cleated=SC

Plastic—Small Smooth Clear=SSC

Plastic—Large Black Smooth=LS

Plastic—Large White Smooth=LWS

Plastic—Large Black Ridged=LR

Plastic—Extra Large Black Smooth=ELBS

Plastic—Extra Large White Smooth=ELWS

Plastic—Extra Large Ridged=ELR (Black)

Plastic—Extra Large Ridged-Spokes=ELRS

Wheel types (top to bottom): SPG, SPS, MG, MS

Wheel types (top to bottom): SS, SSC, SC

Wheel types (top to bottom); LS, LS whitewall

Wheel types (top to bottom): ELBS. ELWS, ELR

Wheel types (top to bottom): ELR whitewall, ELRS whitewall spokes

With the exception of the wheels used for the antique cars, the wheels used on the various vehicles in the Miniature Cars range are the same as are found in the Transport Toys and Miniature Trucks ranges. The one exception is the metal wheels with spokes used on the early cars in the antique car series. According to Rucci, these are wheels that were originally used on some of the vehicles produced in the 1930s.[32] While all of the wheel variations that have been authenticated are listed, there is the possibility that additional wheel variations exist for specific vehicles, particularly for production that occurred in the late-1960s and early-1970s.

Label Variations

A number of different labels were used in the Miniature Cars range. In contrast to the labels used in the Miniature Trucks range, there are no company logos and generic words are limited to the fire, police, and taxi vehicles. Labels such as the numbers and Flower Power are used on multiple vehicle types. The various labels are listed and illustrated in the discussion of each of the five series of Miniature Cars.

Other Characteristics of the Miniature Cars

Aside from the cast lights and steering wheel components that were attached to the early antique cars, the sirens that were attached to the early police and fire cars, and the drivers and passengers that were attached to the racers and sports cars, each of the cars is a single casting. The casting was painted and the wheels, attachments, and labels were attached after the paint had dried. As is the case with all Barclay miniature vehicles, the wheels move and the cars are toys intended for play.

In the years leading up to the date that Barclay ceased operations, the castings for most of the vehicles in the Miniature Cars range were simplified to eliminate attachments to the casting and various cars appeared in the neon colors. As is the case with the other Barclay miniature ranges, examples in the neon colors are scarce to rare.

Antique Cars

The antique cars may have been the first type of miniature car. While it is generally known that there are four distinct castings within the antique car series, the cars are actually based on specific examples of American-made antique vehicles. As illustrated below, the Cadillac has two seats, the Franklin has one seat with a low back, the Stutz has one bucket seat, and the Buick has one seat with a high back.

As will be outlined in detail, there are two separate castings for each of the four varieties and a number of variations in terms of color, accessory detail, wheels, and labels. Although all four varieties were sold in the later 1950s through the mid-1960s, the Franklin variety was the car that was sold in various wheel and color formats, including neon colors, in the later 1960s and early 1970s. With respect to size, the Cadillac and the Stutz are approximately one and three-quarters inches long, whereas the Franklin and the Buick are one and five-eighths inches long.

The first blister packs contained two cars in each pack. The bottom portion of the cardboard identified the four cars in the series; however, this portion of the card was bent under the card and stapled in order to hold the cars within the pack-a very unsatisfactory configuration. The plastic in all other blister backs was glued to the cardboard.

The packages are shown below with a separate card showing the complete packages:

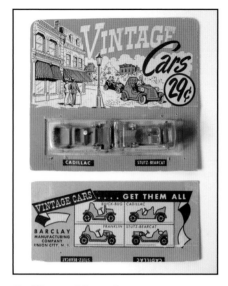

Cadillac and Stutz Bearcat

Buick Bug and Franklin

Cadillac and Stutz Bearcat

Buick Bug and Franklin

Scarcity and pricing is listed in italics after the detailed description for each piece. Due to variations seen in the market, prices are listed in ranges for examples in C-8 (Very Good) and C-10 (Mint) conditions.

Antique Cars						
Type	**Description**	**Casting**	**Colors**	**Wheel**		**Details**
				Mat.	**Type**	
Separate Headlamps						
MC1.1.1	Cadillac-Two Seats	1.1	Blue, Lt. Blue, Green	Metal Plastic	SPG, SPS SC	Separate Lights, Nail Steering Wheel
MC1.1.2	Franklin-One Seat-Low Back	2.1	Lt. Green, Green	Metal	SPG. SPS	Separate Lights, Nail Steering Wheel
MC1.1.3	Stutz-One Bucket Seat	3.1	Red	Metal	SPG. SPS	Separate Lights, Nail Steering Wheel
			Red	Metal	SPS	Separate Lights, Nail Steering Wheel with Nail Painted Red
MC1.1.4	Buick-One Seat-High Back	4.1	Black	Metal	SPG. SPS	Separate Lights, Nail Steering Wheel
Cast Headlamps						
MC1.2.1	Cadillac-Two Seats	1.2	Blue	Plastic	SC	Gold Cast Lights, Metal Steering Wheel
MC1.2.2	Franklin One Seat-Low Back	2.2	Red, Green	Plastic	SSC	Gold Cast Lights, Plastic Steering Wheel
			Green	Plastic	SC	Gold Cast Lights, Nail Steering Wheel
			Orange-Red Neon	Plastic	SSC	Cast Lights-Painted, No Steering Wheel
			Yellow-Neon, Pink-Neon	Plastic-W	LS, ELR	Cast Lights-Painted, No Steering Wheel; Flower Power Label or Plain
			Blue-Metallic	Plastic-W	ELR	Cast Lights-Painted, Plastic Steering Wheel, 147A Labels-Front and Back
			Orange-Neon	Plastic-W	ELR	Cast Lights-Painted, Plastic Steering Wheel, 147A Labels-Front and Back
MC1.2.3	Stutz-One Bucket Seat	3.2	Red	Plastic	SC	Cast Lights-Painted Steering Wheel
MC1.2.4	Buick One Seat-High Back	4.2	Green	Metal	SPG	Gold Cast Lights, Metal Steering Wheel
			Green, Lt. Green	Metal	SPG	Gold Cast Lights, Metal Steering Wheel, Open Lamp Holds
			Green	Plastic	SSC	Gold Cast Lights, Plastic Steering Wheel
			Black	Plastic	SC	Gold Cast Lights, Nail Steering Wheel

Note: (1) No Labels on Antique Cars

MC.1.1.1–MC1.1.4 As is noted above, there are four specific castings and types of antique cars—the Cadillac with two seats, the Franklin with one seat with a low back, the Stutz with one bucket seat, and the Buick with one seat with a high back. These first antique cars had metal wheels with a nail inserted into a hole in the floorboard of the casting that represented a steering wheel. The lights were separate small castings that were mounted on each side of the car by means of a peg that was part of the light casting and which was inserted into holes on each side of the casting. Examples are frequently found missing one or both of the light castings.

The metal wheels were either silver or gold in color and the lights were gold in color. The primary colors were blue for the Cadillac, green for the Franklin, red for the Stutz, and black for the Buick. These vehicles are available; however, locating them in mint condition can be a bit challenging. Sets in the original orange and black blister pack, which identify the various makes for each variation, are rare. Examples of the Cadillac, MC1.1.1, with plastic wheels are both very unusual and rare.

R2/3: MC1.1.1–MC1.1.4, Each Individual Example ($10-12) ($15-20)

R7/10: Set in Orange and Black Blister Pack ($60-70) ($90-300)

MC1.1.1-MC1.1.4 MOC

Cadillac MC1.1.1

Franklin MC1.1.2

Stutz MC1.1.3

Buick MC1.1.4

MC1.2.1–MC1.2.4 Toward the mid-1960s, the antique cars were simplified by altering the castings to include the headlights. The Cadillac and the Stutz have only been authenticated in a single version of this second casting. The Buick includes minor variations, each of which have been found in unopened blister packs; however, the Franklin version of this casting is found in a multiplicity of variations with regard to painting, steering wheel arrangements, wheels and labels. In general, mint specimens of the Franklin in neon and metallic colors are scarce. Mint specimens of the

Franklin with the 147A labels are rare. Although a number of variations of the Franklin from the final year or two before Barclay closed have been authenticated, there is every expectation that additional varieties exists.

R4: MC1.2.1–MC1.2.4 Various Versions–Neither Neon or Metallic ($12-15) ($20-25)
R7/8: MC1.2.1–MC1.2.4 Neon and Metallic Versions ($30-40) ($50-100)
R7/10: Examples with 147A labels ($60-70) ($90-150)

Antique cars with cast lights MOC

Cadillac MC1.2.1

Antique Franklin with whitewall tires in orange-red neon

Franklin MC1.2.2

Franklin MC1.2.2

Franklin Neon MC1.2.2

Buick MC1.2.4

Stutz MC1.2.3

Franklin Neon MC1.2.2 147A label

Franklin Neon MC1.2.2 147A label

Franklin Neon MC1.2.2 147A label

Race Cars

The Barclay race cars are relatively straightforward. There are two basic varieties, a narrow-back version and a wide-back version. The race cars were first introduced in the late 1950s or the early 1960s. Production of a least some of the models of race cars continued up to or shortly before Barclay ceased operations in 1971. As was the case with the other types of vehicles in the Miniature Cars range, the second casting of the two types of race cars eliminated the separate driver component by including the driver as part of the casting of the vehicle. In the case of both types of racers, the cars are almost exactly two inches long.

Scarcity and pricing is listed in italics after the detailed description for each piece. Due to variations seen in the market, prices are listed in ranges for examples in C-8 (Very Good) and C-10 (Mint) conditions.

Race Cars						
Type	**Description**	**Casting**	**Colors**	**Wheel**		**Labels or Details**
				Mat.	**Type**	
Narrow Back, Two-Piece						
MC2.1.1	Large Gold Driver	1	Aqua, Green, White, Silver, Orange, Blue, Purple Met.	Plastic	ELBS, ELWS, ELR	S or R 1-6
MC2.1.2	Large Gold Driver, Silver Trim	1	White	Plastic	ELBS	S
MC2.1.3	Large White Driver	1	Blue, Red	Plastic	ELBS	S or R 1-6
MC2.1.4	Large Pink Driver	1	White	Plastic	ELBS	S 1-6
Narrow Back, One-Piece						
MC2.2	Narrow Back	3	Red, Blue	Plastic	ELR, SSC	None
				Plastic-W	LS	
Wide Back, Two Piece						
MC2.3.1	Large Gold Driver	2	Blue, Green, Red Orange, Silver	Plastic	ELBS, ELWS, ELR	S or R 1-6
MC2.3.2.1	Large Gold Driver	2	Lemon Yellow-Neon, Orange-Neon, Pink-Neon, Blue-Metallic	Plastic-W	ELR	SN Label
MC2.3.2.2	Large Gold Driver	2	Orange-Neon, Yellow-Neon	Plastic-W	ELRS	SN Label
MC2.3.3	Large Gold Driver, Silver Trim	2	Blue	Plastic	ELBS	R
MC2.3.4	Large White Driver	2	Red, Blue	Plastic	ELBS	S
Wide Back, One-Piece						
MC2.4.1	Wide Back	4	Blue, Green, Red, White, Orange	Plastic	ELR	No Label
MC2.4.2	Wide Back	4	Pink-Neon, Red, Silver	Plastic-W	ELR, LS	SN Label or None
MC2.4.3	Wide Back	4	Pink-Neon	Clear	SSC	None

Notes: (1) Logos: R=round, S=square/rectangle, RS=racing strip, SN=strip with number (pink or green on black).
(2) There are two versions of square labels, plain edge and red edge.

Race Car MOC

Race Cars with white rubber wheels MOC

Race Cars in Wheel-a-Rific packaging MOC

MC2.1.1, MC2.1.3–MC2.1.4 Most Common Narrow-Back Race Cars These varieties represent the most common versions of the narrow-back Barclay racers. The MC2.1.1 racers all have a large gold driver and come in various color and tire combinations. The MC2.1.3 racers have a large white driver whereas the MC2.1.4 racers have a large pink driver. Racers sold with the original casting always had numbers, either round or square. Both sets of numbers run from 1 to 6; however, the square numbers appear to be somewhat easier to locate. First casting racers without numbers are common; however, in every case reviewed, the number has either fallen off or been removed.

The white wheels that appear on some examples are the result of the shipment of white rubber wheels that Barclay received in the early to mid-1960s. Rather than return the wheels for the correct black wheels, Barclay went ahead and used the wheels on several different vehicles including these race cars.

R4: Various More Common Narrow-back Racers ($12-15) ($20-25)

Narrow-back with gold driver MC2.1.1

Narrow-back, ELWS wheels MC2.1.1

Narrow-back with white drivers MC2.1.3

Narrow-back, large pink driver MC2.1.4

MC2.1.2 Narrow-Back Racer with Silver Trim There is at least one example of a narrow-back racer with silver trim applied at the factory. In all likelihood, this example represents an experiment and is quite rare.

R7/8: MC2.1.2 Example with Silver Trim ($30-40) ($50-100)

Narrow-back with silver trim MC2.1.2

Narrow-back with silver trim MC2.1.2

MC2.2 Second Casting Narrow-Back Race Cars The major difference between the first casting and the second casting of the narrow-back racers is the fact that the second casting race cars do not have a separate driver component. In contrast to the first casting, the driver is included in the basic casting of the race car. The second casting narrow-back racers appear to have been sold without numbers or logos. Examples of the second casting are somewhat difficult to locate.

R5/6: MC2.2 Racers, Second Casting ($18-35) ($30-80)

MC2.2 narrow-back second casting race car, ELR wheels

MC2.2 narrow-back second casting race car, SSC wheels

MC2.2 narrow-back second casting race car, LS wheels with whitewalls

MC2.3.1, MC2.3.4 Most Common Wide-Back Race Cars These varieties represent the most common versions of the wide-back Barclay racers. The MC2.3.1.1 racers have a large gold driver and come in various color and tire combinations. The MC2.3.4 racers have a large white driver.

Racers sold with the original casting always have numbers, either round or square. Both sets of numbers run from 1 to 6; however, the square numbers are somewhat easier to locate. First casting racers without numbers are common; however, in every case reviewed, the number has either fallen off or been removed.

The white wheels that appear on some examples are the result of the shipment of white rubber wheels that Barclay received in the early to mid-1960s. Rather than return the wheels for the correct black wheels, Barclay went ahead and used the wheels on several different vehicles including these race cars.

R4: Various More Common Racers ($12-15) ($20-25)

MC2.3.1 wide-back race cars with gold driver

MC2.3.4 wide-back race car with white driver

MC2.3.2.1 First Casting Wide-Back Neon Race Cars In the last year or two before Barclay ceased production, a number of race cars were sold in various neon colors with whitewall tires and SN labels. In some cases, a mixture of whitewall and plain tires were used. In general, these cars are very scarce to rare.

R7/10: Various Combinations–Neon Colors, Whitewall Tires, and SN Labels ($60-70) ($90-150)

MC2.3.2.2 First Casting Wide-Back Neon Race Cars with Spokes This variety is the same as MC2.3.2.1 except that the wheels are the whitewall variety with spokes. This variety is rare.

R7/10: Various Combinations–Neon Colors, Whitewall Tires with Spokes, and SN Labels ($80-90) ($125-200)

Wide-body neon race car with spokes (orange racer to the right) MC2.3.2.2

MC2.3.3 Wide-Back Racer with Silver Trim There is at least one example of a wide-back racer with silver trim applied at the factory. In all likelihood, this example represents an experiment and is quite rare.

R7/8: MC2.3.3 Example with Silver Trim ($30-40) ($50-100)

Wide-back racer with silver trim MC2.3.3   *Wide-back racer with silver trim MC2.3.3*

Wide-body neon race cars with whitewall tires MC2.3.2.1

MC2.4.1 Second Casting Race Cars The major difference between the first casting and the second casting of the racers is the fact that the second casting race cars do not have a separate driver component. In contrast to the first casting, the driver is included in the basic race car casting. The initial second casting racers were not sold with numbers or logos. Examples of the early second castings are somewhat difficult to find, particularly in colors such as green, white, and orange.

R5/6: MC2.4.1 Racers, Second Casting ($18-35) ($30-80)

MC2.4.1 second casting wide-back racers

MC2.4.2 Second Casting Race Cars with Whitewall Tires This variety of the wide back racers includes examples of both neon and regular colors with varying sizes of whitewall tires. All examples are very scarce to rare.

R7/10: Various Combinations–Neon Colors, Whitewall Tires, SN or No Labels ($60-70) ($90-150)

MC2.4.2 second casting wide-back racers with LS whitewall tires

MC2.4.3 Second Casting Race Cars This variety of the second casting, wide back racers has SSC Tires. All examples are very scarce to rare.

R7/10: MC2.4.3 Second Casting Wide-Back Race Cars with SSC Tires ($60-70) ($90-150)

MC2.4.3 Second casting racer with clear plastic tires

Wide-back racers with numbers 1 to 6

Sedans

The miniature sedans were patterned after the French Citroën DS-19, which was first introduced at the Paris Auto Show in 1955 to wide-scale acclaim for its engineering and design innovations. The car was designed by Flaminio Bertoni, an Italian sculptor and industrial designer, and André Lefèbvre, a French aeronautical engineer. This futuristic design was produced from its introduction until 1975 and it was recognized in third place in the Car of the Century competition in 1999.[33]

Sedan MOC

The Citroën model is slightly larger than other cars in the Miniature Car range, two and one-eighth inches long. There are three distinct castings of this vehicle. The first or traditional variation is simply the car without a siren. The second casting variation has a siren as part of the casting. The final variation has a cast siren; however, the back window is now solid rather than open. Aside from the different castings, other differences exist with respect to colors, siren attachments, labels, and wheels. As is the case with other cars in the Miniature Cars range, all labels are generic without any reference to a specific company or business; however, label variations exist and are noted in the detailed descriptions.

Scarcity and pricing is listed in italics after the detailed description for each piece. Due to variations seen in the market, prices are listed in ranges for examples in C-8 (Very Good) and C-10 (Mint) conditions.

MC3.1.1 Citroën Cars with Metal Wheels The earliest Citroëns had metal wheels, which suggests that they were first released in the late 1950s or early 1960s. Of the two colors, metallic purple and gold, metallic purple is the more common; however, both are reasonably difficult to locate. This casting is simply the car without attachments or labels.

R5: Metal Wheels–Metallic Purple ($18-25) ($30-40)
R6: Metal Wheels–Gold ($25-35) ($40-80)

MC3.1.1 Earliest Citroën cars–metal wheels

Sedans						
Type	**Description**	**Casting**	**Colors**	**Wheel**		**Labels or Details**
				Mat.	**Type**	
Traditional Casting						
MC3.1.1	Traditional Auto	1	Purple-Metallic, Gold	Metal	-	None
MC3.1.2	Traditional Auto	1	Green, Blue, Orange, Red, Military, Purple-Metallic	Plastic	SC	None
MC3.1.3.1	Traditional Auto-Fire	1	Red	Plastic	SC	Attached Siren, Red Chief on White on Hood, Gold Badge on White on Door
MC3.1.3.2	Traditional Auto-Fire	1	Red	Plastic	SC	Attached Siren, Red Chief on White on Hood, Black Badge on Gold on Door
MC3.1.4	Traditional Auto-Military*	1	Military	Plastic	SC	Large Army, Large Star; Small Army, Small Star
MC3.1.5	Traditional Auto-Police	1	Blue	Plastic	SC	Attached Siren, Red Block Police on Doors, Police Badge on Hood
Cast Siren						
MC3.2.1.1	Fire Chief	2	Red	Plastic	SC	Red Chief on White on Hood, Gold Badge on White on Door
MC3.2.1.2	Fire Chief	2	Red	Plastic	SC	Red Chief on White on Hood Hood, Black Badge on Gold on Door
MC3.2.2	Military	2	Military	Plastic	SS, SC	Large Army, Large Star
MC3.2.3.1	Police**	2	Blue	Plastic	SC	Police Block, Badge on Hood
MC3.2.3.2	Police ***	2	Blue	Plastic	LS	Police Large Logo, Badge on Hood
MC3.2.3.3	Police	2	Blue	Plastic-W	SS	Police Large Logo, Badge on Hood
MC3.2.4	Police Chief	2	Blue	Plastic	SC	Chief on Door, Badge on Hood
MC3.2.5.1	Taxi****	2	Yellow	Plastic	SS, SC, LS	Taxi
MC3.2.5.2	Taxi	2	Orange-Neon	Plastic-W	SS	Striped Logo on Sides
MC3.2.5.3	Taxi	2	Dark Yellow	Plastic	SS	Taxi
Cast Siren, Solid Window						
MC3.3	Traditional Auto With Siren	3	Orange Neon, Green Neon, Pink Neon	Plastic-W	SS	Flower Power or None

*May exist Large Army, Small Star
**Exists MOC with no badge
***Badge on either hood or top
**** Exists MOC with no labels

Notes: (1) An example of MC3.1.5 exists with block letter Police on door, Police Badge on hood and three holes on roof.
(2) A variation of MC3.1.3.1 or 2 exists MOC with a hole in the roof, no attached siren, and no labels.

MC3.1.2 Traditional Casting with Plastic Wheels
This is the most common of the Citroëns with the traditional casting. The most common colors are green, blue, and red. Examples of traditional Citroëns in the military color without logos exist in unopened blister packs.

R4: Traditional Casting–Plastic Wheels ($12-15) ($20-25)

Citroën cars, traditional casting MC3.1.2

MC3.1.4 Citroën Cars with Military Finish and Logos

The military Citroëns using the traditional casting are differentiated only by the paint color and the logos. As noted in the grid, the military logos come in both large and small army and star varieties and were used in various combinations on the military vehicles.

R4: Military Version–Traditional Casting ($12-15) ($20-25)

Citroën Cars, traditional casting with military finish MC3.1.4

MC3.1.3.1–MC3.1.3.2; MC3.1.5 Attached Sirens

The initial police car and fire chief cars, using the first Citroën casting, had a hole in the top of the hood of the car for an attached siren. The component actually used to create the siren was the casting of the headlight used for the antique cars. Label variations with respect to the "badge" on the fire chief car and the "police" label on the police cars are seldom recognized details. While occasionally seen, the police and fire chief cars with attached sirens are difficult to locate.

R6: Police and Fire Chief with Attached Sirens ($25-35) ($40-80)

Fire Chief cars, traditional castings with attached sirens, MC3.1.3.1 and MC3.1.3.2

Police car, MC3.1.5, variation with two extra holes on roof

Police Car, traditional casting with attached siren, MC3.1.5

MC3.2.1.1–MC3.2.5.2 Citroën Cars with Cast Sirens

The second casting for the Citroën series has a cast siren. This variety was used for the fire chief, military, police, police chief, and taxi variations. One should note the differences in the various logos, which create distinct variations. With respect to the police label, it exists in two variations, a smaller block letter version and a larger version. Of the nine different types of cars with cast sirens, there are three variations that are scarce to rare. They are MC3.2.3.3, the police vehicle with whitewall tires; MC3.2.4, the police chief car; and MC3.2.5.2, the orange neon taxi with a striped logo on its side, and the MC3.2.5.3 taxi.

R5: All Variations except Those Listed Below ($18-25) ($30-40)
R6: Taxi Dark Yellow MC3.2.5.3 ($25-35) ($40-80)
R7/10: MC3.2.3.3, MC3.2.4, MC3.2.5.2 ($60-70) ($90-150)

Fire Chief variations, cast sirens, MC3.2.1.1 and MC3.2.1.2

Military finish, cast siren, MC3.2.2

Police variation with block logo on side, MC3.2.3.1

Police variation with large logo on side and badge on hood or roof, MC3.2.3.2

Police variation with large logo and whitewall tires, MC3.2.3.3

Police Chief finish, MC3.2.4

Taxi, dark yellow, MC3.2.5.3

Taxi finish, MC3.2.5.1

MC3.3 Citroën Cars with Solid Windows The third and final casting of the Citroën automobile has a solid back window in contrast to the other castings in this range that have open back windows. Cars with this third casting were all produced near the end of Barclay's existence and all feature neon colors and have either no logo or a Flower Power logo. All are rare.

R7/10: MC3.3 ($60-70) ($90-150)

Citroën cars with solid window, left side view, MC3.3   *Citroën Cars with solid window, right side view, MC3.3*

Sports Cars

The sports cars in the Miniature Cars range were originally issued in the late 1950s or early 1960s. There are two significant body styles: a single-driver casting with tail fins and a driver and passenger ("two passengers") casting with a rounded rear-end. As far as we know, the designs are generic. In all likelihood, the two-passenger style was not produced after the mid-1960s. Certain variations of the one passenger style were manufactured up until the time that Barclay closed in 1971.

The single-passenger style is approximately one and seven-eighths inches in length whereas the two passenger style is slightly less than two inches in length. The sports cars vary in the color of the car, the color of the driver and/or the driver and the passenger, wheel type, and, in some cases, the logos. All of the logos are generic with no reference to a company or type of business.

The final casting variation for this car incorporates the driver in the casting, thus eliminating the need to produce and attach a separate driver component. In general, the versions of the cars in neon colors with whitewall tires are the most difficult to locate.

Scarcity and pricing is listed in italics after the detailed description for each piece. Due to variations seen in the market, prices are listed in ranges for examples in C-8 (Very Good) and C-10 (Mint) conditions.

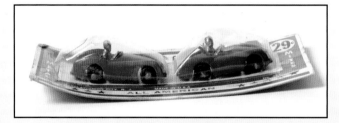

Sport cars MOC

Sports Cars						
Type	**Description**	**Casting**	**Colors**	**Wheel**		**Labels or Details**
				Mat.	**Type**	
Tail Fins, One Driver						
MC4.1.1	One Small Gold Driver	1	Red, Black	Metal	MG, MS	None
MC4.1.2	One Small White Driver	1	Red	Metal	MG, MS	None
MC4.1.3	One Large Gold Driver	1	Red, Green, Orange	Plastic	SC	None
MC4.1.4	One Small Gold Driver	1	Red	Plastic	SC	None
Tail Fins, Racing Stripes						
MC4.2.1	One Small Gold Driver	1	Red, Blue	Plastic	SC	Racing Stripe, R 1-6 Label
MC4.2.2.	One Large Gold Driver	1	Red, Blue, Green	Plastic	SC, SS	Racing Stripe, R 1-6 Label
Tail Fins, Large Wheels						
MC4.3.1	One Large Gold Driver	1	Blue	Plastic	ELR	R 1-6 Label
MC4.3.2	One Large Gold Driver	1	Orange-Neon	Plastic-W	ELR	Flower Power
MC4.3.3	One Large Gold Driver	1	Orange	Plastic-W	SS	Flower Power
Tail Fins Single Piece						
MC4.4	Driver Part of Casting	3	Orange Red-Hot	Plastic-W	SS	Flower Power
Rounded, Driver, Passenger						
MC4.5.1	Gold Driver, Passenger	2	Black, Blue, Green, Silver	Metal	MG, MS	None
MC4.5.2	Gold Driver, Passenger	2	Green, Blue	Plastic	SC	None
MC4.5.3	White Driver, Passenger	2	Blue	Metal	MG, MS	None

Notes: (1) In the latter part of the 1960s, certain sports cars were issued with the single-piece, plastic axle and wheel assembly used on the final version of the modern transport cars.

MC4.1.1–MC 4.1.4 Single Driver

These variations center on the size of the driver (either small or large); however, the color of the wheels may be either silver or gold. These toys came in several colors.

R2/3: Early Single Driver Sports Cars ($10-12) ($15-20)

Sports car with tail fins, small gold driver, SC wheels MC4.1.4

Sports car with tail fins, small gold driver, metal wheels MC4.1.1

Sports car with tail fins, small white driver, metal wheels MC4.1.2

MC4.2.1–MC4.2.2 Single Driver with Racing Stripe
This version of the single-driver sports car had plastic wheels. The car is the same as the earlier cars; however, a sports stripe runs down the hood of the car. One problem with this variation is the tendency for the sports stripe to fall off.

R4: Single Driver with Racing Stripe ($12-15) ($20-25)

Sports car with tail fins, large gold driver, plastic wheels, MC4.2.2

MC4.3.1–MC4.3.3 Single Driver, Large Wheels The basic casting for this group of cars is the same casting used earlier; however, the wheels are enlarged. The initial version, MC4.3.1 has a round numbered label. The other two versions were produced in the final year or two before Barclay closed. The colors are either bright or neon, the tires are whitewall, and the labels are the Flower Power labels. All of these cars are scarce to rare.

R6: MC4.3.1 Large Wheels, Round Numbered Labels ($25-35) ($40-80)
R7/8: Large Whitewall Tires ($30-40) ($50-100)

Sports car with tail fins MC4.3.1 and MC4.3.2, left side view

Sports car with tail fins MC4.3.3, left side view

MC4.4 Single Driver, Driver as Part of Casting This variation has the driver cast as part of the casting for the car eliminating the need to cast and assemble two separate pieces. This casting was created in the later 1960s. Since this variation is painted a neon color, has whitewall tires, and a Flower Power label, it was manufactured shortly before Barclay ceased to operate.

R7/10: Single Driver, Driver as Part of Casting ($60-70)

Sports car with tail fins, single-piece casting, MC4.4, left side view

Sports car with tail fins, single-piece casting, MC4.4, right side view

Sports car with tail fins MC4.3.3, right side view

($90-150)

MC4.5.1–MC4.5.3 Sports Car with Driver and Passenger The second type of sports car has both a driver and a passenger. Unlike the single passenger sports car, the car has no fins and a rounded rear. There is no evidence that this variation was produced beyond the mid-1960s.

Sports car with rounded rear, gold driver and passenger, plastic wheels, MC4.5.2

R2/3: Sports Car for Driver and Passenger ($10-12)

Sports car with rounded rear, gold driver and passenger, metal wheels, MC4.5.1

Sports car with rounded rear, white driver and passenger, metal wheels, MC4.5.3

($15-20)

Volkswagens (VW)

The Barclay Volkswagen series is particularly interesting. As were the Citroën and antique cars, this toy is based on an actual car, the Volkswagen "Beetle," which was extremely popular on college campuses and among younger adults in the late 1950s and throughout much of the 1960s. The scale of the Volkswagens is a slightly larger scale than most of the cars in either the Transport Toys range or the Miniature Cars range, measuring approximately one and seven-eighths inches in length. Since the actual Volkswagen Beetle was a very small car, the scale of the toy is significantly larger than the other toy cars in the various Barclay miniature ranges. While not widely realized, at least a small number of Barclay Volkswagens have painted details that were executed at the factory.

The first Volkswagens were introduced in the late 1950s or very early 1960s with the initial introduction of the Miniature Cars range. In various forms and castings, the Volkswagens continued to be produced until Barclay closed in 1971.

Before focusing on the details of the Volkswagen series, there is an issue as to whether Barclay produced the Volkswagens in more than one size. Through several editions of *O'Briens's Collecting Toy Cars &*

Trucks, including the current 4th Edition, a larger sized Barclay Volkswagen has been listed as "BV 160" with a length of two and three-sixteenths inches. The problem is that no one has ever produced an example, a picture, or any evidence whatsoever that this second Barclay Volkswagen exists. The only purported example of this alleged toy turned out to be a toy Volkswagen Beetle produced by Tootsietoy at approximately the same time as the Barclay Volkswagen Beetle was produced. This particular Tootsietoy toy is approximately two and one-fourth inches in length. Although numerous examples of this smaller Tootsietoy Volkswagen exist and they are generally marked as Tootsietoy on the inside of their roof, this particular size of Volkswagen is not listed in the current O'Brien catalog under Tootsietoy.[34]

Tootsietoy and Barclay nose-to-nose

Tootsietoy on left, Barclay on right

While it is not clear how O'Brien made the apparent mistake concerning the existence of a larger Barclay VW Beetle, there is a reasonable explanation. On first glance, the small Tootsietoy VW Beetle is very similar to the Barclay toy except that it is slightly larger. The first clear indication that this larger VW Beetle was made by Tootsietoy rather than Barclay lies in the wheels and the nub of the axles. Both the wheels (round with cleats) and the nubs (tapered toward the outside) are clearly the wheel and axle construction found on many of the smaller Tootsietoy vehicles in the 1960s. Another problem relates to the Tootsietoy marking on the inside of the roof. Although many of the Tootsietoy VWs of this type are clearly marked as Tootsietoy products, the molds evidently suffered from repeated use and on some examples of these toys the Tootsietoy name as well as "Chicago USA" are completely missing. Although it will never be known why this "larger" Volkswagen Beetle was listed as a Barclay product, to date there is absolutely no proof that Barclay ever produced a product of this nature.

As will be outlined, there are two Volkswagen

Tootsietoy identification on inside of roof

VWs Tootsietoy in back row, Barclay in front row

castings; however, the first casting was used for virtually all of the production of this series. Additional variations were created by changing paint colors and wheel types. Although various labels were used within this series, all labels featured generic numbers or various types of Flower Power logos.

Scarcity and pricing is listed in italics after the detailed description for each piece. Due to variations

Traditional VWs sold with and without numbers

VW				Wheel		Labels or Details
Type	Description	Casting	Colors	Mat.	Type	Labels or Details
Open Back Window						
MC5.1.1.1	Traditional	1	Blue-Steel	Metal	MS	None
MC5.1.1.2	Traditional-Silver Trim	1	Blue-Steel	Metal	MS	None
MC5.1.2	Traditional	1	Blue, Green, Maroon, Orange, Red, Blue-Steel, Red-Metallic	Plastic	SC, LS	None
MC5.1.3	Traditional With Number	1	Blue, Green, Red	Plastic	SC, SS	R or S Number Labels 1-6 on Hood or Door
MC5.1.4	Traditional with Number, Silver Trim	1	Red	Plastic	SS	R 4 on Hood of Known Example
MC5.1.5.1	Traditional, Wheel-O-Rific	1	Pink-Neon, White, Orange-Neon, Yellow-Lemon Neon	Plastic-W	ELR	Flower Power or Plain
MC5.1.5.2	Traditional, Wheel-O-Rific	1	Red-Neon	Plastic-W	ELRS	Flower Power
MC5.1.6	Traditional	1	Orange-Neon	Plastic-W	SS	None
Closed Back Window						
MC5.2		2	Green-Hot	Plastic-W	SS	Flower Power or None

VWs MOC

VWs in Wheel-a-Rific packaging

seen in the market, prices are listed in ranges for examples in C-8 (Very Good) and C-10 (Mint) conditions.

MC5.1.1.1–MC5.1.1.2 Traditional Volkswagen, Metal Wheels The first Volkswagen Beetles use the traditional Beetle casting with metal wheels. The fact that the cars are steel blue with metal wheels suggests that they were, perhaps, produced in the late 1950s, but more likely were produced in the early 1960s. The only difference between these two varieties is the existence of painted bumpers and other details in silver with respect to the MC5.1.1.2 variety. Both of these early Volkswagens are scarce, and the MC5.1.1.2 variety is very scarce to rare.

VWs, metal wheels MC5.1.1.1 (front) and MC5.1.1.2 (rear)

R4/5: MC5.1.1.1, Metal Wheels, No Painted Detail ($12-20) ($20-35)

Early VW with silver trim MC5.1.1.2, side view

Early VW with silver trim MC5.1.1.2, front view

Early VW with silver trim MC5.1.1.2, rear view

R7/8: MC5.1.1.2, Metal Wheels, Painted Detail ($30-40) ($50-100)

MC5.1.2 Traditional Volkswagen, Plastic Wheels The traditional Volkswagens with various types of plastic wheels are by far the most common within this series. Of the various colors, blue, green, and red are the most common. In all likelihood, the red metallic color was manufactured toward the end of production for this series and is the scarcest of this variety.

R2/3: Blue, Green, and Red ($10-12) ($15-20)

VWs, plastic wheels MC5.1.2

R4: Maroon, Orange, Steel Blue ($12-15) ($20-25)
R7/8: Metallic Red ($30-40) ($50-100)

MC5.1.3 Traditional Volkswagens with Numbers This variety is exactly the same as the MC5.1.2 variety except it has a number logo on the hood or, less frequently on the driver's door. The numbers are either round or square and run 1 to 6. Examples with numbers are relatively easy to locate.

Traditional VWs with different number configurations

R2/3: MC5.1.3 ($10-12) ($15-20)

MC5.1.4 Traditional Volkswagens with Numbers and Silver Trim This variety is the same as MC5.1.3 except that it has painted bumpers and other details, the existence of which has been confirmed by examples in unopened blister packs. Examples with painted details are rare.

R7/10: Red with Details Painted in Silver ($30-40) ($75-200)

VW with silver trim

MC5.1.5.1 and MC5.1.5.2 Wheel-O-Rific Volkswagens Barclay Wheel-O-Rific vehicles were a very late attempt to revive sales and bring new interest in the company's products. In all likelihood, these variations were manufactured during the last two or three years of the company's existence. Whether it was the VWs or other Wheel-O-Rific vehicles, Barclay took existing parts and created a new toy. In the case of the Volkswagens, Barclay used the an existing casting; painted the casting a neon color; added oversized wheels; and, in some cases, added a Flower Power label. The cars were sold in redesign blister packs with the Wheel-O-Rific title. The only difference between the MC5.1.5.1 ("ELR" wheels) examples and the MC5.1.5.2 ("ELRS" wheels) examples are the wheels. All Wheel-O-Rific toys are scarce and the MC5.1.5.2 design with six spokes on each wheel is rare.

VW Wheel-O-Rific, MOC   *VW Wheel-O-Rific, MOC*

R7/8: MC5.1.5.1 with ELR Wheels ($30-40) ($50-100)

VW Wheel-O-Rific examples MC5.1.5.1, left side view   *VW Wheel-O-Rific examples MC5.1.5.1, right side view*

*VW Wheel-O-Rific example
with spoke wheels, MC5.1.5.2*

R7/10: MC5.1.5.2 with Six Spoke Wheels ($60-70)
*   ($90-150)*

MC5.1.6 Volkswagen with Neon Paint and Whitewall Tires This variety was produced in the period shortly before Barclay closed. It has neon paint, but unlike the Wheel-O-Rific variety, it has whitewall SS size tires. This variety is very scarce to rare.

VW with neon paint and whitewall tires, MC5.1.6

R7/10: MC5.1.6 Neon Paint and Whitewall Tires ($60-70)
*   ($90-150)*

MC5.2 Volkswagen With Closed Back Window The MC5.2 Volkswagen features a new casting with a closed window. The only color discovered to date is green neon and examples exist with or without Flower Power labels. This version of the Barclay Volkswagen Beetle was manufactured near the time that Barclay ceased doing business and examples are rare.

R7/10: MC5.2 with Closed Back Window ($60-70)
*   ($90-150)*

VW second casting, closed back window MC.5.2

VW second casting, closed back window MC.5.2

Detailed Catalog

Miniature Trains

Background

The Miniature Trains were first introduced in the early 1930s approximately the same time that the first Transport Toys were introduced. In contrast to the other three ranges of miniature Barclay toys, the Miniature Trains were produced in three distinct sizes: large, medium, and small. The Miniature Trains were initially produced by the slush casting method; however, the trains produced after the late 1930s were produced by the die-cast casting method. The Miniature Trains were always produced in sets. With the exception of the single-piece Streamlined Train, the various sets had between three and five pieces connected by couplings of various types.

With a single exception, each piece in the train set is painted a single, standard Barclay color, primarily the basic colors used at the particular time the set was produced. As a consequence, the earlier pieces were painted colors such as black, red, orange, green, and blue. Colors such as silver and gray were introduced later. As with the other ranges of Miniature Toys, neon colors appeared in the years just prior to 1971, when Barclay ceased operations.

Although most Barclay collectors are familiar with the small trains that were produced from the end of the 1930s through 1971, many collectors are not familiar with the older, large- and medium-size trains of the earlier years as well as the variety of trains that were produced in the small size. While the information provided in the section has been carefully researched, there is very little contemporary information regarding the Barclay trains and additional variations of these toys may exist. Identification of these toys is further complicated by the fact that other trains manufactured in the 1930s are sometimes attributed to Barclay even though there is no evidence whatsoever that they were part of the Barclay toy ranges.

Large- and medium-size Trains

Large-Size
Miniature Trains

As far as is known, the first trains produced by Barclay were what we now classify as the large-size Miniature Trains. While the exact dates that each set was introduced is somewhat uncertain, they were probably introduced in 1931 or 1932. The T1.1 passenger set and the T1.2.1 set consist of a combination engine/tinder with four additional cars. Although complete sets of these two train varieties periodically appear, the pieces are more likely to be seen in mixed lots of toy train pieces. All of the pieces were manufactured using the slush casting method and the undersides have the typical Barclay slush casting characteristics. Each of these sets had metal hitches.

The most interesting of the large train sets is the T1.2.2 train set. The engine for this set does not have an attached tender; however, it has the same four cars as the T1.2.1 freight train set. The open question is whether this set had a tender or not. A number of collectors believe that there was an orange tender that was part of this set. While this could be the case, the only orange tenders seen to date are slightly larger than the pieces in the T1.2.1 set and these tenders were not manufactured by Barclay. While a complete six-piece set has yet to be seen, sets with the T1.2.2 engine and the four cars from the T1.2.1 set have periodically appeared. This set as well as both the T1.1 and T1.2.1 train sets have metal hitches. It is not known whether the T1.2.2 train set predated the T1.2.1 set or was produced after the T1.2.1 set was introduced. The T1.2.2 train set also had metal hitches.

While it is not know for certain how the T1.2.2 train set was packaged, both the T1.1 (566) and the T1.2.1 (577) train sets were packaged in lithographed boxes. During the 1930s, toys such as the Transport Toys were attached to flat pieces of heavy cardboard with small triangles cut along the edge. The triangular cuts were used to place rubber bands around the toy to hold the toy to the cardboard piece. In all likelihood, the various five-piece train sets produced during the 1930s were packaged in lithographed boxes, while the three-piece train sets may have been packaged in either lithographed boxes or in a manner similar to the Transport Toys of this period.

We do not know how many years the large-size trains were produced, but production certainly ceased by the late 1930s when Barclay began to move to die-cast casting. Pieces of these train sets do appear both at toy shows and in online auctions so it can be assumed that they were sold in reasonably significant quantities. While pricing for mint condition pieces are given below, it should be kept in mind that original, mint condition pieces of these early trains are almost impossible to find.

Scarcity and pricing is listed in italics after the detailed description for each piece. Due to variations seen in the market, prices are listed in ranges for examples in C-8 (Very Good) and C-10 (Mint) conditions.

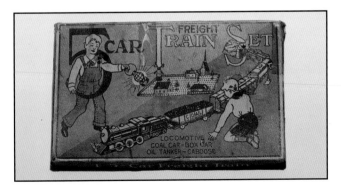

T1.2.2 (577) large-size slush freight set, box open

T1.2.2 (577) large-size slush freight set, top view

Trains—Large Size									
Type	**Ref.**	**Years**	**Characteristics**	**Colors** *Pass.=Passenger; Bag.=Baggage; Cab.=Caboose*					
				Engine/ Tender	**Pass.**	**Bag.**			
T1.1 Slush	566	1930s	Five Car Passenger Train Set. Engine/ Tender Combination, 3 Passenger Cars, 1 Baggage Car. Engine/Tender-10 Metal Wheels Painted Red. Cars-Metal Wheels Painted Black. Metal Hitches. Color Color Combinations Vary. (Train 21 3/8" Long When Connected)	Black (4 3/4")	Red, Orange, Green, Blue (4 3/8")	Red, Orange, Green (4 3/8")			
				Engine/ Tender	**Coal**	**Box**	**Tank**	**Cab.**	
T1.2.1 Slush	577	1930s	Five Car Freight Train Set. Engine/Tender Combination, Coal Car, Box Car, Tank Car, Caboose. Engine/Tender-10 Metal Wheels Painted Red. Cars-Metal Wheels Painted Black. Metal Hitches. Color Combinations Appear to Have Been Consistent (Train 18 1/2" Long When Connected)	Black (4 3/4")	Dark Red/ Black (3 3/4")	Green (3 3/4")	Orange (3 3/4")	Red (Cupola Centered) (3 5/16")	
				Engine	**Tender**	**Coal**	**Box**	**Tank**	**Cab.**
T1.2.2 Slush	Number not known	1930s	Five Car Freight Train Set. Engine, Tender, Coal Car, Box Car, Tank Car, and Caboose. Engine-6 Metal Wheels Painted Red. Cars-Metal Wheels Painted Black. Metal Hitches. Cars Same as T1.2.1. Combinations Appear to Have Been Consistent (Train 17 7/8" Long When Connected)	Black (4 1/8")		Dark Red/ Black (3 3/4")	Green (3 3/4")	Orange (3 3/4")	Red (Cupola Centered) (3 5/16")

Notes: (1) Some collectors and authors believe that the T1.2.2 train with the smaller engine was sold with a separate tender. To date this cannot be confirmed.

T1.1 Five-piece Passenger Train Set (#566) This set consists of a single-piece engine/tender, three passenger cars, and a baggage car. It is not known whether there was a standard color configuration for this train. The engine/tender is always black with red metal wheels. The most common colors for the passenger cars and the baggage cars are red and green. Orange color passenger and baggage cars are scarce and blue cars are extremely scarce or rare. All wheels are metal.

R5: Engine/Tender ($18-25) ($40-50)
R5: Passenger or Baggage Car, Red or Green ($10-15) ($25-35)
R6: Passenger or Baggage Car, Orange ($20-30) ($40-50)
R7/8: Passenger Car, Blue ($30-40) ($50-100)
R7/8: Complete Train ($150-$175) ($200-400)
R9/10: Complete Train in box ($500-700)

T1.1 (566) large passenger set

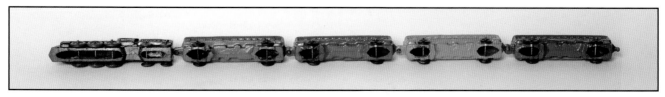

T1.1 (566) large passenger set, underside

T1.1 engine

T1.1 green baggage car

Red baggage car

T1.1 red passenger car

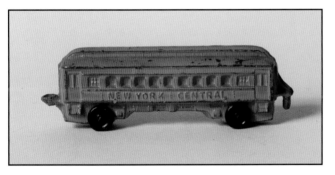

T1.1 orange passenger car

T1.1 blue passenger car

T1.1 red passenger car with red wheels

T1.2.1 Five-piece Freight Train Set (#577) This set consists of the same single-piece engine/tender found in the T1.1 passenger train set as well as a coal car, box car, tank car, and caboose. The car colors of this set are consistent. The one notable aspect of the cars relates to the coal car, which has a dark red body with the load of coal painted black. While this set appears to have been somewhat more popular than the passenger car set, it is still seldom seen complete with all five pieces.

T1.2.1 (577) large freight set

T1.2.1 (577) large freight set, underside

R5: Individual Freight Cars and Caboose ($10-15) ($25-35)
R6: Engine/Tender ($18-25) ($40-50)
R7/8: Complete Train ($125-$150) ($175-350)
R9/10: Complete Train in box ($500-700)

T1.2.1 engine

T1.2.1 coal car   *T1.2.1 tank car*   *T1.2.1 box car*   *T1.2.1 caboose*

T1.2.2 Five-piece Freight Train Set with Small Engine The exact configuration of this set is subject to question. Since the engine pictured is clearly a variation of the T1.1 and T1.2.1 engine without an attached tender, there is an open question as to whether this train variation had a tender, making it a six-piece set, or not. While some collectors have suggested that there is an orange tender that is part of this set, this set has periodically been offered for sale without a tender and to date no one has been able to produce a set that contains a tender. Although there are one or more examples of a slush orange tender, this tender is larger and clearly was not manufactured by Barclay. (See example pictured in the Appendix). Unlike the T1.1 and T1.2.1 sets, there are no known catalog pictures of this set. Until proven otherwise, it is assumed that this set consists of the engine without a tender and the same four cars found on the T1.2.1 set.

T1.2.2 large freight set with small engine

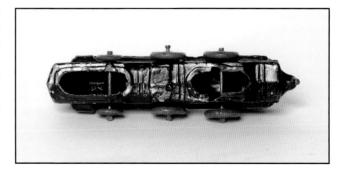

T1.2.2 engine, underside

R5: Individual Freight Cars and Caboose ($10-15) ($25-35)
R6: Black Engine without Tender ($25-35) ($40-50)
R7/10: Complete Train ($150-$200) ($190-$400)

Medium-Size

Miniature Trains

Medium-Size Slush Miniature Trains

Scarcity and pricing is listed in italics after the detailed description for each piece. Due to variations seen in the market, prices are listed in ranges for examples in C-8 (Very Good) and C-10 (Mint) conditions.

It is not clear how early Barclay began production of the medium-size trains; however, the T2.1.1 version was in production in 1934 as seen in one of the Butler Brothers catalogs of that year. It can be safely assumed

Slush Trains—Medium Size				Colors Pass=Passenger; Bag=Baggage; Cab=Caboose					
Type	**Ref.**	**Years**	**Characteristics**						
				Engine	Tender	Pass.	Box	Tank	Cab.
T2.1.1	May be 550; not confirmed	1930s	Five Car Freight Train Set Shown in Butler Brothers Catalog, September 1934. Engine Has Light Powered by a Small Flashlight Battery. Set Includes Engine, Coal Tender, Box Car, Tank Car, and Caboose. All Pieces Have White Rubber Wheels With Red Wooden Hubs. Connected by Metal Hitches. (Train 15 3/4" Long When Connected)	Black (3 3/16")	Black (2 1/16")		Green (most likely) (3 1/4")	Orange (most likely) (3 1/8")	Red (Cupola Centered) (2 3/4")
				Engine	Tender	Pass.	Box	Tank	Cab.
T2.1.2	May be 550; not confirmed	1930s	Five Car Freight Train Set Shown in Butler Brothers Catalog, September 1936. This Train is Exactly Like the T2.1.1 Train Except That the Cars are Connected By Wire Hitches. (Train 16 1/16" Long When Connected)	Black (3 3/16")	Black (2 1/16")		Green (most likely) (3 1/4")	Orange (most likely) (3 1/8")	Red (Cupola Centered) (2 3/4")
				Engine	Tender	Pass.	Box	Tank	Cab.
T2.2	May be 550; not confirmed	1930s	Engine and Tender Casting Same as T2.1.1 , T2.1.2, T2.3.1, and T2.3.2 Except No Light-Hitches are Wire. Cars Same As T2.1.2-Connected By Wire Hitches. All Pieces Have White Rubber Tires Without Hubs. (Train 16 1/16" Long When Connected)	Silver (3 3/16")	Silver (2 1/16")		Green (3 1/4")	Orange (3 1/8")	Red (Cupola Centered) (2 3/4")
				Engine	Tender	Pass.			
T2.3.1	555	1930s	Three Car Passenger Train Set. Engine Has Light Powered by a Small Flashlight Battery. Engine and Tender are Same Casting as T2.1.2. All Pieces Have White Rubber Wheels With Red Wooden Hubs. Connected by Wire Connectors. (Train 9 1/8" Long When Connected)	Black (3 3/16")	Black (2 1/16")	Red (3 3/8")			
				Engine	Tender	Pass.			
T2.3.2	555 (assumed)	1930s	Same as T2.3.1 Except White Rubber Wheels; No Hubs (Train 9 1/8" Long When Connected)	Black (3 3/16")	Black (2 1/16")	Red (3 3/8")			

that the initial versions of the medium-size trains were produced simultaneously with the large-size trains.

In all likelihood, the first two sets of the medium-size trains were the T2.1.1 five-piece train advertised in the Butler Brothers catalog and T2.3.1 three-piece passenger set. In addition to a tender and the cars listed, each had an engine with a light. A flashlight bulb was attached on the front of the engine and was powered by a flashlight battery housed in the inside of the engine casting. In both sets, wheels were white rubber mounted on red wooden hubs,

which were characteristic of many Barclay vehicles in the early 1930s. One difference between the two sets is that the freight train shown in the Butler Brothers catalog has metal hitches whereas the passenger set has wire connectors. The only difference between the T2.1.1 set and the T2.1.2 sets relates to the type of connectors that were used. The T2.2 and the T2.3.2 sets are described below. All of these sets were made by the slush casting method, which places their date of manufacture in the early to mid-1930s.

T2.1.1 Medium-Size Five-piece Freight Train Set
This set is similar to the larger freight car set; however, each piece is smaller in size. The engine has a light on the front powered by a flashlight battery enclosed in the interior of the engine. The wheels are rubber mounted on red wooden hubs and the cars are connected by metal hitches. This particular version of the medium-size Barclay trains is extremely rare.

R7/8: Engine with Light, Wooden Hubs, and Metal Hitch ($75-90) ($100-200)
R7/8: Individual Cars with Wooden Hubs and Metal Hitches ($40-60) ($75-100)
R7/10: Complete Train ($350-425) ($500-750)

Butler Brothers Catalog, September 1934

T2.1.2 Medium-Size Five-piece Freight Train Set
The T2.1.2 set is exactly the same as the T2.1.1 set except for the fact that the engine and cars are connected by wire couplings. This set was shown in the September 1936 Butler Bothers Catalog. This version of the medium-size train is extremely rare.

R7/8: Engine with Light, Wooden Hubs, Wire Coupler ($75-90) ($100-200)
R7/8: Individual Cars with Wooden Hubs, Wire Couplers ($40-60) ($75-100)
R7/10: Complete Train ($350-425) ($500-750)

T.2.1.2 or T.2.3.1 tender

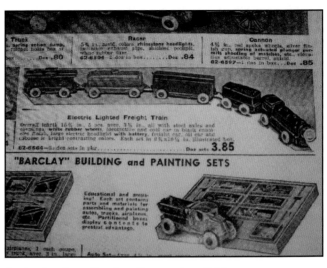

Butler Brothers Catalog, September 1936

T2.2 Medium-Size Five-piece Freight Train Set This set is difficult to locate, but occasionally can be found. The castings are the same as the castings for the T2.1.1 medium-size train except that the engine does not have a light and the couplings are wire. In contrast to the wheels on the T2.1.1 version, the wheels are white rubber without the wooden hubs.

R6: Engine, No Light, White Wheels, Wire Coupler ($25-35) ($50-60)
R6: Individual Cars, White Wheels, Wire Couplers ($25-35) ($50-60)
R7/8: Complete Trains ($200-250) ($350-400)

T2.2 medium-size slush train

T2.2 medium-size slush train, underside

T2.2 engine

T2.2 tender

T2.2 tank car

T2.2 box car

T2.2 caboose

T2.3.1 Medium-Size Three-piece Passenger Set This set has the same engine with a light as the T2.1 set with wheels that are white rubber mounted on red wooden hubs. One difference is that this set has wire hitches. While not as rare as the T2.1 freight train set, this set is quite scarce.

R7: Engine with Wooden Hubs and Wire Couplers ($60-80) ($95-125)
R7: Individual Cars with Wooden Hubs and Wire Couplers ($30-40) ($65-90)
R7/10: Complete Train ($150-225) ($250-350)
R7/10: Complete Train in Box ($300-450)

T2.3.1 set with lithographed box

T2.3.1 medium-size slush passenger train

T2.3.1 medium-size slush passenger train, underside

T2.3.1 engine

T2.3.1 passenger car

T2.3.2 Medium-Size Three-piece Passenger Set This passenger train set is exactly the same as the T2.3.1 set; however, each piece has white rubber tires without hubs. In the mid-thirties, Barclay transitioned many of its vehicles that formerly had rubber tires mounted to the red wooden hubs to simple, white rubber tires without hubs. Although this set was produced slightly later, it is still quite scarce.

R7: Engine with White Rubber Wheels and Wire Couplers ($60-80) ($95-125)
R7: Individual Cars with White Rubber Wheels and Wire Couplers ($30-40) ($65-90)
R7/10: Complete Train ($150-225) ($300-400)

Medium-Size Die-Cast Miniature Trains

In the later part of the 1930s, Barclay began moving from the use of the slush casting method to the die-cast casting method. In the case of the medium-size trains, the basic scale of the trains was retained; however, new molds had to be prepared. Rather than separate engines and tenders, a combined engine/tender was used. Other changes included the addition of a coal car, the movement of the cupola on the caboose to the rear of the caboose casting, and the use of metal couplings on all cars. The initial die-cast trains were produced in the late 1930s or, perhaps, very early 1940s, with white rubber wheels. This train was reissued after the end of World War II with black rubber wheels. This latter version was the only Barclay miniature train manufactured after World War II in any size other than small, which is discussed further in this section.

Scarcity and pricing is listed in italics after the detailed description for each piece. Due to variations seen in the market, prices are listed in Ranges for examples in C-8 (Very Good) and C-10 (Mint) conditions.

Type	Ref.	Years	Characteristics	Engine	Coal	Box	Tank	Cab.
Die-Cast Trains—Medium Size				Colors Cab.=Caboose				
T2.4.1	550	1930s to early 1940s	Five Car Freight Train Set. Engine/Tender, Gondola Car, Box Car, Tank Car, and Caboose. All Pieces Have 4 White Rubber Wheels. Metal Hitches. Each Piece is Marked "550." Train 15 3/8" Long. (Train 15 3/8" Long When Connected)	Silver, Blue, Gray (3 13/16")	Blue (3 3/8")	Green, Light Yellow (3 3/8")	Orange, Light Yellow, Burnt Orange (3 3/8")	Red (Cupola Toward Rear) (2 5/8")
T2.4.2	550	1945 to Early 1950s	Same as T2.4.1 Except Black Rubber Wheels With Exception of Engine/Tender Color, Color Combinations Appear to Have Been Consistent. (Train 15 3/8" Long When Connected)	Black, Blue, Silver (3 13/16")	Blue (3 3/8")	Green (3 3/8")	Orange (3 3/8")	Red (Cupola Toward Rear) (2 5/8")

T2.4.1 Medium-Size Five-piece Die-Cast Freight Train Set As indicated this train has a duel engine/tender, which came in three colors, silver, blue, and gray. Of these colors the silver and the blue are the most common. The gray color is quite scarce. The train has four cars—a coal car, box car, tank car, and caboose. All of the couplings are metal and the cupola on the caboose has been moved toward the rear in contrast to the earlier medium-size trains where the cupola on the caboose is centered. Of the various medium-size trains, this variety is the most common.

R5: Engine/Tender, Silver or Blue ($18-25) ($35-40)
R7/8: Engine/Tender, Gray ($40-50) ($50-100)
R5: Individual Cars ($15-20) ($25-30)
R7/8: Complete Train ($110-170) ($200-275)
R7/8: Box Car-Light Yellow T2.4.1 ($40-50) ($50-100)
R7/8: Tank Car-Light Yellow or Burnt Orange T2.4.1 ($40-50) ($50-100)

T2.4.1 (550) medium-size die-cast freight train—53: silver engine

T2.4.1 (550) medium-size die-cast freight train, underside

T2.4.1 engine/tender, silver

T2.4.1 engine/tender, gray

T2.4.1 engine/tender, blue

T2.4.1 (550) medium-size die-cast freight train—blue engine

T2.4.1 coal car

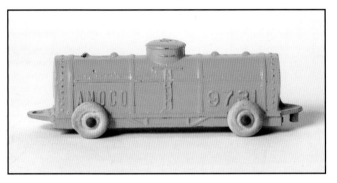

T2.4.1 tank car, orange

T2.4.1 box car, green

T2.4.1 caboose

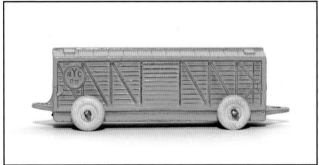

T2.4.1 box car, light yellow

T2.4.2 Medium-Size Five-piece Die-Cast Freight Train Set This set is exactly the same as the T2.4.1 set above; however, each piece has black rubber or plastic tires. These sets were manufactured after World War II. Given the fact that they are very rare, it can be assumed that very limited quantities were sold and that they were produced for a relatively short time. This set was sold in a lithographed cardboard box.

T2.4.1 (550) medium-size die-cast freight

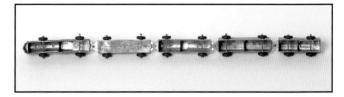

T2.4.1 (550) medium-size die-cast freight, underside

R7/8: Engine/Tender, Black or Blue ($40-50) ($60-100)
R7/10: Medium-size Engine T2.4.2 Silver ($50-70) ($80-150)
R7/8: Individual Cars ($35-40) ($50-70)
R7/10: Complete Train ($100-200) ($300-400)
R7/10: Complete Train in Box ($225-300) ($500-700)

T2.4.1 (550) medium-size die-cast freight, top view

T2.4.1 (550) medium-size die-cast freight lithographed box

T2.4.1 (550) medium-size die-cast freight box, open

T2.4.2 engine

T2.4.2 coal car

T2.4.2 box car

T2.4.2 caboose

Medium-size engine, silver

T2.4.2 tank car

Streamlined Trains

The Barclay streamlined train is a three-car train created from a single slush casting. There is only one casting type and all examples are painted silver with white rubber wheels. The Streamlined Moderne Design evolved from the Art Deco design movement, which originated in the mid-1920s. Streamlined Design emphasized curved forms and horizontal lines. This design movement was very important in the later part of the 1930s and examples are seen in many forms. Among others, examples can be found in architecture, furniture, vehicles, trains, jewelry, household goods, and toys. The design of the train and the use of white rubber wheels suggests that this toy was manufactured in the late 1930s. The toy is scarce and particularly significant given its direct tie to the Streamlined Moderne Design movement.

Scarcity and pricing is listed in italics after the detailed description for each piece. Due to variations seen in the market, prices are listed in Ranges for examples in C-8 (Very Good) and C-10 (Mint) conditions.

Slush Trains—Streamlined				Colors
Type	Ref.	Years	Characteristics	Train
T3	565	Mid- to Late 1930s	Single-piece 3 Car Streamliner. White Rubber Wheels.	Silver (7 3/16")

T3 Streamlined Train This toy is a very simple one-piece slush casting. There are three cars, but all are included in the single casting. The wheels are white rubber. As discussed above, the most distinctive aspect of this toy is the design, which clearly reflects the Streamlined Moderne Design movement at the time. It is very likely that the direct design influence for this toy was New York Central Railroad's 20th Century Limited designed in 1938 by the famed industrial designer, Henry Dreyfuss. This toy is scarce.

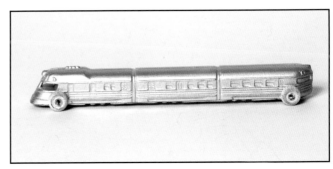

T3 Streamlined train

T3 Streamlined Train from Various Angles:

R7: Complete Train ($85-90) ($125-200)

Front view

Rear view

Rear view

Front view

Small-Size
Miniature Trains

Small-Size Slush Casting Miniature Trains

The small-size trains were first produced in the mid-to late 1930s. The initial trains were produced using the slush casting method. Although very similar in size and scale to the later three-car trains, the slush castings are somewhat different. The engines of the initial version of the three-car train have six wheels in contrast to the second version where the engines have four wheels. Both versions of the slush cast trains are somewhat more detailed than the later die-cast versions. The easiest way to clearly distinguish the slush varieties from the die-cast varieties is that the engines on the slush versions have a single-pane window whereas the engines in the die-cast versions have double-pane windows. In contrast to the metal connectors used in the die-cast varieties, the slush varieties use "s" hook connectors.

Scarcity and pricing is listed in italics after the detailed description for each piece. Due to variations seen in the market, prices are listed in ranges for examples in C-8 (Very Good) and C-10 (Mint) conditions.

Slush Trains-Small Size (335 Series)							
Type	Ref.	Years	Characteristics	Colors *Pass.=Passenger*			
				Wheels	Engine	Tender	Pass.
T4.1	335	1930s	6-Wheel Engine, Open Coal, Passenger, S Hook Connections, Single Pane Windows on Engine (Train 7 5/16" Long When Connected)	Metal	Black (2 3/8")	Black (1 7/8")	Red (2 11/16")
T4.2	335	Late 1930s	4-Wheel Engine, Open Coal, Passenger, S Hook Connections, Single Pane Windows on Engine (Train 7 5/16" Long When Connected)	Metal	Black (2 3/8")	Black (1 7/8")	Red (2 11/16")

T4.1 and T4.2 Small Size, Slush Cast Trains In addition to a black engine with six wheels, the T4.1 set consists of a black tender and a red passenger car. The pieces are connected by means of "s" hooks. The only difference between the T4.1 variety and the T4.2 variety are the number of wheels on the engine. Both of these sets are periodically seen, but scarce.

R5/6: Small Size, Slush Cast Trains ($18-35) ($30-80)

T4.1 small-size slush passenger train

T4.1 small-size slush passenger train, underside

T4.2 small-size slush passenger train

T4.2 small-size slush passenger train, underside

T4.1 and T4.2 small-size slush passenger trains

Small-Size Die-Cast Miniature Trains–Traditional Colors

Scarcity and pricing is listed in italics after the detailed description for each piece. Due to variations seen in the market, prices are listed in ranges for examples in C-8 (Very Good) and C-10 (Mint) conditions.

Die-Cast Trains-Small Size (335 A Series)								
Type	Ref.	Years	Characteristics		Colors *Pass.=Passenger*			
				Wheels	Engine	Tender	Pass.	
T4.3.1	335	1945/ 1950s	4-Wheel Engine, Closed Coal, Passenger, Cast Connections, Double Pane Windows on Engine (Train 6 5/8" Long When Connected)	Metal	Black (2 9/16")	Black (1 3/4")	Red (2 13/16")	
T4.3.2	335	1950s– Early 1960s	4-Wheel Engine, Closed Coal, Passenger, Cast Connections, Double Pane Windows on Engine (Train 6 5/8" Long When Connected)	Metal	Silver (2 9/16")	Black (1 3/4")	Red (2 13/16")	
T4.3.3	335	1950s– Early 1960s	4-Wheel Engine, Closed Coal, Passenger, Cast Connections, Double Pane Windows on Engine (Train 6 5/8" Long When Connected)	Metal	Silver (2 9/16")	Silver (1 3/4")	Red (2 13/16")	
T4.3.4	335	1950s– Early 1960s	4-Wheel Engine, Closed Coal, Passenger, Cast Connections, Double Pane Windows on Engine (Train 6 5/8" Long When Connected)	Metal	Blue (2 9/16")	Blue (1 3/4")	Red (2 13/16")	
T4.4.1	335	1960s	4-Wheel Engine, Closed Coal, Passenger, Cast4-Wheel Engine, Closed Coal, Passenger, Cast Connections, Double Pane Windows on Engine (Train 6 5/8" Long When Connected)	Plastic	Silver (2 9/16")	Black (1 3/4")	Red (2 13/16")	
T4.4.2	335	1960s	4-Wheel Engine, Closed Coal, Passenger, Cast Connections, Double Pane Windows on Engine (Train 6 5/8" Long When Connected)	Plastic	Silver (2 9/16")	Green (1 3/4")	Red (2 13/16")	
T4.4.3	335	1960s	4-Wheel Engine, Closed Coal, Passenger, Cast Connections, Double Pane Windows on Engine (Train 6 5/8" Long When Connected)	Plastic	Gray (2 9/16")	Green (1 3/4")	Red (2 13/16")	
T4.4.4	335	1960s	4-Wheel Engine, Closed Coal, Passenger, Cast Connections, Double Pane Windows on Engine (Train 6 5/8" Long When Connected)	Plastic	Orange (2 9/16")	Green (1 3/4")	Red (2 13/16")	

Shortly after Barclay restarted production after World War II, it introduced a die-cast version of the small train. This version was similar to the pre-war slush version; however, it had several distinctive characteristics. The engines had four wheels similar to the T4.2 engine; however, the engine had a two-pane window. The cars were connected by means of cast connectors. In general, the castings have somewhat less detail when compared to the earlier slush castings. Although the length of the individual pieces are slightly longer than the slush versions, the total length of the trains are slightly shorter than the small slush trains due to the difference in the connector systems of the two types of trains.

T4.3.1-T4.3.4 Small die-cast passenger trains, metal wheels

T4.4.1-T4.4.4 Small die-cast passenger trains, plastic wheels

This variety of the small train was produced and sold continuously from the later 1940s through most of the 1960s. During that period, the earlier trains had the same small metal wheels that were used on most of the miniature toy ranges. During the early to mid-1960s, the wheels were changed to the small rubber or plastic wheels used on the other miniature vehicles. The only other difference in the small trains during this period lies in the color combinations, some of which are scarce to rare.

T4.3.1, T4.3.2, T4.3.3, T4.3.4 Die-Cast Small Trains with Metal Wheels The only difference in these four varieties is the different color combinations. Of the four varieties, the T4.3.2 (silver, black, and red) color combination is by far the most common.

R2: T4.3.2 (Silver, Black, Red) ($8-10) ($15-20)
R4: T4.3.4 (Blue, Blue, Red) ($15-20) ($25-35)
R5: T4.3.3 (Silver, Silver, Red) ($18-25) ($30-40)
R6: T4.3.1 (Black, Black, Red) ($25-35) ($40-80)

T4.3.1 Small die-cast passenger trains, metal wheels

T4.3.2 Small die-cast passenger trains, metal wheels

T4.3.2 Small die-cast passenger trains, metal wheels, underside

T4.3.3 Small die-cast passenger trains, metal wheels

T4.3.2 Small die-cast passenger trains, metal wheels MOC

T4.3.4 Small die-cast passenger trains, metal wheels

T4.4.1, T4.4.2, T4.4.3, T4.4.4 Die-Cast Small Trains with Plastic Wheels, Regular Colors After the plastic wheels were introduced, trains with four different color combinations appeared. In contrast to the final versions of the small trains that had neon colors, these trains were painted traditional Barclay colors. Of these trains, the T4.4.1 (silver, black, and red) is by far the most common.

R2: T4.4.1 (Silver, Black, Red) ($8-10) ($15-20)
R4: T4.4.2 (Silver, Green, Red) ($15-20) ($25-35)
R7/8: T4.4.3 (Gray, Green, Red) and T.4.4.4 (Orange, Green, Red) ($40-50) ($60-100)

T4.4.2 Small die-cast passenger trains, plastic wheels

T4.4.2 Small die-cast passenger trains, plastic wheels MOC

T4.4.3 Small die-cast passenger trains, plastic wheels

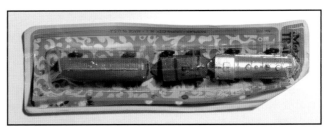

T4.4.2 Small die-cast passenger trains, plastic wheels MOC

T4.4.4Small die-cast passenger trains, plastic wheels

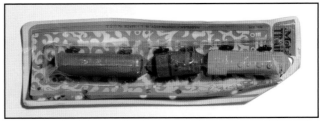

T4.4.4 Small die-cast passenger trains, plastic wheels MOC

T4.4.1 Small die-cast passenger trains, plastic wheels

**Additional Variety: T4.4 Sub-Group: Small-Size
Train** Passenger car, metallic red, plastic wheels.
Listed in "Notes Applicable to All Barclay Trains."

R7/8: ($40-50) ($60-100)

Passenger car, metallic red

Small-Size Die-Cast Miniature
Trains—Neon Colors

In the last year or two before the company closed, Barclay began painting many of its miniature vehicles, including the Miniature Trains, neon colors. As was the case in some other ranges, it is not clear whether there were definite standards with respect to the color combinations used. The only conclusive way to identify an original color combination is to find the particular combination in an unopened blister pack. Colors were created by spraying a white base color and then using neon automobile paint to achieve the desired result. It should be noted that the period when these pieces were produced was the Psychedelic Era of wild design and bright colors. All of these sets are scarce to very rare.

Scarcity and pricing is listed in italics after the detailed description for each piece. Due to variations seen in the market, prices are listed in ranges for examples in C-8 (Very Good) and C-10 (Mint) conditions.

Die-Cast Trains-Small Size (335 A Series—Neon Colors)							
Type	**Ref.**	**Years**	**Characteristics**	**Colors** *Pass.=Passenger*			
				Wheels	**Engine**	**Tender**	**Pass.**
T4.5.1	335 A	1969-70	4-Wheel Engine, Closed Coal, Passenger, Cast Connections, Double Pane Windows on Engine (Train 6 5/8" Long When Connected)	Plastic	Orange Neon (2 9/16")	Yellow-Lemon Neon (1 3/4")	Orange Neon (2 13/16")
T4.5.2	335 A	1969-70	4-Wheel Engine, Closed Coal, Passenger, Cast Connections, Double Pane Windows on Engine (Train 6 5/8" Long When Connected)	Plastic	Pink Neon (2 9/16")	Yellow-Lemon Neon (1 3/4")	Orange-Red Neon (2 13/16")
T4.5.3	335 A	1969-70	4 Wheel Engine, Closed Coal, Passenger, Cast Connections, Double Pane Windows on Engine (Train 6 5/8" Long When Connected)	Plastic	Red Neon (2 9/16")	Yellow-Lemon Neon (1 3/4")	Orange-Red Neon (2 13/16")
T4.5.4	335 A	1969-70	4-Wheel Engine, Closed Coal, Passenger, Cast Connections, Double Pane Windows on Engine (Train 6 5/8" Long When Connected)	Plastic	Yellow Neon (2 9/16")	Green Neon (1 3/4")	Pink Neon (2 13/16")
T4.5.5	335 A	1969-70	4-Wheel Engine, Closed Coal, Passenger, Cast Connections, Double Pane Windows on Engine (Train 6 5/8" Long When Connected)	Plastic	Pink Neon (2 9/16")	Yellow-Lemon Neon (1 3/4")	Orange Neon (2 13/16")
T.4.6	335 A	1970-71	4-Wheel Engine, Closed Coal, Passenger, Cast Connections, Double Pane Windows on Engine (Train 6 5/8" Long When Connected)	Plastic-W	Pink Neon (2 9/16")	Green Neon (1 3/4")	Orange-Red Neon (2 13/16")

T4.5.1-T4.6 Small Size Die-Cast Miniature Trains-Neon Colors The initial versions, T4.5.1-T4.5.5, of the neon trains have plain plastic wheels, which indicate that they were most likely produced in the last years of production. The final version, T4.6, has white side-wall wheels. This final version was most likely produced shortly before Barclay closed. Since in these final years of production it appears that color combinations were put together randomly, it is certainly possible that additional color combinations were sold; however, that can only be confirmed when original blister packs with new color combinations are located. Prices on these sets are somewhat difficult to establish because they are so seldom seen in the antique toy market. Regardless, they are all very scarce to extremely rare.

Neon trains (top to bottom) T4.5.3, 4.5.5, and T4.5.2

R7/10: T4.5.1–T4.6, All Types ($60-90) ($100-300)

Neon trains with T4.4.4 (top to bottom) T4.4.4, T4.5.2, T4.5.5, and T4.6

Notes Applicable

to Barclay Trains

Notes Applicable to All Barclay Trains

(1) Individual pieces were measured from the points of the solid metal of the casting. On the pieces with wire hooks, the hooks were not included in the measurements. When the pieces are hooked together, the length of the train will not equal the sum of the individual pieces.

(2) The color combinations for the 335 A sets only include those sets found in original blister packs.

(3) Additional pieces known to exist, however, the set to which they belong is not known:

Additional Small Size Train Pieces	Engine	Tender	Pass.
T4.3, Metal Wheels	Gold	Red	
T4.4, Plastic Tires	White	Yellow	White
T4.4, Clear Plastic Tires		Red	
Small Size Train-Plastic Whitewall Tires	Silver		Green Neon

T4.3 gold engine

T4.3 red tender

T4.4 white engine

T4.4 yellow tender

T4.4 white passenger

T4.4 red tender with clear tires

Small-size train with whitewall tires

Appendix

The Appendix illustrates variations of various Barclay miniature toys that were not illustrated in the text, larger Barclay vehicles from the post-World War II era, pictures from the Barclay archives, and related material that may be of interest to Barclay collectors.

Red Streamlined Cab From time to time, this version of the Streamlined Series cab is seen at toy fairs and on online auctions. The toy has the same dimensions as the Streamlined Series cab; however, it has black rubber wheels and the hitch is built much higher than the standard Streamlined Series cab. So far as is known, this cab was not part of the Transport Toys range.

Classic and Modern Series Cars Painted Two or More Times As was discussed in the earlier sections of the book, car castings were sometimes painted more than once. We know that this occurred for a number of reasons, such as: coverage of a given casting was not complete, the casting turned over, or the casting fell off the paint pan. When this happened, the casting was often returned to the paint line even when the color of the batch being painted was different from the original color. In some cases, the wheels had been attached already and the casting was repainted with the wheels attached. Most of the examples that have come to light are Classic car examples; however, examples of the Modern cars are found occasionally. While these pieces are not considered as separate varieties, they are interesting and rare.

Classic S3.1.3 yellow outside

Classic S3.1.3 yellow inside

Classic S3.1.3 blue over orange outside

Classic S3.1.3 blue over orange inside

Classic S3.1.1 light green over yellow outside

Classic S3.1.1 light green over yellow inside

Classic CO3.1.1 red over blue outside

Classic CO3.1.1 red over blue inside

Classic S3.1.3 light blue over orange outside

Classic S3.1.3 light blue over orange inside

Classic CO3.1.3 green over pink outside

Classic CO3.1.3 green over pink inside

Classic CO3.1.1 red over red outside

Classic CO3.1.1 red over red inside

Classic CO3.1.3 blue after wheels attached outside

Classic CO3.1.3 blue after wheels attached inside

Classic CO3.1.3 salmon after wheels attached outside

Classic CO3.1.3 salmon afterwheels attached inside

Classic CO3.3 blue over red outside

Classic CO3.3 blue over red inside

Modern S4.1.1 blue after wheels attached outside

Modern S4.1.1 blue after wheels attached inside

Modern CO4.3 dark green over yellow outside

Modern CO4.3 dark green over yellow inside

Miniature Tank Trucks Without Labels It is clear that the MT11.2.2 green trucks were sold with no label as well as with the Sinclair labels. There is evidence that this truck was also sold in the white and yellow colors without labels, but this has not been conclusively proven.

Miniature tank trucks without labels

Barclay Cars for U-Drive-It Toy This toy was manufactured by Northwestern Products Co., St. Louis, Missouri. The toy had wires that attached to the front of classic Barclay cars by connecting the wire to a hole drilled at the front of the hood. By turning the steering wheel, a child could drive the cars. It appears that the game most often used Barclay Classic coupes, but Classic sedans were also used. Both the game and examples of cars used in the game are shown below.

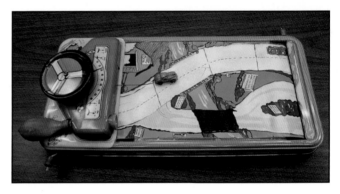

U-Drive-It toy

Barclay Classic coupes used in the U-Drive-It toy

U-Drive-It toy with its box

Post Cereal Promotion Cereal promotions were very common in the 1950s. These promotions normally required submission of one or more box tops and a small amount of money. In this case, the recipient received five Barclay miniature vehicles. The box was purchased with the notation concerning the date of the promotion. The three trucks shown are three of the five vehicles originally included in the box.

Post Cereal promotion addressed box

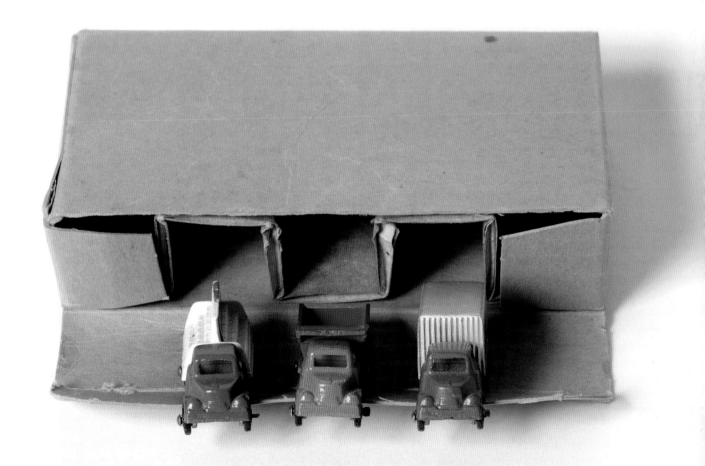

Post Cereal promotion showing partial contents

Barclay Race Track Set The Barclay race track was manufactured in the mid-1960s. It included a ten-foot plastic track and two Barclay race cars. The cars were from the second casting of the race cars with the driver cast as part of the racer. It is an open question how popular this toy was. This toy is only seen as part of an unopened set and is rare.

Barclay race track set MOC, front

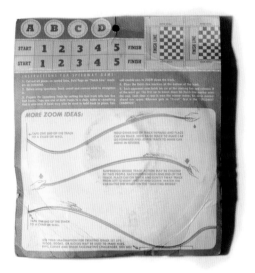

Barclay race track set MOC, back

Barclay Large-size Transport Set The larger Barclay transport set (BV153) was first manufactured in the early 1930s. The transport carries four cars. The sedans are two inches in length and the coupes are two and one-fourth inches in length. The overall length of the set is ten and three-eighths inches. In the set shown below, the metal wheels of the cab and the trailer are painted black. In other sets, the cab and the trailer have white rubber tires mounted on red hubs or white rubber tires without hubs. The cab and the cars were manufactured using the slush casting method whereas the trailer was stamped from steel. While not considered part of the miniature Barclay toy ranges, this set is certainly related to those toys.

Barclay large transport Set

Comparison of cars from large transport and miniature transport sets

Barclay Large-size Pickup Other than a few military toys, Barclay only manufactured two larger size vehicles after World War II–this large pickup and the fire truck shown in the next entry. This pickup (377) is three and five-eighths inches long and two inches high. The earlier version of this vehicle has white rubber tires, which suggests it was first manufactured in the late 1930s or early 1940s. After Barclay reopened in 1945, this toy had black rubber tires. As illustrated below, the large pickup was produced with whitewall tires as well as neon colors. Normally, the pickup was sold with six wooden barrels, which were either painted silver or left unpainted. Both the whitewall wheel version and the black wheel version came in many colors. It has been suggest that his vehicle was originally manufactured by Tommy Toy, which produced metal toys for a short period in Union City, New Jersey, between 1935 and 1939; however, there is no conclusive evidence of this fact.

Standard large-size pickup

Large pickup MOC, neon color

Large pickup MOC, neon color, side view

Large pickup with whitewall tires

Barclay Post-World War II Fire Truck The second larger, non-military vehicle produced by Barclay after World War II was the two-piece hook and ladder fire truck (390) pictured below. The toy was designed by William Rucci, Sr., for which he was reportedly paid a twenty dollar bonus. The toy is five and seven-eighths inches long and was produced for a short period of time in the early 1950s. As the ladder is raised by means of a handle on the driver's side of the ladder component, the fireman climbs

the ladder. The two pieces are connected by means of a round metal hitch that is cast into the back of the cab and that fits into a round hole that is cast into the front of the ladder component. There have been reports that cabs exist with a hole in the back of the cab into which a metal hitch would have to be fitted; however, there have been no reports of a second casting variation of the trailer component that includes a metal hitch. This toy was sold in the lithographed box pictured below.

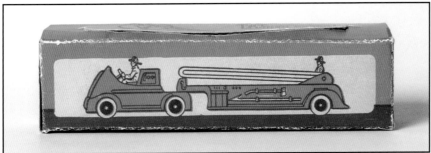

Barclay fire truck box, reverse side

Barclay fire truck box, end

Barclay fire truck box, underside

Barclay fire trucks with lithographed box

Barclay Esso Concept Tank Truck This Esso tank truck was designed in the 1950s or early 1960s; however, it was never produced for sale. The truck is approximately two and three-quarters inches long. The example below was cast in zinc from the original mold.

Esso tank truck, side view

Esso tank truck, front view

Esso tank truck, rear view

Esso tank truck, underside

Orange Tender from Unknown Manufacturer Pictured below is the orange tender that some assume was a part of the large-size Barclay train, T1.2.2. This particular train component is larger than the pieces of the T1.2.2 train and the couplings do not fit the pieces on the T1.2.2 train. The most telling difference between this tender and the Barclay components lies in the casting. This casting is exceedingly rough and does not resemble the Barclay casting in any matter whatsoever. This train component has been seen as part of trains from the 1930s produced by an unknown manufacturer.

Orange tender from unknown manufacturer

Pictures From Barclay Archives Below are a representative group of pictures from a larger group of seventeen photographs from the Barclay archives, which were reportedly discarded when Barclay closed. The lead photograph is marked on the back, "Barclay Mfg. Co. Inc., 316 Palisade Ave., Union City, N.J., #112.

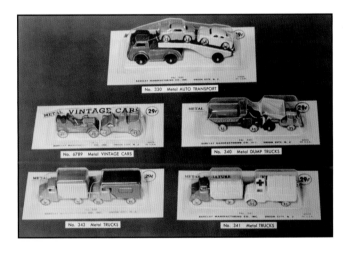
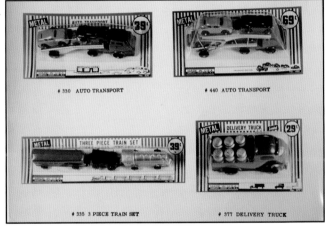

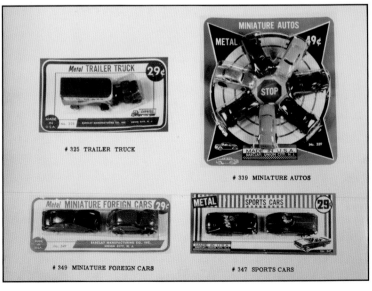

Japanese Miniature Vehicle Sets From Japan The sets of miniature vehicles below are representative of toys produced in Japan in the 1950s and 1960s and sold throughout the United States. They are included here because they are frequently mixed with Barclay toys of those eras and often misattributed to Barclay.

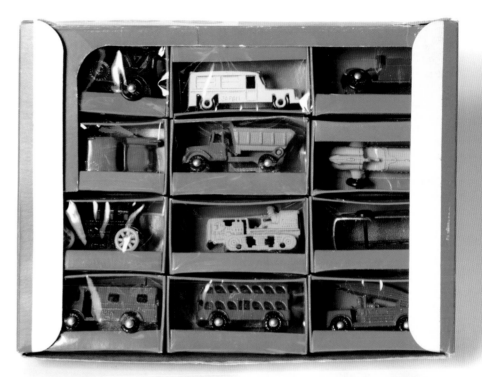

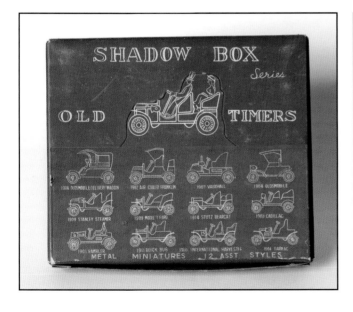

Identification Grids

Type	Ref.	Years	Characteristics	Colors					
				Blue	Green	Green/Blue	Orange/Blue	Red	Red/Blue
First or Vintage Series (Cabs and Trailers)									
C1	(BV152)	1932-37	Cast, white wheels, red hubs, Model A Ford. **See detail listing below.**		■			■	
C1.4	(BV152)	1937	Cast, white wheels, no hubs, Model A Ford. **See detail listing below.**		x				
2T1	(BV152)	1932-37	Steel, white wheels, red hubs, painted			■	x		■
2T2	(BV152)	1937	Steel, white wheels, no hubs, painted			x			

Notes: (1) The 2T2 Trailer appears to be part of an original set with the C1.4 cab; however, it is the same trailer as is found in the Second Series.

Type	Ref.	Years	Characteristics	Colors	
				Green	Red
Model A Cab—Detail of C1 cabs listed above: all cabs cast with wheels having red hubs unless noted as having solid wheels.					
C1.1	(BV152)	1932-37	Plain hood, no hitch bars, plain tank, hubs	x	
C1.2	(BV152)	1932-37	Plain hood, no hitch bars, cross on tank, hubs	x	x
C1.3	(BV152)	1932-37	Plain hood, small hitch bars, cross on tank	x	
C1.4	(BV152)	1932-37	Plain hood, long hitch bars, plain tank, solid wheels	x	
C1.5	(BV152)	1932-37	Hood louvers, small hitch bars, cross on tank, wheels with hubs or solid wheels	x	

Notes: (1) C1.1–1.5 hitches vary in height, flashing on some pieces look like radiator caps.
(2) C1.1–1.5. Although these variations have been identified, it is very likely that additional variations exist.

Type	Ref.	Years	Characteristics	Colors				
				Blue	Green	Orange*	Red	Yellow
First or Vintage Series (Sedans and Coupes)								
S1	(BV152 or 114)	1932-38	Cast, metal wheels, closed windows	x	x	■	x	■
S2	(BV152 or 114)	1932-38	Cast, metal wheels, open windows			■		
CO1.1	(BV152 or 114)	1932-38	Cast, metal wheels, closed windows	x	■	x		
CO1.2	(BV152 or 114)	1932-38	Cast, metal wheels painted black, closed windows		x			
CO2	(BV152 or 114)	1932-38	Cast, metal wheels, open windows		x		■	

Notes: * Exists in two shades: orange and burnt orange.

Type	Ref.	Years	Characteristics	Colors							
			Second or Streamlined Series (Cabs and Trailers)	Blue-Dk.	Blue/Plain	Green	Green/Green	Orange/Red	Red/Plain	Red/Blue	White/White
C2	(BV114)	1938	Cast, white wheels, no hubs, "Trailer" on side			▓					
2T2	(BV114)	1938	Steel, white wheels, no hubs, painted	x	x		x	x	x	x	x

Notes: (1) Related cab variety-C2 in red with built-up hitch. Not considered a part of this series; see Appendix.
(2) A transitional variety cab and trailer with red hubs may or may not be original. Pictures of those seen appear to have been restorations that took place outside of the factory.

Type	Ref.	Years	Characteristics	Colors										
			Third or Classic Series Cabs	Blue	Blue-Lt.	Chocolate	Green-Forest	Green-Lt.	Green-Moss	Gray	Orange	Pink	Red	Salmon
C3.1.1	(BV11)	1939-42	Cast, White Tires, Open Wheel-Wells, Low Hitch, '38 Ford Cab Over Engine		x		▓						▓	
C3.1.2	(BV11)	1939-40	Same as C3.1.1, Except Lights and Grill Mask, Painted Silver										▓	
C3.1.3	(BV11 or 157)	1945-46	Same as C3.1.1, Except Black Tires								x		▓	
C3.2.1	(BV11 or 157)	1945-49	Cast, Black Wheels, Open Wheel-Wells, High Hitch, '38 Ford Cab Over Engine		x								▓	x
C3.2.2	(BV11 or 157)	1945-46	Same as C3.2.1, Except White Tires										▓	
C3.3.1	(BV11 or 157)	1950	Cast, Black Wheels, Half Open Wheel-Wells, High				▓							
C3.3.2	(BV11 or 157)	1950	Same as C3.3.1, Except Reinforced									x		
C3.4.1	(BV11 or 157) (330 or 440)	1950-65	Cast, Black Wheels, Closed Wheel-Wells, High Hitch, '38 Ford Cab Over Engine, Smooth Wheels	▓	▓			x	▓	▓	▓	▓		
C3.4.2	(BV11 or 157) (330 or 440)	1965	Same as C3.4.1, Except Ridged Wheels	x	x		x		▓		x		▓	
C3.4.3	(BV11 or 157) (330 or 440)	1960s	Same as C3.4.1, Except White Rubber Wheels										▓	

Note: (1) Classic cabs in yellow may exist, but an example has not yet been authenticated.

Type	Ref.	Years	Characteristics	Colors				
				Unpainted	Blue-Light	Orange	Yellow	Red
Third or Classic Series Two-Car Trailers								
2T3.1.1	(BV11)	1939-42	Cast, white wheels, painted					x
2T3.1.2	(BV11)	1945-46	Cast, black wheels, painted			x	x	x
2T3.1.3	(BV11)	1945-46	Cast, black wheels, painted, reinforced tabs					
2T3.2.1	(BV11)(330) (BV75)(330)	1945-65	Aluminum, black weels				x	
2T3.2.2	(BV11)	1945-46	Aluminum, white wheels					
		1960-66		x				
2T3.2.3	(BV11)	1945-46	Copper plated steel, black wheels		x			
2T3.2.4	(BV11)	1945-46	Steel, Black Wheels					
2T3.3	(BV11)(330) (BV75)(330)	1965-70	Aluminum, Ridged Black Tires					

Type	Ref.	Years	Characteristics	Colors
				Unpainted
Third or Classic Series Four-Car Trailers				
4T3.1.1	(BV157)(440)	1945-64	Aluminum, smooth black wheels, tab hole, separate steel or aluminum tab in place	
4T3.1.2	(BV157)(440)	1945-46	Same as 4T3.1.1, but smooth white tires	
		1960-66		x
4T3.1.3	(BV157)(440)	1945-46	Same as 4T3.1.1, but copper plated steel	
4T3.1.4	(BV157)(440)	1945-46	Same as 4T3.1.1, but steel	
4T3.1.5	(BV157)(440)	1960s	Aluminum, smooth black wheels, tab hole with lower tab unbent and scoring across the tab	
4T3.1.6	(BV157)(440)	1960s	Aluminum, smooth black wheels, tab hole on both lower and upper platform. No scoring.	
4T3.1.7	(BV157)(440)	1965-70	Same as 4T3.1.1, but ridged tires	
4T3.2.1.1	(BV157)(440) (BV107)(440)	1965-70	Aluminum, no tab hole, back tab bent up, ridged black tires	
4T3.2.1.2	(BV157)(440) (BV107)(440)	1965	Aluminum, no tab hole, back tab bent up, smooth black tires	x
4T3.2.2	(BV157)(440) (BV107)(440)	1965-70	Aluminum, no tab hole, back tab not bent up, ridged black tires	

Notes: (1) The variety listed as 4T3.1.6.1 in *Barclay Toys* most likely was not a product of the factory. This "variety" appears to have resulted from purchasers bending the back tabs up after having lost the small movable tab.
(2) Additional variety–4T3.2.2 axle with nubs at both ends.
(3) Additional variety–4T3.1.4 one steel and one aluminum platform.
(4) Additional variety–4T3.1.1 aluminum platforms with copper plated steel connectors.
(5) Additional variety-Four-Car Trailer with aluminum platforms and copper-steel connectors.

Type	Years	Characteristics	Blue	Blue-Lt.	Blue-Steel	Brown-Light	Camel	Chocolate	Clay	Flesh	Gold	Gray	Green-Aqua	Green-Forest	Green-Lt.	Green-Moss	Orange	Pink	Red	Salmon	Silver	Tan	Yellow	Yellow-Lemon
Third or Classic Sedans (BV11 or 157) (440 or 330)																								
Plain Sedans																								
S3.1.1	1939-50s	Cast, plain grill, open wheel-wells, unpainted metal wheels, two door handles; perhaps '39 Buick																						
S3.1.2	1939	Same as 3.1.1 except painted wheels	x																					
S3.1.3	1950s-65	Same as 3.1.1 except closed wheel-wells			x					x			x											
S3.1.4.1	1957-65	Same as 3.1.1 except gold-colored wheels																						
S3.1.4.2	1957-65	Same as 3.1.3 except gold-colored wheels					x		x													x		
S3.1.5	1965	Same as 3.1.3 except dull, cleated rubber tires	x																x					
Parking Light Sedan																								
S3.2.1	1939	Cast, plain grill, open wheel-wells, unpainted metal wheels, sq. parking light left front, die-cut left back, two door handles, dipping wind shield, flat headlights	x																					
S3.2.2	1939-50s	Same as 3.2.1 except painted wheels																					x	
S3.2.3	1950s-65	Same as 3.2.1 except closed wheel-wells							x	x	x				x									
S3.2.4	1965	Same as 3.2.3 except dull, cleated rubber tires																						
Grill Bars Sedan																								
S3.3.1	1950s-65	Cast, vertical grill, closed wheel-wells, metal wheels, four door handles, partial left front parking light, rounded trunk							x	x					x									
S3.3.2	1950s-65	Same as S3.3.1 except gold-colored wheels					x																	

Notes: (1) Although a number of classic sedans repainted black exist, to date no genuine example has been found.

(2) Examples of S3.2.3 (red) exist with a small hole in the hood. These were part of the older versions of the game, U-Drive-IT.

Additional Varieties (Examples of Cars Painted Multiple Colors Can Be Found in the Appendix)

(1) S3.1.3 Double painted. Light blue over orange.

(2) S3.1.2 Double painted. Lt. green example painted solid green inside.

(3) S3.1.2 Double painted. Blue example painted yellow inside and over painted blue on the outside.

(4) S3.1.1 Solid yellow on inside.

(5) S3.1.2 Orange with 5 cent sticker.

Type	Years	Characteristics	Colors																									
Third or Classic Coupes (BV11 or 157) (440 or 330)			Blue	Blue-Lt.	Blue-Steel	Brown	Camel	Clay	Cream	Flesh	Gray	Gold	Green-Aqua	Green-Forest	Green-Lt.	Green-Moss	Khaki	Lilac	Orange	Orange-Burnt	Pink	Red	Salmon	Silver	Tan	Turquoise	Yellow	Yellow-Lemon
Plain Coupes																												
CO3.1.1	1939-50s	Cast, wide body, open wheel-wells, unpainted metal wheels, full grill, smooth cast, wide body; perhaps '39 Plymouth																										
CO3.1.2	1939	Same as 3.1.1 except painted wheels	x																									
CO3.1.3	1950s-65	Same as 3.1.1 except closed wheel-wells			x							x	x					x		x						x		
CO3.1.4	1957-65	Same as 3.1.3 except gold-colored wheels																										
CO3.1.5	1965	Same as 3.1.3 except cleated rubber tires						x				x		x	x													
Crooked Line Coupe																												
CO3.2.1	1950s-65	Cast, narrow body, closed wheel-wells, metal wheels, crooked line on right grill, tapered backend; perhaps '37 Willys or '37 Studebaker																										
CO3.2.2	1957-65	Same as 3.2.1 except gold wheels																										
No-Line Coupe																												
CO3.3	1950s-65	Cast, Mid-Width Body, Closed Wheel-Wells, Metal Wheels, Headlight and Three Grill Bars on Left Side, No Headlight and One Grill Bar on Right Side, Later Version had no Headlight or Grill on Left Side, Rounded Backend															x											

Notes: (1) Although a number of classic coupes repainted black exist, to date no genuine example has been found.
(2) Examples of CO3.1.3 (red, blue), CO3.2.1 (red), and CO3.3 (red) exist with a small hole in the hood.
   These were part of the older versions of the game, U-Drive-It.

Additional Varieties (Examples of Cars Painted Multiple Colors Can Be Found in the Appendix)
(1) CO3.1.3 Double painted. Light green over pink.
(2) CO3.3 Double painted. Blue over red-solid blue wheels.
(3) CO3.1.2 Blue with painted wheels and front axles crimped on both ends.

Type	Ref.	Years	Characteristics	Colors											
				Blue	Green-Forest	Green-Lt.	Orange	Orange-Red Neon	Pink-Neon	Red	Red-Metallic	Salmon	Yellow	Yellow-Neon	Yellow- Lemon-Neon
Fourth or Modern Series Cabs															
C4.1	(BV75 or 107) (330 or 440)	1960s	Cast, black wheels, '58 Ford cab—over engine truck		x	x		x	x	x	x		x	x	
C4.2	(BV75 or 107) (330 or 440)	1970-71	Cast, black wheels with white sidewalls; '63 Ford				x								x

Notes: (1) C4.2 May exist or may not exist in either light blue or light blue neon.
(2) In *Barclay Toys*, the yellow color was identified as "hot-yellow."

Type	Ref.	Years	Characteristics	Colors
				Unpainted
Fourth or Modern Series Two-Car Trailers				
2T4.1	(BV75) (330)	1965-70	Same as 2T3.3	
2T4.2	(BV75) (330)	1970-71	Same as 2T3.3 with white sidewalls	

Type	Ref.	Years	Characteristics	Colors
				Unpainted
Fourth or Modern Series Four-Car Trailers				
4T4.1	(BV107) (440)	1965-70	Same as 4T3.2.1.1	
4T4.2	(BV107) (440)	1965-70	Same as 4T3.2.2	
4T4.3	(BV107) (440)	1970-71	Same as 4T3.2.1 with white sidewalls	

Type	Years	Characteristics	Colors																									
Fourth or Modern Series Sedans (BV75 or 107) (440, 330, or 331)			Aqua	Black	Beige	Blue	Blue-Lt.	Blue Steel	Brown	Brown-Lt.	Chocolate-Metallic	Clay	Cream	Gray	Green-Forest	Green-Lt.	Green-Moss	Magenta	Orange	Orange-Neon	Pink	Pink-Bright	Red	Salmon	Silver	Tan	White	Yellow	Yellow-Lemon
S4.1.1	1957-65	Cast, metal wheels and axles, marked 1-8, open back window, eyelet axle holder; perhaps '51 Packard	x	x	x			x	x	x							x							x					
S4.1.2	1960-65	Same as S4.1.1 except gold wheels			x		x												x					x					
S4.2.1.1	1965-70	Same as S4.1.1 except with cleated rubber or plastic vinyl tires, metal axles make from pins crimped at one end, forked or eyelet wheel assembly, open back window													x		x											x	
S4.2.1.2	1965-70	Same as S4.2.1.1 except closed back window		x															x						x				
S4.2.2.1	1966-70	Same as S4.2.1.1 except axle nub at both ends																							x				
S4.2.2.2	1966-70	Same as S4.2.1.2 except axle nub at both ends																							x				
S4.2.3	1966-70	Same as S4.2.1.2 except with small smooth rubber tires, metal axle made from pin crimped at one end, forked axle holders, closed back wndow		x											x							x			x				

Notes: (1) Examples of Cars Painted Multiple Colors Can Be Found in the Appendix.

Type	Years	Characteristics	Colors																									
S4.3 Fourth or Modern Series Sedans (BV75 or 107) (330, 440, or 331)			Black	Blue	Blue-Metallic	Blue-Neon	Cinnamon-Metallic	Copper	Gold	Green-Forest	Green-Metallic	Green-Neon	Maroon	Olive-Metallic	Orange	Orange-Neon	Orange-Red Neon	Pink-Neon	Purple-Neon	Red	Red-Metallic	Red-Neon	Silver	Tan	Violet	White	Yellow	Yellow Lemon-Neon	Yellow-Lemon
S4.3.1	1970-71	Cast, plastic wheels, plastic axles						x						x															
S4.3.2	1970-71	Same as S4.3.1 with flower power label																											
S4.3.3	1970-71	Same as S4.3.1 with small, round number label on top of car														x			x									x	
S4.3.4	1970-71	Black paint over gold paint	x																										

Type	Years	Characteristics	Colors																									
Fourth or Modern Series Coupes (BV75 or 107) (440, 330, or 331)			Aqua	Black	Blue	Blue-Lt.	Blue-Steel	Clay	Coral	Cream	Gray	Green-Forest	Green-Lt.	Green-Metallic	Green-Neon	Gold	Orange	Orange-Burnt	Orange-Neon	Pink	Pink-Bright	Red	Red-Neon	Salmon	Silver	Tan	Yellow	Yellow-Lemon
CO4.1.1	1957-65	Cast, metal wheels and axles, marked 1-8, open back window, eyelet axle holder; perhaps '51 Packard.		x						x	x																	
CO4.1.2	1957-65	Same as CO4.1.1 except closed back window																										
CO4.1.3	1960-65	Same as CO4.1.1 except gold wheels																		x	x	x		x				
CO4.2.1	1965-70	Same as CO4.1.1 except with cleated rubber or vinyl plastic tires, metal axle made from pin crimped at one end, forked or eyelet wheel assembly, closed back window						x	x										x									
CO4.2.2	1966-70	Same as CO4.2.1 except axle nub at both ends													x													
CO4.2.3	1966-70	Same as CO4.2.1 except with small smooth rubber tires, metal axle made from pin crimped at one end, forked axle holders, closed back window		x	x							x										x		x	x			
CO4.2.4	1966-70	Same as CO4.2.1 except large smooth plastic tires															x				x						x	

Notes: (1) CO4.1.1 Blue over red with solid wheels.
(2) CO4.1.1 Orange with solid orange wheel painted over gold wheels.

Type	Years	Characteristics	Colors																							
CO4.3 Fourth of Modern Series Coupes (BV75 or 107) (330, 440, or 331)			Black	Blue	Blue-Metallic	Copper	Gold	Green-Forest	Green-Metallic	Green-Neon	Maroon	Orange	Orange-Burnt	Orange-Red	Orange-Red Neon	Pink-Neon	Purple-Metallic	Purple-Neon	Red	Red-Neon	Red-Metallic	Silver	Tan	White	Yellow	Yellow-Lemon	Yellow-Lemon-Neon
CO4.3	1970-71	Cast, plastic wheels and axles								x		x					x					x				x	

Notes: (1) Additional variations: C4.3.1–black over gold and black over yellow.

Bottle Delivery Truck

Type	Description	Cab Casting	Cab Color	Body Casting	Body Color	Wheel Mat.	Type	Logo— Side/Top
MT1.1.1	Traditional cab, bottle del. body	1.2	Green		Red	Metal	—	None
MT1.1.2	Traditional cab, bottle del. body	1.2	Aqua		Red	Metal	—	None
MT1.1.3	Traditional cab, bottle del. body	1.2	Red		Red	Metal	—	None
MT1.1.4	Traditional cab, bottle del. body	1.2	Blue		White	Metal	—	None
MT1.2.1	Traditional cab, bottle del. body	1.2	Blue		White	Metal	—	Cola
MT1.2.2	Traditional cab, bottle del. body	1.2	Blue		White	Plastic	SC	Cola
MT1.3.1	Traditional cab, bottle del. body	1.3	Yellow		Yellow	Plastic	SS, LS	Coca-Cola
MT1.3.2	Traditional cab, bottle del. body	1.3	Yellow		Yellow	Plastic-W	LS	Coca-Cola
MT1.3.3	Traditional cab, bottle del. body	2	Yellow		Yellow	Plastic	LS	Coca-Cola
MT1.4	Traditional cab, bottle del. body	1.2	Blue		White	Metal	—	Pepsi-Small
MT1.5.1	Traditional cab, bottle del. body	1.3	Blue		White	Plastic	SC, LS, SS	Pepsi
MT1.5.2	Traditional cab, bottle del. body	1.3	Red		White	Plastic	SC	Pepsi
MT1.6	Traditional cab, bottle del. body	1.3	Cream		Cream	Plastic	SS, LS	YooHoo
MT1.7	Modern cab, bottle del. body	2	Yellow-Lemon		Yellow-Lemon	Plastic-W	LS	None
MT1.8	Modern cab, bottle del. body	2	Yellow		Yellow	Plastic-W	LS	Coca-Cola likely

Box Van-Front of Box Cut-Out

Type	Description	Cab Casting	Cab Color	Body Casting	Body Color	Wheel		Logo— Side/Top
						Mat.	Type	
MT2.1.1	Traditional cab, body with front cut-out, flat sides	1.1	Red	1	Aluminum	Metal	—	—
MT2.1.2	Traditional cab, body with front cut-out, flat sides	1.1	White	1	White	Metal	—	—

Box Van—Square Box, Ribbed Sides

Type	Description	Cab Casting	Cab Color	Body Casting	Body Color	Wheel		Logo— Side/Top
						Mat.	Type	
MT2.2.1	Traditional cab, square body, ribbed sides	1.2	Red	2	Aluminum	Metal	—	None
MT2.2.2	Same as 2.2.1	1.2	Green	2	Aluminum	Metal	—	None
MT2.3.1	Same as 2.2.1	1.2	Green	2	Aluminum	Metal	—	Hertz—Yellow On Black
MT2.3.2	Same as 2.2.1	1.2	Green	2	Aluminum	Plastic	SC	Hertz—Yellow On Black
MT2.3.3	Same as 2.2.1	1.2	Yellow	2	Yellow	Plastic	SC	Hertz—Black On Yellow

Box Van-Square Box, Flat Sides

Type	Description	Cab Casting	Cab Color	Body Casting	Body Color	Wheel Mat.	Wheel Type	Logo– Side/ Top
MT2.3.1	Traditional cab	1.3	Red	3	Aluminum	Plastic	SC, SS, LS	A&P
MT2.3.2	Modern cab	2	Red	3	Aluminum	Plastic	LS	A&P
MT2.3.3	Modern cab	2	Red-Metallic	3	Aluminum	Plastic	LS	A&P
MT2.4.1	Traditional cab	1.2	Blue	3	Aluminum	Metal	-	Avis–4 sides
MT2.4.2	Traditional cab	1.3	Blue	3	Aluminum	Plastic	LS	Avis–4 sides
MT2.4.3	Traditional cab	1.3	Blue	3	Aluminum	Plastic	SS	Avis–6 sides
MT2.4.4	Modern cab	2	Blue	3	Aluminum	Plastic	LS	Avis–6 sides
MT2.4.5	Modern cab	2	Red	3	Aluminum	Plastic	LS	Avis–6 sides
MT2.4.6	Modern cab	2	Blue	3	Aluminum	Plastic	LS	Avis–4 sides
MT2.5.1	Traditional cab	1.3	Green	3	Aluminum	Plastic	SC	Hertz
MT2.5.2	Traditional cab	1.3	Orange	3	Aluminum	Plastic	LS	Hertz
MT2.5.3	Traditional cab	1.3	Red	3	Aluminum	Plastic	SC	Hertz
MT2.5.4	Traditional cab	1.3	Yellow	3	Aluminum	Plastic	SC, LS	Hertz
MT2.5.5	Modern cab	2	Yellow	3	Aluminum	Plastic	LS	Hertz
MT2.5.6	Modern cab	2	Yellow	3	Aluminum	Plastic-W	LS	Hertz
MT2.6.1	Traditional cab	1.3	Military	3	Military	Plastic	SS, LS	Large Army/ large star
MT2.6.2	Modern cab	2	Military	3	Military	Plastic	LS	As Above
MT2.7	Traditional cab	1.3	White	3	White	Plastic	SC	Stuart
MT2.8.1	Traditional cab	1.3	Cream	3	Aluminum	Plastic	SC, SS, LS	U-Haul
MT2.8.2	Modern cab, square body	2	Cream	3	Aluminum	Plastic	LS	U-Haul
MT2.9	Modern cab	2	White	3	White	Plastic	LS	None
MT2.10	Traditional cab	1.2	Blue	3	Blue	Plastic	SC	None

Canvas Covered Transport

Type	Description	Cab Casting	Cab Color	Body Casting	Body Color	Wheel Mat.	Wheel Type	Logo– Side/Top
Wide Body								
MT3.1.1	Traditional cab, wide body	1.1	White	1	White	Metal	—	Red Cross–painted
MT3.1.2	Traditional cab, wide body	1.1	White	1	White	Metal	—	Red Cross–label
MT3.1.3	Traditional cab, wide body	1.1	Military	1	Military	Metal	—	None
Narrow Body								**(Only Labels Below)**
MT3.2.1	Traditional cab, narrow body	1.2	White	2	White	Metal	—	Red Cross
MT3.2.2	Traditional cab, narrow body	1.3	White	2	White	Plastic	SS, SC, LS	Red Cross
MT3.2.3	Modern cab, narrow body	2	White	2	White	Plastic	LS	Red Cross
MT3.3.1	Traditional cab, narrow body	1.2	Military	2	Military	Metal	—	None
MT3.3.2	Traditional cab, narrow body	1.2	Military	2	Military	Plastic	SC	Small Army–small star
MT3.3.3	Traditional cab, narrow body	1.3	Military	2	Military	Plastic	LS	None
MT3.3.4	Traditional cab, narrow body	1.3	Military	2	Military	Plastic	SS, SC	Large Army–large star
MT3.3.5	Modern cab, narrow body	2	Military	2	Military	Plastic	LS	Large Army–large star or none

Dump Truck-Long Body

Type	Description	Cab Casting	Cab Color	Body Casting	Body Color	Wheel Mat.	Wheel Type	Logo– Side/Top
MT4.1.1	Traditional cab, long body	1.1	Red		Blue	Metal	—	None
MT4.1.2	Traditional cab, long body	1.1	Red		Blue-Lt.	Metal	—	None
MT4.1.3	Traditional cab, long body	1.1	Red		Blue-Steel	Metal	—	None
MT4.1.4	Traditional cab, long body	1.1	Red		Blue	Plastic	SC	None
MT4.2.1	Traditional cab, long body	1.2	Red		Blue	Metal	—	None
MT4.2.2	Traditional cab, long body	1.2	Blue-Lt.		Blue-Lt.	Metal	—	None
MT4.3.1	Traditional cab, long body	1.3	Red		Yellow	Plastic	LS	None
MT4.3.2	Traditional cab, long body	1.3	Red		Blue	Plastic	SC LS	None

Dump Truck: Small Dump

Type	Description	Cab Casting	Cab Color	Body Casting	Body/ Dump Color	Wheel Mat.	Wheel Type	Logo– Side/ Top
MT5.1.1	Narrow undercarriage, dump	1	Blue	1	Orange	Met/Pla	ELBS	None
MT5.1.2	Narrow undercarriage, dump	1	Blue	1	Yellow-Lemon	Met/Pla	ELBS	None
MT5.1.3	Narrow undercarriage, dump	1	Lt. Blue	1	Cream	Met/Pla	ELBS	None
MT5.1.4	Narrow undercarriage, dump	1	Lt. Blue	1	Yellow	Met/Pla	ELBS	None
MT5.1.5	Narrow undercarriage, dump	1	Mint	1	Orange	Met/Pla	ELBS	None
MT5.1.6	Narrow undercarriage, dump	1	Lt. Blue	1	Red	Met/Pla	ELBS	None
MT5.2.1	Wide undercarriage, dump	2	Mint	2	Orange	Met-Pla	ELR	None
MT5.2.2	Wide undercarriage, dump	2	Mint	2	Orange	Met-Pla	ELWS	None
MT5.2.3	Wide undercarriage, dump	2	Black	2	Yellow	Plastic	ELR, LS	None
MT5.2.4	Wide undercarriage, dump	2	Blue	2	Orange	Plastic	ELR, SC	None
MT5.2.5	Wide undercarriage, dump	2	Blue	2	Yellow	Plastic	ELR, LS	None
MT5.2.6	Wide undercarriage, dump	2	Green	2	Orange	Plastic	ELR, SC	None
MT5.2.7	Wide undercarriage, dump	2	Green	2	Yellow	Plastic	ELR, LS	None

Notes: Met/Pla=Metal/Plastic

Flatbed-Log Carrier

Type	Description	Cab Casting	Cab Color	Body Casting	Body/ Dump Color	Wheel Mat.	Wheel Type	Logo– Side/ Top
MT6.1	Traditional cab, flatbed body	1.2	Red		Blue	Metal	—	None
MT6.2.1	Traditional cab, flatbed body	1.3	Red		Green	Plastic	SS, SC, LS	None
MT6.2.2	Traditional cab, flatbed body	1.3	Red		Red	Plastic	SC, LS	None
MT6.2.3	Traditional cab, flatbed body	1.3	Yellow		Yellow	Plastic	LS	None
MT6.3.1	Modern cab, flatbed body	2	Red		Green	Plastic	LS	None
MT6.3.2	Modern cab, flatbed body	2	Red		Red	Plastic	LS	None
MT6.3.3	Modern cab, flatbed body	2	Red		Green	Plastic-W	LS	None

Moving Van

Type	Description	Cab Casting	Cab Color	Body Casting	Body/ Dump Color	Wheel Mat.	Wheel Type	Logo– Side/ Top
MT7.1.1	Traditional cab, moving van	1.1	Green		Red	Metal		None
MT7.1.2	Traditional cab, moving van	1.1	Green-Lt		Red	Metal		None
MT7.1.3	Traditional cab, moving van	1.1	Green		Green	Metal		None
MT7.1.4	Traditional cab, moving van	1.1	Red		Red	Metal		None

Open Bed

Type	Description	Cab Casting	Cab Color	Body Casting	Body/ Dump Color	Wheel		Logo— Side/Top
						Mat.	Type	
MT8.1.1	Traditional cab, open bed body	1.2	Red		Red	Metal	—	None
MT8.2.1	Traditional cab, open bed body	1.3	Green		Red	Plastic	SC	None
MT8.2.2	Traditional cab, open bed body	1.3	Yellow		Yellow	Plastic	LS	None
MT8.3.1	Traditional cab, open bed body	1.3	Military		Military	Plastic	SC, LS	Large Army/ large star or large Army/ small star
MT8.3.2	Modern cab, open bed body	2	Military		Military	Plastic	LS	Large Army/ star
MT8.4.1	Traditional cab, open bed body	1.3	Yellow		Yellow	Plastic	LS	Euclid
MT8.4.2	Modern cab, open bed body	2	Yellow		Yellow	Plastic	LS	Euclid
MT8.5.1	Modern cab, open bed body	2	Lemon Yellow		Lemon Yellow	Plastic-W	LS	Flower Power
MT8.5.2	Modern cab, open bed body	2	Red- Orange Neon		Red- Orange Neon	Plastic-W	LS	Flower Power
MT8.5.3	Modern cab, open bed body	2	Red-Neon		Red-Neon	Plastic-W	LS	Flower Power

Refuse

Type	Description	Cab Casting	Cab Color	Body Casting	Body/ Dump Color	Wheel		Logo— Side/ Top
						Mat.	Type	
MT9.1.1	Traditional cab, refuse carrier	1.1	Red		Blue	Metal		None
MT9.1.2	Traditional cab, refuse carrier	1.1	Red		Lt. Blue	Metal		None

Semi-Trailer Sets Group 1:
Axle Holder on Trailer-Either Eyelet or Forked

Type	Description	Cab Casting	Cab Color	Body Casting	Body/ Dump Color	Wheel Mat.	Wheel Type	Logo— Side/Top
MT10.1	Traditional cab, eyelet	1.2	Lemon Yellow	1	Yellow-Lemon	Plastic	SC	None
MT10.2	Traditional cab, eyelet	1.2	Red	1	Aluminum	Metal	-	Barclay
MT10.3.1	Traditional cab, forked	1.3	Orange	2	Orange	Plastic	SS, SC	Allied
MT10.3.2	Traditional cab, forked	2	Orange	2	Orange	Plastic	LS	Allied
MT10.3.3	Traditional cab, forked	2	Orange	2	Orange	Plastic-W	LS	Allied
MT10.3.4	Traditional cab, forked	2	Orange-Neon	2	Orange	Plastic-W	LS	Allied
MT10.3.5	Traditional cab, forked	2	Orange-Red Neon	2	Orange	Plastic-W	LS	Allied
MT10.3.6	Traditional cab, forked	2	Red-Neon	2	Orange	Plastic-W	LS	Allied
MT10.3.7	Traditional cab, forked	2	Green-Neon	2	Orange	Plastic-W	LS	Allied
MT10.3.8	Traditional cab, forked	2	Pink-Neon	2	Orange	Plastic-W	LS	Allied
MT10.3.9	Traditional cab, forked	2	Lemon-Neon	2	Orange	Plastic-W	LS	Allied
MT10.4.1	Traditional cab, eyelet	1.2	Black	1	Aluminum	Plastic	SC	Hertz
MT10.4.2	Modern cab, forked	2	Orange-Red Neon	2	Yellow	Plastic-W	LS	Hertz
MT10.4.3	Modern cab, forked	2	Lemon Yellow	2	Yellow	Plastic-W	LS	Hertz
MT10.4.4	Modern cab, forked	2	Lemon Yellow	2	Aluminum	Plastic-W	LS	Hertz
MT10.4.5	Modern cab, forked	2	Orange	2	Yellow	Plastic-W	LS	Hertz
MT10.4.6	Modern cab, forked	2	Pink-Neon	2	Yellow	Plastic-W	LS	Hertz
MT10.5.1	Traditional Cab, Forked	1.3	Red	2	Green	Plastic	SS, LS	Railway Exp.
MT10.5.2	Traditional Cab, Forked	1.3	Yellow	2	Green	Plastic	SC	Railway Exp.
MT10.5.3	Modern cab, forked	2	Red	2	Green	Plastic	LS	Railway Exp.
MT10.5.4	Modern cab, forked	2	Red	2	Green	Plastic-W	LS	Railway Exp.
MT10.5.5	Modern cab, forked	2	Red-Neon	2	Green	Plastic-W	LS	Railway Exp.
MT10.5.6	Modern cab, forked	2	Orange-Red Neon	2	Green	Plastic-W	LS	Railway Exp.
MT10.5.7	Modern cab, forked	2	Yellow Neon	2	Green	Plastic-W	LS	Railway Exp.
MT10.5.8	Modern cab, forked	2	Pink Neon	2	Green	Plastic-W	LS	Railway Exp.
MT10.5.9	Modern cab, forked	2	Orange Neon	2	Green	Plastic-W	LS	Railway Exp.
MT10.5.10	Modern cab, forked	2	Metallic Red	2	Green	Plastic	LS	Railway Exp.

Note: (1) Railway Exp.=Railway Express

Semi-Trailer Sets Group 2:
Axle Holder on Trailer-Either Eyelet or Forked

Type	Description	Cab Casting	Cab Color	Body Casting	Body/ Dump Color	Wheel		Logo— Side/Top
						Mat.	Type	
MT10.6.1	Traditional cab, eyelet	1.2	Red	1	Blue	Metal	—	U.S. Mail
MT10.6.2	Traditional cab, forked	1.3	Red	2	Blue	Plastic	SC, LS, SS	U.S. Mail
MT10.6.3	Traditional cab, forked	1.3	Blue	2	Blue	Plastic	SC	U.S. Mail
MT10.6.4	Traditional cab, forked	1.3	Pale Red	2	Blue	Plastic	LS	U.S. Mail
MT10.6.5	Modern cab, forked	2	Red	2	Blue	Plastic	LS	U.S. Mail
MT10.6.6	Modern cab, forked	2	Red	2	Blue	Plastic-W	LS	U.S. Mail
MT10.6.7	Modern cab, forked	2	Pink-Neon	2	Blue	Plastic-W	LS	U.S. Mail
MT10.6.8	Modern cab, forked	2	Red-Neon	2	Blue	Plastic-W	LS	U.S. Mail
MT10.6.9	Modern cab, forked	2	Orange-Red Neon	2	Blue	Plastic-W	LS	U.S. Mail– Four Sides
MT10.6.10	Modern cab, forked	2	Yellow-Neon	2	Blue	Plastic-W	LS	U.S. Mail– Four Sides
MT10.7.1	Traditional cab, eyelet	1.2	Red	1	Aluminum	Metal	—	Woolworth
MT10.7.2	Traditional cab, eyelet	1.2	Red	1	Blue	Metal	—	Woolworth
MT10.7.3	Traditional cab, eyelet	1.2	Aqua	1	Blue	Metal	—	Woolworth
MT10.7.4	Traditional cab, forked	1.3	Red	2	Green	Metal	—	Woolworth
MT10.7.5	Traditional cab, forked	1.3	Red	2	Green	Plastic	SC	Woolworth
MT10.7.6	Traditional cab, forked	1.3	Green	2	Green	Plastic	SC	Woolworth
MT10.8.1	Traditional cab, forked	1.3	Pink-Neon	2	Pink-Neon	Plastic-W	LS	Flower Power
MT10.8.2	Modern cab, forked	2	Blue	2	White	Plastic	LS	None
MT10.8.3	Modern cab, forked	2	Green-Neon	2	Pink-Neon	Plastic	LS	None
MT10.8.4	Modern cab, forked	2	Pink-Neon	2	Pink-Neon	Plastic-W	LS	None
MT10.9	Modern cab, forked	2	Unknown	2	Aluminum	Plastic-W	LS	U-Haul

Notes: (1) Various pieces have double nub axle.
(2) MOC examples exist with a mixture of white-wall and plain wheels.
(3) MOC examples exist with different wheels on the trailer and cab in the same set.

Tank Truck

Type	Description	Cab Casting	Cab Color	Body Casting	Body/ Dump Color	Wheel Mat.	Wheel Type	Logo– Side/Top
MT11.1	Traditional cab, tank truck	1.2	Red		Blue	Metal	—	None
MT11.2.1	Traditional cab, tank truck	1.3	Red		Aqua	Plastic	SC	None
MT11.2.2	Traditional cab, tank truck	1.3	Green		Green	Plastic	LS	None
MT11.3.1	Traditional cab, tank truck	1.2	Military		Military	Metal	—	None
MT11.3.2	Traditional cab, tank truck	1.3	Military		Military	Plastic	SS, SC	Large Army/ large star
MT11.3.3	Traditional cab, tank truck	1.3	Military		Military	Plastic	SC	Small Army/ large star
MT11.4.1	Traditional cab, tank truck	1.3	White		White	Plastic	LS	Elsie
MT11.4.2	Traditional cab, tank truck	1.3	Yellow		Yellow	Plastic	LS	Elsie
MT11.5.1	Traditional cab, tank truck	1.3	Yellow		Yellow	Plastic	SS, LS	Shell
MT11.5.2	Modern cab, tank truck	2	Yellow		Yellow	Plastic	LS	Shell
								Sinclair Logo
MT11.6.1	Traditional cab, tank truck	1.3	Green		Green	Plastic	SC	White 1-piece
MT11.6.2	Traditional cab, tank truck	1.3	Green		Green	Plastic	SS, LS	White 2-piece
MT11.6.3	Traditional cab, tank truck	1.3	Green		Green	Plastic	SC	Brown 1-piece
MT11.6.4	Modern cab, tank truck	2	Red		Green	Plastic	LS	Brown 1-piece
MT11.6.5	Modern cab, tank truck	2	Green		Green	Plastic	LS	White 2-piece
MT11.7.1	Traditional cab, tank truck	1.3	Blue		Silver	Plastic	LS, SS	Sunoco
MT11.7.2	Modern cab, tank truck	2	Blue		Gray	Plastic	LS	Sunoco
MT11.8.1	Modern cab, tank truck	2	Red-Neon		Red-Neon	Plastic-W	LS	Flower Power
MT11.8.2	Modern cab, tank truck	2	Orange-Neon		Orange-Neon	Plastic-W	LS	Flower Power
MT11.8.3	Modern cab, tank truck	2	Green-Neon		Green-Neon	Plastic-W	LS	None
MT11.8.4	Modern cab, tank truck	2	Red-Neon		Yellow-Neon	Plastic-W	LS	Flower Power

Notes: (1) MT11.2 in solid yellow and solid white without labels may have been manufactured and sold by Barclay.

Antique Cars						
Type	**Description**	**Casting**	**Colors**	**Wheel**		**Details**
				Mat.	**Type**	
Separate Headlamps						
MC1.1.1	Cadillac-Two Seats	1.1	Blue, Lt. Blue, Green	Metal Plastic	SPG, SPS SC	Separate Lights, Nail Steering Wheel
MC1.1.2	Franklin-One Seat-Low Back	2.1	Lt. Green, Green	Metal	SPG. SPS	Separate Lights, Nail Steering Wheel
MC1.1.3	Stutz-One Bucket Seat	3.1	Red	Metal	SPG. SPS	Separate Lights, Nail Steering Wheel
			Red	Metal	SPS	Separate Lights, Nail Steering Wheel with Nail Painted Red
MC1.1.4	Buick-One Seat-High Back	4.1	Black	Metal	SPG. SPS	Separate Lights, Nail Steering Wheel
Cast Headlamps						
MC1.2.1	Cadillac-Two Seats	1.2	Blue	Plastic	SC	Gold Cast Lights, Metal Steering Wheel
MC1.2.2	Franklin One Seat-Low Back	2.2	Red, Green	Plastic	SSC	Gold Cast Lights, Plastic Steering Wheel
			Green	Plastic	SC	Gold Cast Lights, Nail Steering Wheel
			Orange-Red Neon	Plastic	SSC	Cast Lights-Painted, No Steering Wheel
			Yellow-Neon, Pink-Neon	Plastic-W	LS, ELR	Cast Lights-Painted, No Steering Wheel; Flower Power Label or Plain
			Blue-Metallic	Plastic-W	ELR	Cast Lights-Painted, Plastic Steering Wheel, 147A Labels-Front and Back
			Orange-Neon	Plastic-W	ELR	Cast Lights-Painted, Plastic Steering Wheel, 147A Labels-Front and Back
MC1.2.3	Stutz-One Bucket Seat	3.2	Red	Plastic	SC	Cast Lights-Painted Steering Wheel
MC1.2.4	Buick One Seat-High Back	4.2	Green	Metal	SPG	Gold Cast Lights, Metal Steering Wheel
			Green, Lt. Green	Metal	SPG	Gold Cast Lights, Metal Steering Wheel, Open Lamp Holds
			Green	Plastic	SSC	Gold Cast Lights, Plastic Steering Wheel
			Black	Plastic	SC	Gold Cast Lights, Nail Steering Wheel

Note: (1) No Labels on Antique Cars.

Race Cars						
Type	**Description**	**Casting**	**Colors**	**Wheel**		**Labels or Details**
				Mat.	**Type**	
Narrow Back, Two-Piece						
MC2.1.1	Large Gold Driver	1	Aqua, Green, White, Silver, Orange, Blue, Purple Met.	Plastic	ELBS, ELWS, ELR	S or R 1-6
MC2.1.2	Large Gold Driver, Silver Trim	1	White	Plastic	ELBS	S
MC2.1.3	Large White Driver	1	Blue, Red	Plastic	ELBS	S or R 1-6
MC2.1.4	Large Pink Driver	1	White	Plastic	ELBS	S 1-6
Narrow Back, One-Piece						
MC2.2	Narrow Back	3	Red, Blue	Plastic	ELR, SSC	None
				Plastic-W	LS	
Wide Back, Two Piece						
MC2.3.1	Large Gold Driver	2	Blue, Green, Red Orange, Silver	Plastic	ELBS, ELWS, ELR	S or R 1-6
MC2.3.2.1	Large Gold Driver	2	Lemon Yellow-Neon, Orange-Neon, Pink-Neon, Blue-Metallic	Plastic-W	ELR	SN Label
MC2.3.2.2	Large Gold Driver	2	Orange-Neon, Yellow-Neon	Plastic-W	ELRS	SN Label
MC2.3.3	Large Gold Driver, Silver Trim	2	Blue	Plastic	ELBS	R
MC2.3.4	Large White Driver	2	Red, Blue	Plastic	ELBS	S
Wide Back, One-Piece						
MC2.4.1	Wide Back	4	Blue, Green, Red, White, Orange	Plastic	ELR	No Label
MC2.4.2	Wide Back	4	Pink-Neon, Red, Silver	Plastic-W	ELR, LS	SN Label or None
MC2.4.3	Wide Back	4	Pink-Neon	Clear	SSC	None

Notes: (1) Logos: R=round, S=square/rectangle, RS=racing strip, SN=strip with number (pink or green on black).
(2) There are two versions of square labels, plain edge and red edge.

Sedans						
Type	**Description**	**Casting**	**Colors**	**Wheel**		**Labels or Details**
				Mat.	**Type**	
Traditional Casting						
MC3.1.1	Traditional Auto	1	Purple-Metallic, Gold	Metal	-	None
MC3.1.2	Traditional Auto	1	Green, Blue, Orange, Red, Military, Purple-Metallic	Plastic	SC	None
MC3.1.3.1	Traditional Auto-Fire	1	Red	Plastic	SC	Attached Siren, Red Chief on White on Hood, Gold Badge on White on Door
MC3.1.3.2	Traditional Auto-Fire	1	Red	Plastic	SC	Attached Siren, Red Chief on White on Hood, Black Badge on Gold on Door
MC3.1.4	Traditional Auto-Military*	1	Military	Plastic	SC	Large Army, Large Star; Small Army, Small Star
MC3.1.5	Traditional Auto-Police	1	Blue	Plastic	SC	Attached Siren, Red Block Police on Doors, Police Badge on Hood
Cast Siren						
MC3.2.1.1	Fire Chief	2	Red	Plastic	SC	Red Chief on White on Hood, Gold Badge on White on Door
MC3.2.1.2	Fire Chief	2	Red	Plastic	SC	Red Chief on White on Hood Hood, Black Badge on Gold on Door
MC3.2.2	Military	2	Military	Plastic	SS, SC	Large Army, Large Star
MC3.2.3.1	Police**	2	Blue	Plastic	SC	Police Block, Badge on Hood
MC3.2.3.2	Police ***	2	Blue	Plastic	LS	Police Large Logo, Badge on Hood
MC3.2.3.3	Police	2	Blue	Plastic-W	SS	Police Large Logo, Badge on Hood
MC3.2.4	Police Chief	2	Blue	Plastic	SC	Chief on Door, Badge on Hood
MC3.2.5.1	Taxi****	2	Yellow	Plastic	SS, SC, LS	Taxi
MC3.2.5.2	Taxi	2	Orange-Neon	Plastic-W	SS	Striped Logo on Sides
MC3.2.5.3	Taxi	2	Dark Yellow	Plastic	SS	Taxi
Cast Siren, Solid Window						
MC3.3	Traditional Auto With Siren	3	Orange Neon, Green Neon, Pink Neon	Plastic-W	SS	Flower Power or None

*May exist Large Army, Small Star
**Exists MOC with no badge
***Badge on either hood or top
**** Exists MOC with no labels

Notes: (1) An example of MC3.1.5 exists with block letter Police on door, Police Badge on hood and three holes on roof.
(2) A variation of MC3.1.3.1 or 2 exists MOC with a hole in the roof, no attached siren, and no labels.

Sports Cars						
Type	**Description**	**Casting**	**Colors**	**Wheel**		**Labels or Details**
				Mat.	**Type**	
Tail Fins, One Driver						
MC4.1.1	One Small Gold Driver	1	Red, Black	Metal	MG, MS	None
MC4.1.2	One Small White Driver	1	Red	Metal	MG, MS	None
MC4.1.3	One Large Gold Driver	1	Red, Green, Orange	Plastic	SC	None
MC4.1.4	One Small Gold Driver	1	Red	Plastic	SC	None
Tail Fins, Racing Stripes						
MC4.2.1	One Small Gold Driver	1	Red, Blue	Plastic	SC	Racing Stripe, R 1-6 Label
MC4.2.2.	One Large Gold Driver	1	Red, Blue, Green	Plastic	SC, SS	Racing Stripe, R 1-6 Label
Tail Fins, Large Wheels						
MC4.3.1	One Large Gold Driver	1	Blue	Plastic	ELR	R 1-6 Label
MC4.3.2	One Large Gold Driver	1	Orange-Neon	Plastic-W	ELR	Flower Power
MC4.3.3	One Large Gold Driver	1	Orange	Plastic-W	SS	Flower Power
Tail Fins Single Piece						
MC4.4	Driver Part of Casting	3	Orange Red-Hot	Plastic-W	SS	Flower Power
Rounded, Driver, Passenger						
MC4.5.1	Gold Driver, Passenger	2	Black, Blue, Green, Silver	Metal	MG, MS	None
MC4.5.2	Gold Driver, Passenger	2	Green, Blue	Plastic	SC	None
MC4.5.3	White Driver, Passenger	2	Blue	Metal	MG, MS	None

Notes: (1) In the latter part of the 1960s, certain sports cars were issued with the single-piece, plastic axle and wheel assembly used on the final version of the modern transport cars.

VW						
Type	**Description**	**Casting**	**Colors**	**Wheel**		**Labels or Details**
				Mat.	**Type**	
Open Back Window						
MC5.1.1.1	Traditional	1	Blue-Steel	Metal	MS	None
MC5.1.1.2	Traditional-Silver Trim	1	Blue-Steel	Metal	MS	None
MC5.1.2	Traditional	1	Blue, Green, Maroon, Orange, Red, Blue-Steel, Red-Metallic	Plastic	SC, LS	None
MC5.1.3	Traditional With Number	1	Blue, Green, Red	Plastic	SC, SS	R or S Number Labels 1-6 on Hood or Door
MC5.1.4	Traditional with Number, Silver Trim	1	Red	Plastic	SS	R 4 on Hood of Known Example
MC5.1.5.1	Traditional, Wheel-O-Rific	1	Pink-Neon, White, Orange-Neon, Yellow-Lemon Neon	Plastic-W	ELR	Flower Power or Plain
MC5.1.5.2	Traditional, Wheel-O-Rific	1	Red-Neon	Plastic-W	ELRS	Flower Power
MC5.1.6	Traditional	1	Orange-Neon	Plastic-W	SS	None
Closed Back Window						
MC5.2		2	Green-Hot	Plastic-W	SS	Flower Power or None

Trains—Large Size

Type	Ref.	Years	Characteristics	Colors Pass.=Passenger; Bag.=Baggage; Cab.=Caboose					
				Engine/Tender	Pass.	Bag.			
T1.1 Slush	566	1930s	Five-Car Passenger Train Set. Engine/Tender Combination, 3 Passenger Cars, 1 Baggage Car. Engine/Tender-10 Metal Wheels Painted Red. Cars-Metal Wheels Painted Black. Metal Hitches. Color Color Combinations Vary. (Train 21 3/8" Long When Connected)	Black (4 3/4")	Red, Orange, Green, Blue (4 3/8")	Red, Orange, Green (4 3/8")			
				Engine/Tender	Coal	Box	Tank	Cab.	
T1.2.1 Slush	577	1930s	Five-Car Freight Train Set. Engine/Tender Combination, Coal Car, Box Car, Tank Car, Caboose. Engine/Tender-10 Metal Wheels Painted Red. Cars-Metal Wheels Painted Black. Metal Hitches. Color Combinations Appear to Have Been Consistent (Train 18 1/2" Long When Connected)	Black (4 3/4")	Dark Red/ Black (3 3/4")	Green (3 3/4")	Orange (3 3/4")	Red (Cupola Centered) (3 5/16")	
				Engine	Tender	Coal	Box	Tank	Cab.
T1.2.2 Slush	Number not known	1930s	Five-Car Freight Train Set. Engine, Tender, Coal Car, Box Car, Tank Car, and Caboose. Engine-6 Metal Wheels Painted Red. Cars-Metal Wheels Painted Black. Metal Hitches. Cars Same as T1.2.1. Combinations Appear to Have Been Consistent (Train 17 7/8" Long When Connected)	Black (4 1/8")		Dark Red/ Black (3 3/4")	Green (3 3/4")	Orange (3 3/4")	Red (Cupola Centered) (3 5/16")

Notes: (1) Some collectors and authors believe that the T1.2.2 train with the smaller engine was sold with a separate tender. To date this cannot be confirmed.

Slush Trains—Medium Size

Type	Ref.	Years	Characteristics	Colors Pass=Passenger; Bag=Baggage; Cab=Caboose					
				Engine	Tender	Pass.	Box	Tank	Cab.
T2.1.1	May be 550; not confirmed	1930s	Five-Car Freight Train Set Shown in Butler Brothers Catalog, September 1934. Engine Has Light Powered by a Small Flashlight Battery. Set Includes Engine, Coal Tender, Box Car, Tank Car, and Caboose. All Pieces Have White Rubber Wheels With Red Wooden Hubs. Connected by Metal Hitches. (Train 15 3/4" Long When Connected)	Black (3 3/16")	Black (2 1/16")		Green (most likely) (3 1/4")	Orange (most likely) (3 1/8")	Red (Cupola Centered) (2 3/4")
				Engine	**Tender**	**Pass.**	**Box**	**Tank**	**Cab.**
T2.1.2	May be 550; not confirmed	1930s	Five-Car Freight Train Set Shown in Butler Brothers Catalog, September 1936. This Train is Exactly Like the T2.1.1 Train Except That the Cars are Connected By Wire Hitches. (Train 16 1/16" Long When Connected)	Black (3 3/16")	Black (2 1/16")		Green (most likely) (3 1/4")	Orange (most likely) (3 1/8")	Red (Cupola Centered) (2 3/4")
				Engine	**Tender**	**Pass.**	**Box**	**Tank**	**Cab.**
T2.2	May be 550; not confirmed	1930s	Engine and Tender Casting Same as T2.1.1, T2.1.2, T2.3.1, and T2.3.2 Except No Light-Hitches are Wire. Cars Same As T2.1.2-Connected By Wire Hitches. All Pieces Have White Rubber Tires Without Hubs. (Train 16 1/16" Long When Connected)	Silver (3 3/16")	Silver (2 1/16")		Green (3 1/4")	Orange (3 1/8")	Red (Cupola Centered) (2 3/4")
				Engine	**Tender**	**Pass.**			
T2.3.1	555	1930s	Three-Car Passenger Train Set. Engine Has Light Powered by a Small Flashlight Battery. Engine and Tender are Same Casting as T2.1.2. All Pieces Have White Rubber Wheels With Red Wooden Hubs. Connected by Wire Connectors. (Train 9 1/8" Long When Connected)	Black (3 3/16")	Black (2 1/16")	Red (3 3/8")			
				Engine	**Tender**	**Pass.**			
T2.3.2	555 (assumed)	1930s	Same as T2.3.1 Except White Rubber Wheels; No Hubs (Train 9 1/8" Long When Connected)	Black (3 3/16")	Black (2 1/16")	Red (3 3/8")			

Die-Cast Trains—Medium Size

Type	Ref.	Years	Characteristics	Colors Cab.=Caboose				
				Engine	Coal	Box	Tank	Cab.
T2.4.1	550	1930s to early 1940s	Five-Car Freight Train Set. Engine/Tender, Gondola Car, Box Car, Tank Car, and Caboose. All Pieces Have 4 White Rubber Wheels. Metal Hitches. Each Piece is Marked "550." Train 15 3/8" Long. (Train 15 3/8" Long When Connected)	Silver, Blue, Gray (3 13/16")	Blue (3 3/8")	Green, Light Yellow (3 3/8")	Orange, Light Yellow, Burnt Orange (3 3/8")	Red (Cupola Toward Rear) (2 5/8")
T2.4.2	550	1945 to Early 1950s	Same as T2.4.1 Except Black Rubber Wheels With Exception of Engine/Tender Color, Color Combinations Appear to Have Been Consistent. (Train 15 3/8" Long When Connected)	Black, Blue, Silver (3 13/16")	Blue (3 3/8")	Green (3 3/8")	Orange (3 3/8")	Red (Cupola Toward Rear) (2 5/8")

Slush Trains—Streamlined					
Type	Ref.	Years	Characteristics	**Colors**	
				Train	
T3	565	Mid- to Late 1930s	Single-piece 3-Car Streamliner. White Rubber Wheels.	Silver (7 3/16")	

Slush Trains-Small Size (335 Series)							
Type	Ref.	Years	Characteristics	**Colors** *Pass.=Passenger*			
				Wheels	**Engine**	**Tender**	**Pass.**
T4.1	335	1930s	6-Wheel Engine, Open Coal, Passenger, S Hook Connections, Single Pane Windows on Engine (Train 7 5/16" Long When Connected)	Metal	Black (2 3/8")	Black (1 7/8")	Red (2 11/16")
T4.2	335	Late 1930s	4-Wheel Engine, Open Coal, Passenger, S Hook Connections, Single Pane Windows on Engine (Train 7 5/16" Long When Connected)	Metal	Black (2 3/8")	Black (1 7/8")	Red (2 11/16")

Die-Cast Trains-Small Size (335 A Series)							
Type	Ref.	Years	Characteristics	**Colors** *Pass.=Passenger*			
				Wheels	**Engine**	**Tender**	**Pass.**
T4.3.1	335	1945/ 1950s	4-Wheel Engine, Closed Coal, Passenger, Cast Connections, Double Pane Windows on Engine (Train 6 5/8" Long When Connected)	Metal	Black (2 9/16")	Black (1 3/4")	Red (2 13/16")
T4.3.2	335	1950s– Early 1960s	4-Wheel Engine, Closed Coal, Passenger, Cast Connections, Double Pane Windows on Engine (Train 6 5/8" Long When Connected)	Metal	Silver (2 9/16")	Black (1 3/4")	Red (2 13/16")
T4.3.3	335	1950s– Early 1960s	4-Wheel Engine, Closed Coal, Passenger, Cast Connections, Double Pane Windows on Engine (Train 6 5/8" Long When Connected)	Metal	Silver (2 9/16")	Silver (1 3/4")	Red (2 13/16")
T4.3.4	335	1950s– Early 1960s	4-Wheel Engine, Closed Coal, Passenger, Cast Connections, Double Pane Windows on Engine (Train 6 5/8" Long When Connected)	Metal	Blue (2 9/16")	Blue (1 3/4")	Red (2 13/16")
T4.4.1	335	1960s	4-Wheel Engine, Closed Coal, Passenger, Cast4- Wheel Engine, Closed Coal, Passenger, Cast Connections, Double Pane Windows on Engine (Train 6 5/8" Long When Connected)	Plastic	Silver (2 9/16")	Black (1 3/4")	Red (2 13/16")
T4.4.2	335	1960s	4-Wheel Engine, Closed Coal, Passenger, Cast Connections, Double Pane Windows on Engine (Train 6 5/8" Long When Connected)	Plastic	Silver (2 9/16")	Green (1 3/4")	Red (2 13/16")
T4.4.3	335	1960s	4-Wheel Engine, Closed Coal, Passenger, Cast Connections, Double Pane Windows on Engine (Train 6 5/8" Long When Connected)	Plastic	Gray (2 9/16")	Green (1 3/4")	Red (2 13/16")
T4.4.4	335	1960s	4-Wheel Engine, Closed Coal, Passenger, Cast Connections, Double Pane Windows on Engine (Train 6 5/8" Long When Connected)	Plastic	Orange (2 9/16")	Green (1 3/4")	Red (2 13/16")

Die-Cast Trains-Small Size (335 A Series—Neon Colors)

Type	Ref.	Years	Characteristics	Colors *Pass.=Passenger*			
				Wheels	Engine	Tender	Pass.
T4.5.1	335 A	1969-70	4-Wheel Engine, Closed Coal, Passenger, Cast Connections, Double Pane Windows on Engine (Train 6 5/8" Long When Connected)	Plastic	Orange Neon (2 9/16")	Yellow-Lemon Neon (1 3/4")	Orange Neon (2 13/16")
T4.5.2	335 A	1969-70	4-Wheel Engine, Closed Coal, Passenger, Cast Connections, Double Pane Windows on Engine (Train 6 5/8" Long When Connected)	Plastic	Pink Neon (2 9/16")	Yellow-Lemon Neon (1 3/4")	Orange-Red Neon (2 13/16")
T4.5.3	335 A	1969-70	4-Wheel Engine, Closed Coal, Passenger, Cast Connections, Double Pane Windows on Engine (Train 6 5/8" Long When Connected)	Plastic	Red Neon (2 9/16")	Yellow-Lemon Neon (1 3/4")	Orange-Red Neon (2 13/16")
T4.5.4	335 A	1969-70	4-Wheel Engine, Closed Coal, Passenger, Cast Connections, Double Pane Windows on Engine (Train 6 5/8" Long When Connected)	Plastic	Yellow Neon (2 9/16")	Green Neon (1 3/4")	Pink Neon (2 13/16")
T4.5.5	335 A	1969-70	4-Wheel Engine, Closed Coal, Passenger, Cast Connections, Double Pane Windows on Engine (Train 6 5/8" Long When Connected)	Plastic	Pink Neon (2 9/16")	Yellow-Lemon Neon (1 3/4")	Orange Neon (2 13/16")
T.4.6	335 A	1970-71	4-Wheel Engine, Closed Coal, Passenger, Cast Connections, Double Pane Windows on Engine (Train 6 5/8" Long When Connected)	Plastic-W	Pink Neon (2 9/16")	Green Neon (1 3/4")	Orange-Red Neon (2 13/16")

Notes Applicable to All Barclay Trains

(1) Individual pieces were measured from the points of the solid metal of the casting. On the pieces with wire hooks, the hooks were not included in the measurements. When the pieces are hooked together, the length of the train will not equal the sum of the individual pieces.

(2) The color combinations for the 335 A sets only include those sets found in original blister packs.

(3) Additional pieces known to exist, however the set to which they belong is not known:

Additional Small Size Pieces	Engine	Tender	Pass.
T4.3, Metal Wheels	Gold	Red	
T4.4, Plastic Tires	White	Yellow	White
T4.4, Clear Plastic Tires		Red	
Small Size Train-Plastic Whitewall Tires	Silver		Green Neon

A Resting Place for

Barclay Miniature Toys

Pictures from Robert E. Wagner's Barclay Junkyard

Endnotes

1. O'Brien, Richard, *Collecting American-Made Toy Soldiers: Identification and Value Guide,* 3rd Edition. Florence, AL: Books Americana, 1997, 61. O'Brien, Karen, *O'Brien's Collecting Toy Cars & Trucks,* 4th Edition. Iola, WI: Krause Publications, 2005, 54 [hereinafter cited as O'Brien's 4th Edition]. Stephen, E. A., *O'Brien's Collecting Toys* 10th Edition, Iola, WI: Krause Publications, 2001, 610.
2. Interview with William ("Bill") Rucci, Sr., Former Senior Barclay Employee and Toy Designer, in Wanaque, NJ (May 16, 2005) [hereinafter cited as "Rucci Interview"].
3. O'Brien, R., 60; Rucci, Interview. Various Conversations (2002–2014) with William Lango, Collector and Author, [hereinafter cited as "Lango Discussions"].
4. Rucci Interview.
5. Rucci Interview.
6. Rucci Interview.
7. Lango Discussions.
8. Rucci Interview.
9. Rucci Interview.
10. Rucci Interview.
11. Rucci Interview.
12. The term "Shoebox" car is attributed to Robert E. Wagner.
13. Rucci Interview.
14. Lango Discussions.
15. Rucci Interview.
16. Rucci Interview.
17. Rucci Interview.
18. Rucci Interview.
19. Rucci Interview.
20. Rucci Interview.
21. Rucci Interview.
22. Various Conversations, Documents, and Notes (2004–2011) with Douglas Ehrenhaft, Collector and Researcher.
23. The terms "parking light sedan," "grill bars sedan," "crooked line coupe," and "no-line coupe" are attributed to Robert E. Wagner.
24. Rucci Interview.
25. Rucci Interview.
26. Rucci Interview.
27. Rucci Interview.
28. Rucci Interview.
29. Rucci Interview.
30. Rucci Interview.
31. Rucci Interview.
32. Rucci Interview.
33. Law, Alex, "Car of the Century," Auto123.com, December 22, 1999.
34. O'Brien's 4th Edition, 71, 596.

Bibliography

The following references are provided for those seeking additional information concerning the Barclay Manufacturing Company, Inc., and the vehicles manufactured by the company.

Publications

Alekna, Stan. "Barclay Car Carriers or Transports," pp. 26-29. *Old Toy Soldier,* 26-1, Spring 2002.

_____. "Barclay's Fire Engines," pp. 38-40. *Old Toy Soldier* (Volume and Date Unknown).

_____. "Barclay's Little Cars and Trucks from the 1960's," pp. 56-59. *Old Toy Soldier* 27-1, Spring 2003.

_____. "Barclay's Trains," pp. 19-21. *Old Toy Soldier* (Volume and Date Unknown).

de Courtivron, Gail and Lara. *de Courtivron's Collectible Coca-Cola Toy Trucks: An Identification & Value Guide*, pp. 64, 67, and 215. Collector Books, Paducah, KY, 1995.

Melton, Howard W., and Robert E. Wagner. *Barclay Toys: Transports & Cars 1932-1971.* Schiffer Publishing Ltd., Atglen, PA, 2004.

O'Brien, Karen. *O'Brien's Collecting Toy Cars & Trucks: Identification and Value Guide 4th Edition*, pp. 54-72. KP Books Imprint, F + W Publications, Iola, WI, 2005.

O'Brien, Richard. *Collecting American-Made Toy Soldiers: Identification and Value Guide,* 3rd Edition, pp. 60-65 and 107-121. KP Books Imprint, Books of America, Inc., Florence, AL, 1997.

_____. *Researching American-Made Toy Soldiers: Thirty-Two Years of Articles.* Ramble House, 2009.

_____. *The Barclay Catalog Book: Material From The Barclay Archives.* Port Murray, NJ, 1985.

_____. *The Second Catalog Book.* Port Murray, N.J., 1986.

Pielin, Don, Norman Joplin, and Verne Johnson. *American Dimestore Toy Soldiers and Figures*, pp. 5-10. Schiffer Publishing Lid., Atglen, PA, 2000.

Unpublished Articles, Research, and Interviews:

Information, observations, and insights regarding the toys covered in this book have been contributed by many collectors and other individuals in addition to those listed above.

Ehrenhaft, Douglas, collector and researcher. Multiple discussions and unpublished research, 2004–2011.

Evangelist, Joe, collector and researcher. Multiple discussions, 2004–2015.

Lango, William, collector and author. Multiple discussions and unpublished research, 2002–2015.

Rappaport, Dave, collector and author. "The Small Barclay Diecast Auto Transport," unpublished article, Woodside, NY, August, 1984.

Rucci, William ("Bill") Sr., senior Barclay employee and toy designer. Interview, Wanaque, NJ, May 16, 2005.

Wagner, Robert E., collector, researcher, and collaborator. Multiple discussions and unpublished research, 2001–2015.